JUMPING THROUGH HOOPS

PERFORMING GENDER IN THE NINETEENTH-CENTURY CIRCUS

BETSY GOLDEN KELLEM

THE FEMINIST PRESS
AT THE CITY UNIVERSITY OF NEW YORK
NEW YORK CITY

Published in 2025 by the Feminist Press
at the City University of New York
The Graduate Center
365 Fifth Avenue, Suite 5406
New York, NY 10016

feministpress.org

First Feminist Press edition 2025

Copyright © 2025 by Betsy Golden Kellem

All rights reserved.

This book is made possible by the New York State Council on the Arts with the support of the Office of the Governor and the New York State Legislature.

No part of this book may be reproduced, used, or stored in any information retrieval system or transmitted in any form or by any means, electronic, mechanical, photocopying, recording, or otherwise, without prior written permission from the Feminist Press at the City University of New York, except in the case of brief quotations embodied in critical articles and reviews.

First printing June 2025

Cover design by Tree Abraham
Text design by Drew Stevens

Library of Congress Cataloging-in-Publication Data is available for this title.
ISBN 978-1-55861-344-7

PRINTED IN THE UNITED STATES OF AMERICA

JUMPING THROUGH HOOPS

For Isabel

CONTENTS

INTRODUCTION *Step Right Up!*   1

CHAPTER 1 *Media and Sources in an Era of Connection*   17

CHAPTER 2 *Building the Nineteenth-Century Big Top*   29

CHAPTER 3 *Womanhood, Real and True*   47

CHAPTER 4 *The Queen of Beauty and the Armless Wonder*   59

CHAPTER 5 *Women Take Flight*   81

CHAPTER 6 *Invisible Girls and Electric Women*   101

CHAPTER 7 *Circassian Beauties in the American Sideshow*   119

CHAPTER 8 *The Remarkable Life of Millie-Christine McKoy, the Two-Headed Nightingale*   137

CHAPTER 9 *The Splendor and Terror of Bearded Ladies*   155

CHAPTER 10 *Ella Zoyara, the "Boy-Girl"*   173

CHAPTER 11 *New Women Join the Circus*   191

CONCLUSION *Taming Savage Beasts*   205

Acknowledgments   217

Notes   221

Bibliography   249

At the circus, women jump
clean through hoops;
in society,
they jump into them
and stick there.

—*The Adams Sentinel*,
September 19, 1865

INTRODUCTION

Step Right Up!

People used to run away with the circus. Some days, I wonder whether this would not be the right thing to do. After all, when a circus comes to town, everything else stops for a while. Why worry about laundry, or the electric bill, or what's for dinner, when you can see someone soar and flip on the flying trapeze? With a bucket of popcorn in your lap, you can watch human beings fly through the air, eat fire, tame wild beasts, and make solid objects seem like quantum fiction. The circus finds the world's best athletes, conjurers, weirdos, and comedians and asks: What if we took all of this ability and placed it in service of nothing less than pure joy? Sure, it is possible to dismiss a circus as childish or outmoded, but in the end, the circus—like magic, automata, carnivals, dime museums, girlie shows, stupid human tricks, and any number of ephemeral and popular entertainments—exists for one reason and for one reason only: to play. This is why I love the circus more than anything else.

Circus is not simply a genre or a venue. Yes, the things that make up a typical circus are real enough—swaths of silk and canvas, greasy fuel smells swirling around trucks and trains, performers putting on spangles and greasepaint in small, backstage alleys. But circus is so much more than the sum of its logistics and cast. Circus is a malleable social space and a laboratory for self-exploration. Down the midway and under a tent, people seek out curiosities, thrills, dangers, and dramatic tales to reinforce or disrupt the ways we see the world. Sometimes this is dark medicine: Monstrosity reinforces individual feelings of normalcy. Danger boosts the feeling of being alive. At the same time, the experience of the circus is joyful, uplifting, even defiant. In a world that too often insists that we wear work-appropriate clothing, eat our vegetables, and keep up with various Joneses, the circus tells us that it is perfectly acceptable and even beautiful to wear sequins at all times of day, to be different, to do something simply because it is possible and not simply productive. People go to the circus for a particular sort of escape, drawn to a place where things outside the everyday norm are conceivable. As an audience member, you are not simply there to watch, but to notice what happens in your heart and head when people juggle, ride, talk to wild beasts, and fly. You are asked to take these things back outside with you to cherish once the tent has been rolled up and sent down the line somewhere else. Circus ruptures the passive gaze. Disrupting the everyday—showcasing a vast spectrum of human lives and bodies and experiences—is the entire point. Plus, IT SELLS POPCORN!

I was born with six toes on my right foot, a fact that, at some point in human history, would probably have gotten me tossed in a river as a very bad sign for the upcoming harvest or possibly publicized with the most underwhelming sideshow poster ever: *Buying Shoes Is Hard!* (I say underwhelming, but it may well have made for decent employment had I been born in a different century: A 1784 engraving of an otherwise conventional and fusty-looking gentleman named Benjamin Jarrat celebrates him as a curiosity "born with six toes on each foot," and an entire 1813 pamphlet devotes itself to the curious wonder of a performing Vermont family with "supernumerary fingers and toes."[1])

But a mild sideshow tendency is not the only reason I have always thought the circus was coming for me. Somehow, it's always been there. In the late 1980s one Thanksgiving, when I was supremely bored and wanted neither to help Grandma pack up green bean casserole nor to join the men in yelling at the Detroit Lions, I picked up three plush Happy Meal toys and learned to juggle. And my mother still reminds me that, when she signed up to help the PTA at my high school, she had no idea that she would be recruited to help put on a fundraiser involving a traveling carnival. She vividly remembers renting a dumpster for elephant poop; I remember riding the elephant. In college, freed from the rules and pressures of being a high school overachiever, I followed a tiny, unexpected voice that told me I should join the circus arts club. I showed up the first day with my juggling clubs and a timid expression. I was immediately welcomed by a woman with perfect jet-black bangs who jiggled a coffee can of lighter fluid in my direction and asked: *Can you breathe fire?* Better still, she leaned in and conspired: *Do you want to?* Or maybe it was simply meant to be: In an old photo, I am a year and a half old in my parents' arms. It is Halloween, and I am smiling in a cone-shaped hat and homemade ruffly suit of mint-green gingham. All three of us are dressed as clowns.

To quote E. E. Cummings: "By this time, my worthy readers have doubtless decided that I myself am a salaried member of that branch of the circus which comprises 'the strange people.'"[2]

Maybe it was inevitable I would be drawn to the circus again and again. Or maybe it has nothing to do with my sideshow feet and propensity to juggle fruit at otherwise dignified occasions. Maybe it is a natural reaction, when the world appears to be on fire at every turn, to choose color and thrill and glorious impossibility with a side of cotton candy. It may even be the only rational decision. The show, after all, must go on. In another age, when people ran away with the departing wonder, maybe I would have, too.

Even if you are not a circus aficionado, there is no doubt a scene in your mind by now. The famous circus march—"Entrance of the Gladiators"—bobs jauntily. There's pink lemonade for sale, ringmasters turning on patent leather heels as their red tailcoats fly behind them. Strongmen lift iron weights in their leopard onesies, and big cats paw at brandished chairs from atop a barrel. Perhaps a steam calliope hoots joyfully in the distance. Amid acres of striped canvas tents, pitchmen bark about the world's smallest man or the alligator girl, standing just outside the tantalizing dark spaces scented with popcorn and wet grass. This is the American circus with its own script, a common cultural and visual shorthand. Like any convenient device, this script is a little bit reductive, a little bit embellished, and a little bit true.

Indulging my fascination with the circus, I spent years researching P. T. Barnum, the impresario and entertainment icon who is arguably the key to understanding not just circus but American popular culture itself. Authors writing about the circus have repeated the mythology of Barnum over and over again—the "Great and Only" showman of the era, a Great American Man spinning gold from everything in his path. But the more I learned about Barnum's winking tomfoolery and his love affair with American mass media, the more the story felt incomplete. There were museums, circuses, entrepreneurial flourishes and failures, and the occasional giant. Every moment of Barnum's rhapsodic Yankee life was memorialized in advertisements, criticism, colorful lithographs, and his autobiography, which he obligingly updated annually for his fans like the world's slowest social media feed. Well, *almost* every moment.

P. T. Barnum was surrounded by women—two wives, three surviving daughters, performers, friends, activists—but for all the newsprint dedicated to Barnum's life, these women only appear in wisps and mentions. My research showed this was true in the broader circus narrative, too. By the twentieth century, women were common in circus. The Ringling Brothers and Barnum & Bailey Circus of 1952 featured an armless girl, a variety of lady equestrians, women performing with trained dachshunds, "sixty lovely lissome lassies aloft" in an aerial ballet, trick roller skaters in blue sequined skirts, a "Miniature Lana Turner," a fire dancer, and Muriel Eagle, allegedly the "World's Smallest Woman."[3] By then, the phrase "circus woman" meant something, calling to mind some mix of the girl next door, a pinup, an Olympic athlete, and a daredevil.

But in 1879, there were neither so many women in the circus nor as many roles for them to fill. A circus ad that year advertised "twelve lady riders" alongside a "twenty-foot Giraffe in Harness," implying that each was as much an uncommon curiosity as the other.[4] Somewhere in the wide-ranging history of the circus, women went from being rare birds to full participants in circus life. This change would not have been possible if not for a few strange and intrepid ladies who were willing to go first and blaze a trail. How did circus women find their way from obscurity to spangled archetype? I was not sure.

And then I learned about Patty Astley.

ooooo

The summer of 1772 was dry and warm in London. On any given evening, people out for a pleasant warm-weather walk followed the whistle of the fife, the thud of hoofbeats and drum—not to mention the unmistakable wafting aroma of a stable—to Philip Astley's Riding School, an open-air structure on the eastern side of the Thames near Westminster Bridge. By day, the venue was indeed a school: Philip Astley, a cabinetmaker's son and veteran of the Seven Years' War, was a gifted horseman who ran a sort of "driver's education" program for everyday riders, teaching them to ride capably and avoid accidents on horseback. For military clients, he was just the man to ensure war horses were reliably trained to ignore the sounds of gunfire or to lie down on command. After the day's schedule of riding lessons, Astley would put on his military uniform and blow off steam by performing stunts in the yard for passersby, galloping around the ring on his white horse, Gibraltar. Word spread, crowds grew, and the riding school became an honest-to-goodness theatrical destination known as "Astley's Amphitheatre."

The school was a modest, white-washed building with covered seating and a broad outdoor riding ring, and for a few coins in admission price, spectators were invited to watch grand evening displays of trick riding, acrobatics, and comedy. On a warm summer night, spectators eagerly came to see Astley and his riders stand on their heads in the saddle, balance with one foot on each of a pair of galloping horses, and swing from their seats to pluck tiny handkerchiefs and coins from the dusty ground.[5] Astley added theatrical entertainers like clowns and acrobats to fill in the gaps between acts and featured an absolutely charming trained pony named Billy who could count, play dead, and fire a pistol. To give audience members good sight lines onto the action, he placed performances within a ring, settling on a circle forty-two feet in diameter to allow riders to benefit from centrifugal forces as they leapt and tumbled on horseback. With such wondrous displays of horsemanship, spectacle, and comedy, the show was a fantastic night out. It appealed to high society as much as everyday Londoners.

Astley was a natural performer and a relentless advertiser. He would stand on Westminster Bridge as crowds walked past, posing cocksure in his handsome red uniform and handing out playbills to anyone whose eyes lingered long enough. This tactic had even drawn the attention of King George III, who passed by in his carriage one day and promptly arranged for a private performance. "Amphi-Philip" Astley would go on to open more than a dozen theaters throughout Europe. Due to his innovations in structure and performance, Astley is known today as the "father of the modern circus."

But Philip Astley was not a single parent. The London press, advertising Astley's summer lineup, in fact gave top billing to a different member of the family: his wife, Patty. In 1768, when Astley's Riding School was in its infancy, advertisements described the dazzling athleticism of Patty's act: In addition to doing handstands on a moving horse and executing military riding maneuvers, Mrs. Astley would stand across a pair of racing horses with one foot on each bobbing saddle. She would then guide the animals over jumps at full speed and triumphantly fire a pistol into the air. Crowds adored her, and so did Mr. Astley. After walking Gibraltar through an elegant routine, he would end the show with a booming shout: "When you have seen all my bill exprest, My wife, to conclude, performs the rest."[6]

Nor did she limit herself to maneuvers from the standard equestrian repertoire. Patty Astley jumped on the back of a horse "with a Swarm of Bees in the following Manner: Mrs. Astley with a Swarm on her Arm, imitating a Lady's Muff."[7] Working with beekeeper Daniel Wildman, Patty had learned how to wear a swarm of bees as an accessory and walk away unharmed. When she was done, she would command the insects to march across a tabletop, at which point the bees would reassemble themselves on Mr. Wildman's head in the fashion of a wig.[8] When the bees returned to their hive, Mrs. Astley would delight audiences with stunt riding every bit as impressive as her husband's—sometimes with her five-year-old son, John, joining her in the saddle. Though the historical record predominantly describes the men who were involved in the circus's early days, women were

Patty Astley on horseback (center, top row), sword held aloft.
Astley Amphitheatre scrapbooks, volume 1. Image courtesy of the Kenneth Spencer Research Library at the University of Kansas.

indeed there from the beginning. The strange and dazzling public performance of an eighteenth-century working mother, along with a few thousand buzzing assistants, is part of the foundation of the modern circus.

Patty Astley's act was astounding and confusing for a variety of reasons. During her era, women occupied a variety of roles and relationships, to be sure, but there was a general assumption that women were naturally subordinate to men and best suited for a safe and well-appointed domestic life. If you asked a traditional English gentleman, there was no reason to expose women to matters of politics, learning, or public authority. Mary Wollstonecraft, in the pages of her 1792 book *Vindication of the Rights of Woman*, raged that "this is the condition in which one-half of the human race should be encouraged to remain with listless inactivity and stupid acquiescence?"[9] So for Patty Astley to have a visible public occupation at all was unusual for a woman of her time, to say nothing of the incredible nature of her performances.

As the Astleys' visibility increased (and as competitors, including other female riders, emerged to seek a share of the audience), Patty continued to delight audiences and the press with her talent and discipline. She was advertised as "the only one of her sex that ever had that honour" of performing for royalty, and journalists concluded that she was only getting better with time: "We hear she was much admired when exhibited before her Majesties last summer," wrote one reporter, "but now she is greatly improved in several feats of her horsemanship."[10]

Astley's troupe continued to perform, staging grand variety shows throughout the constellation of Astley amphitheaters in England, Ireland, and on the European continent. Amid all this activity, Patty Astley's printed narrative starts to fade. It is at this point that, as her biographer Vanessa Toulmin writes, "the memory of her early performances and the role she played with her husband vanishes from the public consciousness and then from the historical narratives." Toulmin, an English scholar with an entertainment family pedigree, sees Astley as an important figure to be "deliberately reintroduced into the text as part of a reshaping of the originating narrative of circus."[11] It is not an easy task: At best, the record often shows Patty described simply as "the wife of Philip" or "the mother of John," making it difficult to fully document her life. Numerous sources converge on the fact that she likely died in her sixties in 1803, but further detail is difficult to gather.

If we remember Philip Astley as the father of the circus, then Patty Astley should be considered its mother. A skilled rider, a charismatic performer, and a surprisingly modern working parent, she lived an unconventional life at a time when no one would have envisioned or desired it for a woman. By doing this, she paved the way for generations of performing women to come. While carrying an armload of bees.

ooooo

In part because they sat outside typical social structures, fields like circus, sideshow, magic, and stunt performance were more open to nineteenth-century women than other vocations. This is not to say it was an easy road or that anyone was especially welcoming right away. The circus may have sat outside the norm, but it wasn't immune to social realities. Early circus women were doing more than just performing a tightrope act or a magic trick when they stepped into the spotlight in the early years of commercialized entertainment: They were challenging long-held ideas of feminine ability and propriety. And though women may have been celebrated by circus posters and fans, progress and integration were slow going. In *The Circus Age*, her pivotal study of the American circus at its height, historian Janet M. Davis explains that "the circus's celebration of diversity was often illusionary, because the circus used normative ideologies of gender, racial hierarchy, and individual mobility to explain social transformations and human difference."[12] A woman looking at a life in the circus could not expect an easy road, but there was at least the opportunity to try something new and freeing. It was one thing for proper society to tell a woman that she could not become a doctor or an actuary; in that case, there was social machinery that could actually bar the doors to entry. Under the circus tent, though, it was far harder to tell a woman what she could not do. You could offer, for a start, that she couldn't wire walk across Niagara Falls, but it would have been very hard for her to hear you over all that rushing water.

Whether they chose the spotlight or found themselves pushed into it, performing women in the long nineteenth century walked an unusual path through the thickets of social expectation. To do something curious, absurd, or groundbreaking—and to make a living in the process—was to cast aside business as usual, which had both benefits and consequences. Women like Maria Spelterini, who took that famous high-wire stroll over Niagara, knew that the bar was set doubly high, and perfection was the fee they paid for bucking the rules. Others simply figured that they would take advantage of an audience calibrated to underestimate them and do anything a man could do, better. This was the case for performers like Lulu Hurst, stronger than a volleyball team's worth of Victorian gentlemen, and Aimee Austin, a ceiling walker known as the "Human Fly."

Matters of appearance were equally complicated. Finding success required women to be extraordinary but relatable, alluring but appropriate, thrilling but also unthreatening all at once. Sideshow performers, riders, strongwomen, and aerialists in the 1800s often showed off their bodies in ways that were unconventional or even scandalous outside the venue, courting both awe and disapproval. When athletic female performers used their highly trained bodies to show off impressive skill—as when the strongwoman Charmion removed her Victorian dress to perform a sporty trapeze routine for Thomas Edison's camera—they were often accused of being unseemly, unladylike, or little better than prostitutes.

The rise and widespread adoption of mass media in the nineteenth century both helped and hindered circus women. On the one hand, the opportunity for increased publicity helped these women grow and lengthen their careers. It is because of mass media that we know about them today. But the same media that elevated remarkable performers could be used to cut them down, particularly if they undercut gendered expectations about ability, strength, modesty, status, race, and speech. An unnamed male circus executive, speaking to reporters in 1905, wanted a few things noted on the record about ladies in (or aspiring to) the business. Women "are comparatively few in number," he commented, and, if not born to a circus family, wouldn't be hired unless "accompanied by some male relative." Second, "dissipation"—promiscuous behavior or alcohol use—"is an impossibility among circus women." And anyway, he said, "Circus women are most devoted wives and mothers, who take life seriously and soberly," who "appreciate and enjoy the comforts and blessings of a home."[13] Whether it was true or not, making audiences believe that they loved darning socks in their spare time was often the price of flight for circus women.

It's important to note that not every woman performed by choice or under her own terms. For nonwhite and disabled performers, whose bodies were too often treated as commodities, the circus could legitimize gawking. The narratives put out by circus press and marketing often expressly tried to confirm audience biases. While the Swiss bearded lady Madame Clofullia was considered a curiosity fit for high society, Julia Pastrana, a hirsute woman of Mexican Indigenous descent, was pathologized and billed as a "bear woman" or a "baboon." Miss La La, a mixed-race "iron jaw" performer immortalized in a painting by Edgar Degas, was a skilled aerialist but was most often marketed with respect to her skin color.

This is a book about the often-forgotten women of the circus who changed entertainment and inspired others to be their authentic selves. These women—conjurers, aerialists, sideshow marvels, wire walkers, queens, and beauties from all walks of life—used circus to break gender stereotypes and revolutionize show business. These performers rejected popular attitudes about femininity, defied traditional rules about clothing and body image, and pushed at the bounds of possibility and expectation in their acts. It's tempting to think that today's performers who play with gender identity and expression are walking through unexplored territory, but the present moment is a flowering of seeds that were planted long ago by many different pioneers. By choice or by force, women who engaged in peculiar entertainments during the 1800s grasped the collective attention for a brief window of profitability and fame, and over time, they normalized the idea of a performing career for generations of women to come. Whether or not it was their intention, women and gender-expansive performers in the nineteenth-century American circus helped to challenge, shape, and expand the possibilities for what women and, by extension, all people, could do. The stories in this book illuminate the lives and contributions of what the sleight-of-hand artist and historian Ricky Jay called "curious characters"; performers whose lives and art sat within the liminal outside but nonetheless commented on society's vast center.[14]

Their legacies still echo today, and they still call us to ask: What does it mean for a woman to stand out?

ooooo

When researching the lives and accomplishments of performing women, it's clear that the historical record is incomplete. When it comes time to write things down or to save them for future generations, the voices of marginalized groups—women, queer folks, people with disabilities, racial minorities—have not historically been prioritized. Public discourse "has always included the power to ignore, trivialize, and indifferently destroy the evidence of lives deemed not worth preserving for the future."[15] Primary sources in a subject's own voice or contemporary to their time are often scarce, and secondary commentary does not always accurately relate an individual's achievements, identity, or thoughts. And since primary sources are limited, in researching this book I have often had to rely disproportionately on male voices to frame women's stories. Acknowledging these constraints, my goal is to understand as much as I can and to talk *with* historic women, not *for* them. My aim is to expand the narrative of the historic circus and to examine the social structures and power dynamics that have historically molded women's stories.

Even though the women in this book largely lived and worked within the nineteenth century, a spillover in both directions is necessary and worthwhile. It's rarely easy to talk neatly about a historical century. Trends and social movements do not pay attention to strict timelines and round numbers. The late 1700s provided important kindling for the circus century to come, and it's hard to talk about the golden age of the American tented circus without considering how it would influence and interact with coming attractions in vaudeville, cinema, theater, and other arts. The scope of this book will be what historians call the "long nineteenth century," which is generally agreed to run roughly from the French Revolution in 1789 to the start of World War I in 1914. The American long nineteenth century sits like a gangly, eager adolescent between the analog history of entertainment and a modern era in which the lines between life and content creation seem to get blurrier with every passing day. For precisely this reason, it is a fascinating period of mass-media experimentation and social self-definition.

Since the body is the first and foremost tool of circus, this project involves looking at the human body in an open and expansive way. Depending on who you are and how you grew up, any number of social expectations may factor into your idea of what makes a body typical or attractive. For most of American history, individuals have been peppered with messaging about how to align their physical self to popular ideas of propriety, fashion, sex appeal, size, shape, athleticism, skin color, or decoration. Society is typically eager not only to categorize people but to value some categories more than others. The problem with this approach is that, as Audre Lorde said, "we do not develop tools for using human difference as a springboard for creative change within our lives. We speak not of human difference but of human deviance."[16] Though social, political, and media structures work to tell us that there is a clear and attainable "good" or "normal" body type, the human body in its infinite diversity suggests that the only consistent trait is variety. Difference and (dis)ability are therefore best understood on a continuum of embodied individual experience in appropriate personal, social, and historical context. This approach avoids value judgment, treating human bodies as "the 'same only different' from every other," in the lovely words of disability scholar Chris Mounsey.[17] Circus presents variable humanity, which spectators can experience either as a matter of curiosity and expansion or of fear and insularity. The first option not only seems more fun, but it invites broader thinking.

The unusual nature of circus performances and circus people invites not only escape but investigation. In the words of Rosemarie Garland-Thomson, "Triggered by the sight of someone who seems

Group of American Museum performers, including Circassian women Zalumma Agra and Zuruby Hannum, little person Lizzie Reid, and "fat lady" Hannah Battersby.
Image courtesy of the Beinecke Rare Book and Manuscript Library at Yale University.

unlike us, staring can begin an exploratory expedition into ourselves and outward into new worlds."[18] In the long nineteenth century, the circus tent was a fluid space in which different manifestations of gender were alternately both exploited and encouraged. Social inversion and behavior that would otherwise be considered socially questionable were briefly permitted within the realm of show business, allowing audience members to see things that fell outside the norm and contemplate whether similarly extraordinary things might exist within themselves. At the circus, bearded ladies, strongwomen, leggy chorus girls, and bareback riders in drag were all celebrated under one canvas ceiling. We cannot know the full truth and experience of these performers' identities and personal expression based on the historical record, but their careers challenged mainstream perceptions and expectations of the feminine body. Each of them asked, through visual presentation and kinetic performance: What can a body do? Who is it for? Whose gaze does it invite? Who, in the end, says what is feminine?

Language deserves a moment of attention, too. In this book, I frequently use the word "women," and I intend it to include people we would today understand to be cisgender women, transgender women, and drag performers when performing in a female persona. Terminology we use today within and about the LGBTQ+ community was not used in nineteenth-century America, even though LGBTQ+ people of course existed. It is still possible to invoke the idea of queerness to talk about individuals who, as writer Wendy Rouse says, "challenged gender and sexual norms in their everyday lives and, if they were alive today, might identify as LGBTQ+."[19]

Primary sources about the historical circus often contain offensive or distasteful language. To remove this language from the record would be to imply that it was not used, and that potentially harms marginalized people through erasure. Rather than censoring or removing any such language, I will contextualize it or place it in quotations.

As for circus itself, the term is very often used to refer to a core set of performing arts that comprise the traditional global discipline—things like acrobatics and aerialist acts, equestrian performances, clowning, juggling, and object manipulation. In this book, I use the word "circus" as a broader umbrella concept, encompassing not only that established body of arts but many of its natural cousins in the related universe of allied arts and entertainments, including magic, sideshow, animal acts, and stunt work. They are natural bedfellows and undeniably part of the same concept and experience. This book is not a history of the circus itself, nor is it completist as to the many shows, acts, and individuals who performed in the United States over the long nineteenth century.

There have always been women in the performing arts. However, due to contemporary values and social attitudes or simply the hungry march of time, many have been underdocumented or their stories have simply been lost to recorded history. Even the incredible Patty Astley might have been forgotten if not for one scholar's dedication. The long nineteenth century is special in that it was the first time when women seized center-stage positions in entertainment with significant frequency. Established theatrical traditions had a history of including women, though much less than men and usually only in nameless archetypical roles. As the authors of *The Great Parade* said about sixteenth-century troupes in commedia dell'arte, "Unlike the men's roles, these were not really stock characters. All that was required was to be pretty and have a lovely voice."[20]

To understand the women in this book, who were far more than just looks and a voice, it will help to understand more about American media culture, circus, and gender roles in the long nineteenth century.

CHAPTER 1

Media and Sources in an Era of Connection

During the long nineteenth century, America grew from a colonial upstart into a global power with political, commercial, and cultural influence. And though products of popular culture may seem frivolous or unimportant, during a century of massive development, they offer a perfect lens through which to view how Americans experienced their changing nation. There are few better indicators of where a society is headed than where folks are eager to spend their free time and pocket money. American recreation during the 1800s featured themes of fraud, deception, individual rights, diversity, and the centuries-long, uniquely American dance between belief and truth. As America grew in population, size, diversity, and innovation during the 1800s, the nation was increasingly connected and shared more common experience. Society changed rapidly and irrevocably as a result, and forms of amusement like the circus followed suit.

The women in this book lived through a period of fast-moving change in American culture during which an increasingly large and diverse population had more income, more options, and increased opportunity for shared entertainment experience. When P. T. Barnum was born in 1810, many of the founding fathers were still alive, and his native state of Connecticut was hanging on to state-sponsored

Puritan religion like an itchy security blanket. When he died in 1891, the global, industrialist Gilded Age was in full swing, and America was a sneeze away from inventing cars and wireless radio. In the middle was a brash, often ham-fisted era of individualism in which entertainers—especially circuses—acted as laboratories of individuality, exploration, delight, and manipulation. The historical and social context of this fast-moving century and its technological changes is critical to understanding the women in this book and the shows in which they performed.

GROWTH AND CONNECTION

The long nineteenth century was a period of massive growth in America, and that began with the literal population count.[1] The 1790 federal census was undertaken by Constitutional mandate to figure out how taxes and House representation would work in the new nation, and it recorded about 3.9 million people. By 1920, thanks to changes in birth and death rates, massive immigration, and natural population growth, that figure was over 106 million and included far greater racial and ethnic diversity. America rapidly expanded its physical footprint over the century, too, beginning with Thomas Jefferson's Constitution-stretching approval of the half-billion-acre Louisiana Purchase in 1803. President James Monroe further stoked the nation's territorial appetite during his 1823 annual message to Congress when he made clear that, if anyone was going to undertake colonialist activity in the Western Hemisphere, it would be the United States; other nations need not apply.[2] Advocates of "manifest destiny" used their belief in inevitable American control of the North American continent to justify relentless westward expansion.[3] They were aided not only by the massive expansion of American territory but also the industrial technologies to enable its exploration and submission. Seeking opportunity, land, destiny, material resources, and more—"great and terrible things" alike—half a million Americans went westward to see what could be done on the frontier.[4]

Industrialization also dramatically altered the nation during the 1800s. Into the Civil War years and beyond, the rapid growth

May Lillie with gun aimed at camera.
Photograph by Frederick Whitman Glasier.
Image courtesy of the Tibbals Learning Center and Circus Museum
at the John and Mable Ringling Museum of Art.

of technology and industry changed the face of work and the labor force, stratifying Americans into a working class, a middle class, and a wealthy elite. It also altered the physical landscape: As more and more workers moved to cities for factory jobs, demands on infrastructure increased. This raised obvious challenges around public health, sanitation, crowding, and overdevelopment. Infrastructure had to try to keep pace with rapid national growth, no small task since, even into the 1830s, most Americans were accustomed to a largely agrarian and analog society. There was no electric light, no rail or long-range telegraph, no telephones or typewriters, no photography or affordable sewing machines. Americans rose and went to bed with the sun, worked and lived with the assistance of candles and analog machinery, and communicated at the pace of gossip and horse traffic. All of that started to change in the mid-1800s, and fast.[5]

American expansion and development opened a 2,000-mile swath of wide West to settlement and connected it more effectively with the populated East. Before the 1860s, people would spend six months or more on bumpy wagons to cross the nation, waited weeks or months for news to trickle from state to state, and relied on artists to draw an image if something was newsworthy. By the end of the Civil War, commercial telegraph could send a message cross-country in a flash. Any number of eager freight and mail delivery companies would carry letters or business stock wherever they needed to go, quickly. (Some of our largest modern financial institutions trace their lineage back to this time and industry. Messrs. Henry Wells, William Fargo, and John Butterfield founded American Express in 1850 as a shipping courier for the eastern United States. When AmEx balked at the idea of expanding westward into California, William and Henry forged ahead anyway and formed Wells Fargo & Co.) The Railroad Act of 1862 drove postwar American rail construction, with the transcontinental railroad linking up at Promontory, Utah, for coast-to-coast service on May 10, 1869. Frontier expansionists, gold rushers, businessmen, the postal service, the military, and political stakeholders all had reasons to cheer for a railroad connecting the Mississippi River with the Pacific West. Afterwards, people and messages could go nearly anywhere in the nation in a matter of mere days.

Innovations in printing and rising literacy rates meant that, from 1790 to 1840, the number of newspapers per capita in America increased ninefold.[6] Daguerreotype photography was invented in 1839, allowing images of real life to be frozen in time. Commentators raved that it was "as great a step in the fine arts as that of the steam-engine in the mechanical arts."[7] Businesses jumped on each innovation as an opportunity to increase their reach, efficiency, and profits.

Early pioneers of mass entertainment culture were aided by the rise of the so-called "penny press," a raft of cheap sensational papers that took America by storm in the run-up to the Civil War. Taking advantage of massive urban population growth, increasing literacy, and low-cost newsprint, publishers and pundits gleefully printed a cavalcade of snappy headlines about crime, politics, and entertainment with little regard for partisanship or fact-checking. These journalists were playing with a new form and needed to meet daily deadlines, which meant they very often resorted to (or gladly covered) gossip, hoaxes, and winking tricks known as "humbugs" in these new daily papers. This dissident spirit could be seen as playful or reckless, depending on who you asked and whether the shenanigans bore any consequences. Either way, the antiauthoritarian humbug was emblematic of America's cultural growing pains in the dynamic nineteenth century.

All this transformation meant that America started to seem both more sprawling and smaller at the same time. Everything was becoming connected—vast swaths of land, people, goods, money, opinions, images, and news. In addition to being geopolitically important, all of this was new grist for the entertainment mill. For the first time in American history, after all, consumers had choices. When people's purchases don't have to be based solely on availability and utilitarian need, they can instead gratify something itchier and more thrilling. A specific nineteenth-century combination of circumstances empowered entertainers and marketers in new and special ways. Rising literacy rates and an increase in media outlets made it easier to spread a message. Transportation developments meant that entertainment could go beyond urban centers. Young America's engagement with democracy and individualism not only fostered the growth of celebrity culture but also created audiences who were increasingly eager to engage with their culture. With increased population and a growing middle class, people had more money and free time to spend it. All of this together grew the entertainment industry, with promoters, performers, audiences, and media critics powering a new and endless loop of common experience like a waterwheel. American mass-media pop culture was being born. (What separates popular culture from plain old recreation? In the words of entertainment historian LeRoy Ashby, it's the ticket price: "Its creators and/or disseminators seek to profit from it; they are in the business of merchandising entertainment."[8])

Approaching mid-century, the commercial theater emerged as a midway point between white-glove opera houses and the seedy places in which no respectable man, woman, or child would be caught dead. In the stereotypical public theater of the era, the infamous "third tier" was reserved for prostitutes—often with its own discreet side entrance—and performances were commonly raucous, even violent. Audiences might shout and applaud if they liked a show and routinely tossed eggs or vegetables if it didn't meet with their approval. (Not only was boozing and prostitution a risk at lower-class joints, but at one Shakespearean performance in 1840s Cincinnati, the audience tossed half a dead sheep onstage in displeasure.[9])

Celebrity culture expanded the idea of fame beyond a precious few figures in the arts or politics. No longer did a person need to be remarkable and dead to ascend to a secondary personality in the public consciousness. Aided by media and culture, figures could cultivate and grow their reputation while still living, speak to their audiences' needs and whims, and encourage parasocial relationships. Some stars, like Oscar Wilde or Mark Twain, relished their roles as tastemakers and "intimate strangers"[10] for the public. Others, perhaps, less so: The nineteenth-century poet Henry Wadsworth Longfellow grew such a devoted fandom that he received more than six thousand fan letters over his life and had to turn a woman away from his doorstep when she turned up, luggage in hand, claiming to be his destined wife.

There was more still. The mid-1800s birthed grand department stores, with the logic that a clean, well-curated festival of fun and products under one roof was not only enticing but would be a safe and respectable place for women to spend their time and discretionary income unattended by men. Photographic technology evolved beyond the fiddly daguerreotype mid-century. This enabled mass production of both realistic portraits and fantastic imagery. On the one hand, this gave the nation a common understanding of the unfolding Civil War in a way never before experienced. On the other, it meant people could collect, collage, and fawn over photos of their family, friends, and famous crushes. All these technologies and innovations allowed creators to make—and audiences to experience and discuss—a different reality than the everyday. Audiences now demanded far more from their entertainments than watching a horse jump, however skillfully done.

AMERICAN INDIVIDUALISM

As the United States moved from colonial experiment into the work of nation-building, it grew in size, diversity, and social complexity. But not everyone was happy with these changes. As far as many everyday Americans were concerned, they had fought for a free country, and that involved the right and duty to do largely as they pleased with minimal interference from government or elite authority. As a result, a certain noisy individualism emerged in religion, science, and the arts in the first half of the century. Jacksonian Democracy elevated the sovereign rights of the (white, male, vocal) common man: rights to land, equality, and a government that didn't get too nosy about one's business.

The religious revival known as the Second Great Awakening encouraged and amplified new prophetic voices of spiritual authority outside traditional Protestant structures. Revivalism enabled charismatic leaders to start communities including the Latter Day Saints, the Shakers, the polyamorous Oneida cult, and William Miller's "Millerites," who were absolutely certain the end times would kick off on October 22, 1844.[11] In antebellum America, even art and culture were increasingly seen as matters for active referendum: The 1849 Astor Place Riot in New York was tipped off by angry populist toughs who preferred an American Shakespearean actor over his traditionalist British counterpart. Ralph Waldo Emerson rhapsodized about the peace to be found only in self-reliance. With the nation "brutally, madly, perplexingly split" through the century over what freedom and integrity meant in a nation scarred by enslavement, it makes sense that people would look to themselves rather than to fragile or fractious institutions.[12]

The concept of scientific knowledge also seemed up for redefinition in this individualist era. Throughout the century, amateur researchers and true believers engaged with aspiring sciences like mesmerism, electrobiology, spiritualism, and phrenology, arguing for them as evidence-based disciplines.[13] Since America was a young nation without long-established academic structures, everyday people felt as entitled to be a part of scientific and intellectual inquiry as the so-called professionals. One newspaper in 1842 declared: "People nowadays, when a new and startling theory is brought up, do not wait for the wise men and the doctors to analyze and investigate it, before they can venture an opinion on its merits or demerits; but they take up the subject at once for themselves; they reason it over in their own mind, and discuss it among their neighbors."[14]

HOAX AND HUMBUG

Few people loved the nascent mass media as much as Phineas Taylor Barnum, who credited his success to "a persistent, liberal, and judicious use of printer's ink."[15] Certainly no one did as much as he to advance the concept of American popular entertainment. Though Barnum is perhaps best known today for the circus that still bears his name, he initially rose to fame on the success of his American Museum in New York. The museum opened under Barnum's name in 1842, and under his management, it became the nation's center of popular entertainment. One biographer estimates that Barnum's first American Museum "sold more tickets in proportion to the population than did Disneyland during its first 23 and a half years in operation."[16] Barnum understood better than most that, as the public's attention span shrank, keeping his name and his offerings in the budding American media would be the key to fame and success.

Humbugs and hoaxes were a way to play out the era's broader American dialogue about populism, individualism, and agency. They were also often responsible for confusing or terrifying readers who weren't used to being skeptical where the news was concerned. Some people indeed believed what they read in the papers: Had scientists discovered unicorn goats and bat-men on the moon in 1859, or was it early science fiction? Did P. T. Barnum really show off a buxom mermaid at the American Museum in 1842, or was the "Fejee Mermaid" a monkey-fish taxidermy hybrid? Was "What Is It?" a missing link between men and apes, or a Black man in a coarse suit put onstage to embody the national tension over evolution, race, slavery, and citizenship?[17] The truth did not stop people from arguing over their belief in the possibilities.

Barnum was a virtuoso of humbug. He was careful to suggest much and guarantee little, leaving his audiences to draw the conclusions that best suited their whims and deductive reasoning, an exchange which Barnum scholar Neil Harris elegantly labeled the "operational aesthetic" and which Barnum himself less elegantly summarized by saying that "persons who pay their money at the door have a right to form their own opinions after they have got upstairs."[18] Barnum himself loved a humbug and openly insisted that the public not only enjoyed the ongoing dance between showman and customer but craved it. The people, he said, *want* to be hoodwinked. It was important, though, to do no harm: For all his reputation as a huckster, Barnum considered outright fraud extremely distasteful and promised he would deliver more than enough edification and enjoyment to take the sting out of a harmless joke.[19] Any magician can tell you about the radical honesty at the heart of what are usually called arts of deception: Very simply, you get up in front of people, tell them you're going to fool them, and then you do it. Bonus points if they then gladly pay to come back and learn how the game is played.

The historian Warren Susman describes this attitude as a national shift from a culture of character to a culture of personality. Where a culture of character is quiet and self-effacing, focused on how an individual can contribute to moral and social order, the culture of personality is a hungry extrovert. This sort of society, Susman argues, values "items that could be best developed in leisure time and that represented in themselves an emphasis on consumption. The social role demanded of all in the new culture of personality was that of a performer. Every American was to become a performing self."[20]

READING CIRCUS IN A WINKING ERA

This performance-focused culture, newly connected by a web of infrastructure and mass media, presented a new opportunity to tell stories. As it increased in size and connection, nineteenth-century America embraced mythmaking. Horatio Alger stories dangled before readers the possibility of a self-made rags-to-riches transformation, Washington Irving playfully rewrote New York history in the fictitious persona Diedrich Knickerbocker, and any number of pulpy fictions glorified the adventure of white American settler culture.[21] In an era of increasing media and connection, people wanted not just news and rhetoric but something that stoked the imagination, too. Even better if these stories could be written quickly and shared widely.

The circus took advantage of this hunger for story and reinvention, writing exciting origin stories for the performers who would sweep into town once a year in a flurry of spangles and sawdust. Certain tropes emerged: This performer was alleged to be an aristocrat or a foreign princess of noble birth; that one an exotic representative of a dying culture. The giantess, why, she was a walking tall tale and came from a town just like your own. Captivity narratives were common, particularly among tattooed performers who swore up and down that their body art was the result of torturous corporal punishment in a savage land.[22] Performers had their pick of wild and conveniently unverifiable stories, choosing a new name and background to suit (and help cultivate) the immersive mystery of the big top. These stories, contrived in private and touted in public, were designed to be enticing to audiences.

Performers of all types and talents often sold souvenirs to supplement their income, from small carte-de-visite photographs to biographical pamphlets, and while images and written narratives can tell us a lot about a given performer, they were generally produced by or in cooperation with press agents and, in many cases, may have been paid for by showmen. This reflects a complicated relationship between story, reality, and advertising. Likewise, newspaper reporters were not always as concerned with veracity as with selling papers, and early syndication practices could result in a giant newspaper-led game of Telephone. In theory, they were reporting the news and factually describing people and events. In reality, they could be filling column inches on a slow day or misreporting something they had heard thirdhand.

By the late nineteenth century, the largest of the big circuses employed entire public relations teams. Dedicated advertising staff in their own train cars would handle advance distribution of photographs, posters, signage, media releases, and other promotional materials before the circus came to town. Bill-posters might hang as many as ten thousand circus posters in a day, sticking them with flour paste on any available surface from store windows to sheds, fences, and billboards. Like A-list rappers today, major circus impresarios would duke it out in the local and national press, crowing about their superior offerings and trashing their competitors in public ads called "rat sheets." Sometimes honestly fought and other times contrived, a good public tussle had the benefit of boosting both parties' businesses.

Surviving sources of circus-related information include playbills, pamphlets, and photographs; grand color lithographs created to stoke excitement in quiet towns; scrapbooks full of yellowed news clippings. Most of these materials were produced with an ear to the clink of cold, hard cash rather than any sense of truth or eye toward posterity. And since much of it was intended just as ephemera for promotion or sale, only some of these materials have survived. What this means for researchers and readers is that circus history must be approached with skepticism and a very malleable Barnumesque sense of truth.

Nineteenth-century media culture took an explosively growing nation, plugged it into a wall outlet, soaked it in ink and speculation, and told every person they were invited to poke around inside the social clockworks. This was the environment in which circus became America's dominant form of entertainment. This level of social electricity and national egotism, combined with the natural propensity of the circus to stretch reality for its patrons' delight, means one thing for sure: Circus history is a slippery discipline. It is a field in which sources must earn your trust. In the archive, details are suggestive but not always definitive. There are almost always credibility questions. Even something like private correspondence cannot always be taken at face value in the realm of the nineteenth-century circus—after all, in the age of humbug, what circus impresario could pass up a good press leak or a tall tale deployed as a publicity strategy?

The rise of mass media in the long nineteenth century turbocharged a new American popular culture premised on common experience, shiny archetype, and escalating excitement. This was most evident in the way the circus grew from humble beginnings into a dazzling, dominant, uniquely American institution.

CHAPTER 2

Building the Nineteenth-Century Big Top

P art of the charm of the circus is that it seems ageless. Was there ever a time in human history when watching a flying acrobat or a sword swallower wasn't a thrill? It is exhilarating to put aside everyday obligations and watch a motley troupe of energetic humans transcend the idea of rules and limits. Also, the adrenaline rush goes perfectly with a good salty snack.

What we might think of as the rough antecedents of modern circus developed over centuries across the world. The human desire to perform and watch seemingly impossible feats spans time, culture, and geography. History is fairly littered with stories from around the globe of trick riders, puppeteers, jugglers, dancers, unusual people, and apparent sorcery. Two thousand years ago, performers in China during the Han dynasty presented the "hundred entertainments," which involved juggling, pole climbing, acrobatics, and balancing acts. Bronze Age daredevils leaped over charging bulls and left evidence of their feats in grand Minoan frescoes. Even Plato admitted in *The Republic* that he liked a good sleight-of-hand show, that "the art of conjuring and deceiving by light and shadow" has "an effect upon us like magic."[1]

Circus acts may be centuries old, but circus only really became an industry during the long nineteenth century. During this time, circuses combined and built on previous traditions such as fairs, menageries, curiosity culture, theatrical traditions, and equestrian craft, creating a cultural juggernaut that moved from the immoral fringe to mass acceptance in just a few decades. For most of the century, in fact, you couldn't go anywhere in the United States without tripping over a circus, whether it was a one-ring "gilly show" or a giant popcorn wonder belching calliope music for miles.[2] (Not kidding about the calliope, which circus folks pronounce "cal-ee-ope" in defiance of sensible phonics: A steam calliope has no volume control and runs at about a hundred decibels, which is equivalent to standing next to a candy-colored jet engine.)

Though circus historians can and do squabble about where to place the exact tent stakes, there is a rough general agreement that circus came to the Americas in the late eighteenth century and reached its "golden age" from the late nineteenth century into the early twentieth. In colonial America, a circus may have been an itinerant wagon-drawn affair or a small company playing to a few hundred people in a makeshift wooden arena. By World War I, though, almost any American could draw a circus in shorthand: an expansive big top tent, elephants on parade, multicolored posters, dozens of intrepid men and spangled women performing wild and wondrous acts. Circus Day had become a massive and transcendent experience that drew spectators by the thousands and temporarily shut down life, business, and schools in any given town or city.

The circus entered the long nineteenth century as a collection of scrappy, small-scale outfits driven by a few dedicated performers. It was fundamentally an offshoot of the British circus, and most Americans, if they weren't sitting in the bleachers, viewed it as part of the immoral fringe. As the nation developed, though, circus did too, and it acquired a distinctly American identity. Circus is, after all, always a mirror of its time and place. Over the years of the Civil War and through Reconstruction, shows navigated the birth of celebrity culture, underwent a crucial transition to family-friendly entertainment, and grappled with the nation's unavoidable questions of race, class, and patriotism. By the 1870s, the American circus had become as culturally dominant as its country. It entered the twentieth century as an increasingly industrial, capitalist spectacle literally performing American ambition, self-image, and exceptionalism.

Beautiful, bewitching belles in feats of graceful daring.
Image courtesy of the Prints and Photographs Division at the Library of Congress.

To understand the women who performed in the unusual entertainments of the long nineteenth century, it's important to understand where their art came from, how the circus coalesced and grew in the United States over that time, and how national trends both shaped and were shaped by these entertainments.

ANCESTORS AND ANTECEDENTS

American circus amalgamated a handful of disciplines and amusements that were already well established abroad by the dawn of the long nineteenth century. In addition to Astley's model of equestrian display, the circus drew from fairs, menageries, and curiosity culture.

One thread in the woven tapestry of the modern circus emerged from the local fairs that entertained people in the late medieval and early modern periods. Then, as now, fairgrounds offered people a welcome diversion with an irresistible combination of commerce, entertainment, and snack foods. The original meaning of the word "juggle" emerged at this time: From Latin root words meaning "to jest," the term throughout history could refer to any of a handful of itinerant amusements, everything from actually tossing balls in the air to sleight of hand, conjuring, or clowning. Early English-language magic textbooks tell us that fairground entertainers delighted crowds by making a cut rope whole again, or they might separate patrons from their wits or money with a shell-game trick.[3] Comedians and clowns were popular on the fairground, as were mountebanks hawking various tonics with magic tricks and elaborate spiels. Giants, people with dwarfism, and individuals with unusual bodies or talents also often displayed themselves as part of fairs or festivals. Their remarkable performances invited the public to enter a space outside of daily life, a space informed by wonder and the continuing cultural fascination with "monstrosity"—that is, any body that deviated from what was perceived as being in line with the natural order.[4]

Exotic animals are another important piece of circus ancestry. Menageries have been documented as symbols of status and wealth for millennia, appearing in royal courts or wealthy estates. But the modern idea of a zoo as a public commercial entity started to emerge in eighteenth-century Europe largely because of developing international trade routes and colonialist intervention in the non-Western world. With an increased supply of exotic animals and demand on the rise, promoters were all too happy to open previously private menagerie gates to the broader public. In the late 1700s, the impresario Gilbert Pidcock was an example of this new sort of promoter. Pidcock exhibited a variety of animals at the Exeter Exchange in London, calling spectators to marvel at a rhinoceros, a cockatoo, an honest-to-goodness elephant, and even a two-headed cow. For a public used to seeing rock doves and river eels, this was a revelation. Around the same time, the Jardin des Plantes in Paris opened its zoo menagerie, and the Schönbrunn Zoo in Vienna received an elephant. The United States welcomed its first pachyderms as traveling curiosities not long after, and a Yankee entrepreneur named Hachaliah Bailey toured an elephant known as "Old Bet" around New England from a base in Somers, New York.[5] Encounters with live animals like these continued to draw slack-jawed wonder from patrons, leading the *New York Times* to remark in 1862 that "nothing creates so great an interest as a zoological collection."[6]

   Curiosity culture is also woven into the development of the circus. "Curiosity" can refer to either an object or something one exercises, and both concepts are relevant to entertainments that deal in wonder, novelty, danger, or aspiration. In the poetic words of scholar Barbara Benedict, curiosity is a means of "seeing your way out of your place. It is looking beyond."[7] In the early modern era "cabinets of curiosity"—literally, glassed-in boxes or entire rooms full of unusual bits and bobs—served exactly this purpose. These cabinets were common among wealthy and educated individuals who wanted to display the world's wonders in artful microcosm for friends or patrons. A typical cabinet might be crowded with bones, furs, and feathers; studded with shells or minerals; giving a place of honor to scientific instruments, art, and antiquities; or even housing allegedly magical or alchemical artifacts. The display was intended to telegraph the owner's knowledge and cultivate a sense of awe at the breadth of creation (in German, it was a "wunderkammer," a chamber of wonders). Collecting artifacts and positioning them in an unusual decorative space could be considered a very early form of social media, a controlled way to make sense of the world and one's place in it.

In the eighteenth and early nineteenth centuries, America lacked the wealthy patrons, strong scientific community, and high-quality artifacts that sustained European galleries. As a result, collectors realized private salons were not enough: They would need to sell tickets to sustain themselves. And to keep the doors open and bring in repeat visitors, the cabinet itself would need to grow. Artist Charles Willson Peale opened America's first natural history museum in 1786 in Philadelphia and later expanded to Baltimore and New York with the cooperation of his sons Rubens and Rembrandt (two of the *seventeen* children Peale named after favorite artists and scientific figures). Aware that a solid box office did more for ongoing business than scientific integrity, over time the younger Peales added public entertainments to the cabinet-style exhibits that father Charles had frankly preferred. These included popular lectures, oddities, one-man bands, and demonstrations of new technology.[8]

Though they were undeniably in it for the ticket revenue, promoters emphasized the edifying nature of their work. In 1812, the *New-York Evening Post* published an article asserting that many visitors to fairs, theaters, and dime museums were simply looking for a fun distraction from daily life, but shame on them if they, confronted with object lessons "beautiful as nature and valuable as truth," overlooked the opportunity to learn a thing or two. This was particularly true for children, and the *Post* raved that curiosity was an excellent teacher: "A young person can scarcely engage in a more delightful study, or one better calculated to enrich the mind, or to shew the wisdom and goodness of the great Author of the Universe."[9]

EARLY AMERICAN CIRCUS

The American circus is generally agreed to have its beginnings with John Bill Ricketts, an English equestrian who emigrated to Philadelphia in 1792 with the intention of establishing a riding school and circus in Philip Astley's model. Ricketts's circus held its debut performance on April 3, 1793, and was quickly successful among all echelons of society—one Philadelphia paper informed readers that

"The President of the United States and family are to honor the Circus with their company."[10] As Astley had done before him, Ricketts responded to audience demand by adding grander feats and a wider variety of acts, from clowns and dancers to rope-walkers and performing animals. People loved it. The circus was a welcome break from the routines and pressures of daily life.

In the coming decades, Joshua Purdy Brown popularized traveling menageries in America, and in 1825, Brown crucially decided to hold performances under a canvas tent rather than in the wooden theaters and arenas typically associated with British and early American circuses. This innovation released the show from urban centers, making every small town and frontier outpost a potential new audience. Circus historian Stuart Thayer confirms that, by 1830, "the large cities no longer were the exclusive entertainment centers."[11] The canvas tent made the circus a thing of transportation, both literally and figuratively: The show could appear, perform, and move on down the road in a day. In terms of experience, the tent was also valuable. The canvas sidewalls concealed and then welcomed audiences into a space outside reality in which the impossible revealed itself possible and the to-do list waited until tomorrow. In these first decades of the nineteenth century, circus became more flexible, more mobile, and accessible to more people.

By the 1840s, most urban centers had a dime museum, and traveling circuses frequently arrived in far-flung towns to offer a pop-up distraction from everyday life. Historian William Slout estimates that, by 1859, there were between fifteen and eighteen wagon shows in the United States and a handful of others moving by boat or train.[12] Circuses were scrappy, but it was nonetheless a tough business. A bad season—poor ticket sales, problems with horses, nasty weather— could doom a show. Some shows followed Civil War movements in the hope of catering to soldiers on leave, as showman Peter Conklin did in 1862, when he claimed to have made $10,000 in a single day ("all soldiers, blue coats and brass buttons").[13] Others stuck to the cities, since the Union economy was doing decently in the middle 1860s, and, once the initial shock waves of secession and war had dissipated, people were eager to escape reality with some good entertainment.

COURTING RESPECTABILITY

For some people, the distraction of a traveling circus was welcome and exciting—a visual and emotional spectacle. The poet E. E. Cummings described his own heart when the circus came to town: "At the very thought of 'circus,'" he wrote, "a swarm of long-imprisoned desires breaks jail. Armed with beauty and demanding justice and everywhere threatening us with curiosity and Spring and childhood, this mob of forgotten wishes begins to storm the supposedly impregnable fortifications of our Present."[14] For others, the distraction was insidious and far less welcome. In the first half of the nineteenth century, circus had to work hard to shake the idea that it was not fit for decent people.

Political and religious authorities have long sworn that dime museums, fairgrounds, circuses and the like are idle entertainments that trample good manners and civic virtue. Circus has often been criticized as unsavory: immoral, greedy, unnecessarily sexualized, and too likely to encourage the likes of drinking and fights amongst the showgoing public. (Plus, the costumes tend to be skimpy.) Many of the American colonies considered traveling entertainment such bad news for public order that they passed legislation to curb the practice. In the fall of 1774, the Continental Congress passed the Articles of Association to boycott trade with Britain in the wake of the Intolerable Acts (themselves a retaliatory measure after the Boston Tea Party).[15] In an effort to emphasize frugality and good citizenship, the terms specifically urged signatories to avoid "exhibitions of plays, shows and other expensive diversions and entertainments" like circuses. Steady, Puritan Connecticut outlawed "Plays, Tricks, Jugling or unprofitable Feats of uncommon Dexterity and Agility of Body" well into the 1800s.[16] Even as late as 1860, books like *The Circus Girl and Sunday-School Scholar* proclaimed that religious folks "do not go to such places, because their presence there would not be consistent with their duties as Christians."[17]

Though the circus evokes friendly, colorful entertainment to modern audiences, the antebellum American circus was not directed toward children. Kids were certainly welcome to attend—many did, and there was plenty of joy in a glass of lemonade and some first-rate

A circus performer stands on a galloping horse.
Image courtesy of the Prints and Photographs Division at the Library of Congress.

spectacle. However, in these early American decades, the circus was primarily oriented toward an adult audience, with an emphasis on horsemanship, leggy ladies, and political humor.

In these shows, clowns were quick-witted comedians, outsider figures who played a gadfly role versus the ringmaster's "straight man." They regularly lampooned everyday culture, engaging in political satire and telling dirty jokes. Sometimes the punch lines were more working-class dad jokes; one typical circus joke went: "Why is our tent pole like a hundred-dollar bill? Because they are both difficult to get up."[18] (You had to be there.) The adult appeal of the circus was enhanced by the combination of dangerous aerial and equestrian acts, as well as the often-racy costumes. The equestrienne in particular was a routinely sexualized act, performing athletic entertainments on horseback in a manner that virtually invited male spectators to lean in for a glance upskirt: "Officially the pitch was skill, vigor, and beauty: come see our talented performers," writes historian David Carlyon. "However, theatre and circus implicitly invited one to leer at legs."[19]

One of the biggest factors in the dominance of circus in American entertainment culture was its successful transition to family-friendly entertainment. Some of this was thanks to the groundwork laid by dime museums such as P. T. Barnum's American Museum in New York, which eagerly presented an evergreen selection of curiosities, live entertainments, animals, and arts under one roof. Dime museums welcomed patrons of all ages for a low admission price and presented themselves as both respectable and educational. Many, including Barnum's, embraced an anti-alcohol temperance agenda. The dime museum was new and novel precisely because it brought a variety of amusements—a "single, 'walk-through' entertainment, suitable for the entire family"—under one roof.[20] Dime museums provided visitors with an immersive entertainment experience, a cavalcade of attractions aimed to overwhelm, delight, and instruct the viewer all at once. They also assured spectators that the experience would be safe, moral, and educational. Offering an assurance of safety and propriety for respectable families ultimately meant more ticket sales for these dime museums, and circuses took note.

EVERYTHING'S A PERFORMANCE

In the mid-century decades, as Americans adjusted to common experiences of public and political events, the lines between life and entertainment began to blur. In years prior, the concept of fame had generally been reserved for individuals such as artists or statesmen, and then only *maybe* while they were still alive. In the long nineteenth century, and especially in the stages and center rings of entertainment venues, a new type of celebrity emerged. This version of fame drew its energy from an ongoing dialogue among audiences, media, and famous figures. Each of the three drew from and elevated the others, increasing the overall sense among the masses that everyone was entitled to access something extraordinary. A celebrity was someone you could admire, hate-watch, even imagine to be your friend. Oscar Wilde, Dan Rice, P. T. Barnum, Jenny Lind, Sarah Bernhardt, and many more nineteenth-century entertainers became larger than life in this climate. They could have a private persona and a public one, and build an entire career on the carefully crafted excess of the latter. In the early nineteenth century, the appeal of the circus may have been simply to watch some first-class riding or to laugh at a clown's saucy jokes. But as time went on, society spoke to the circus—and the circus talked back.

Politics borrowed from entertainment, too. We see this in the person of Charles Blondin, a French wire walker who became nationally famous in America when he crossed Niagara Falls on a thin rope in 1859. He did not simply walk across the roaring foam: Blondin's acts included carrying another man on his shoulders while walking, or even pushing a wheelbarrow with a tiny stove on which he would cook an omelet while suspended on the wire. Passengers watched in disbelief from the *Maid of the Mist* tourist boat below as the acrobat obligingly lowered a plate of eggs to the deck on a rope. In a nineteenth century characterized by growing muscular masculinity, men like Blondin (never mind that he was French) became avatars of white American male exceptionalism. More than one editorial cartoon in the 1860s depicted President Lincoln walking the tightrope in similarly grand and precarious fashion. One such illustration in *Frank Leslie's Budget of Fun* explained that the president found the circus metaphor useful, "that he was like Blondin on the tightrope, with all that was valuable in America, the Union, in a barrow."[21] The circus clown Dan Rice became wildly famous as an orator, performer, comedian, and horseman. A quintessential circus clown, Rice drew huge crowds with his quick wit. His biographer notes that "if brand-name recognition had been a common concept at the time Rice would have been Coca-Cola."[22] With his striped pants, signature goatee, and top hat, he is often rumored to be part of the inspiration for US national symbol Uncle Sam.

Politics took on the metaphor and language of circus. The exchange ran in reverse, too. In 1853, P. T. Barnum put up a production of *Uncle Tom's Cabin*, based on the emotional antislavery novel Harriet Beecher Stowe claimed to have written in a trancelike state of divine inspiration. Barnum's version of the story, rewritten by playwright H. J. Conway, invented a happy ending and effectively neutered the message. It was a calculated move: By centering the drama around compromise, Barnum avoided polarizing (and thereby limiting) his audience. He allowed viewers the escapist luxury of not having to think too hard about things that made them uncomfortable and made his theater a space in which families of all political persuasions could relax without worrying about protest or violence.

AN AMERICAN BEHEMOTH

The golden-age American circus arrived in the public consciousness as a juggernaut of family entertainment. Gone was the chaos of the early traveling circus with its vulgar jokes and wagon-borne spectacle. Steam power and miles of track invited the circus to expand, to roam, and to grow as never before. This was not an open-and-shut matter—at first, moving a circus by rail was prohibitively expensive, and any show that came by train typically had to cut corners. Maybe the tent was smaller, or there was no menagerie. "Railroad circus" was not originally a compliment. But the connection of transcontinental rail in the 1860s, along with the proliferation of local railways, opened the United States to travel and connection at previously unavailable speed and cost efficiency. Dan Costello and W. C. Coup, the circus entrepreneurs who would coax P. T. Barnum out of retirement to create what would eventually become The Greatest Show on Earth, were among the first to take advantage. Not only did they travel out West with full shows to the delight of frontier audiences (and the equal delight of their bank accounts), but Coup eventually realized that a system of railroad flatcars would make loading and transporting shows possible at giant scale. Circus responded by growing not just its production but the support structures to make it possible: an entire back-office crew of managers, press agents, railroad contractors, routing teams, strategists, bankers, and more.[23]

From the 1870s on, shows increased in spectacle wherever possible. Tents got larger, holding tens of thousands of spectators. Why have only one performance ring when two or three are possible? Parade wagons became more common and more ornate, and after the 1855 patent invention of the steam calliope, a handful of circuses adopted this new, extremely loud means of advertising their presence.[24] Elephants became an increasingly common and plentiful sight in menageries.[25] These are only a few examples.

By the 1870s, Circus Day now arrived in an American town as a prepackaged public holiday, a complete and unavoidable corporate disruption of usual norms and routines. Circus was broadly considered a wholesome and worthwhile entertainment, but it could still be regarded as socially dangerous: Like the theater, it gave performers and audiences a temporary permission slip to question or even break normal constraints imposed by gender, class, power, or respectability.

Despite popular notions that the circus was a frivolous, outsider form of entertainment, the late nineteenth-century circus was the emblem of big business. P. T. Barnum's big show made $400,000 in its inaugural 1871 season—the equivalent of roughly ten million dollars today.[26] At the beginning of the nineteenth century, circuses were wagon-drawn affairs, so-called "mud shows" that made a living grinding their way from one town to another. But just decades later, at its height, the American circus spent and earned the modern equivalent of hundreds of millions of dollars. It employed thousands of workers and dealt with the business and regulatory realities of any major corporation, all with the added pressure of transporting itself over state lines quickly and often.

The largest railroad shows of the late nineteenth century brought together a dazzling variety of amusements in one grand, immersive experience. A show would arrive by train in the morning gloam, quickly build a nine-acre tented city, and be ready to welcome thousands to the grounds by early afternoon. A visit would begin at the ticket wagons and continue through a long broad avenue called the "midway," with concessions and amusements on each side. With its bannerline of brightly colored paintings, the midway funneled spectators toward the "big show" in the main tent. The soaring big top might span a footprint of a hundred thousand square feet.[27] Along the way, visitors might be tantalized by detours into sideshow or museum tents, pause to take in the menagerie, listen to the sideshow band, or visit concession sellers ("candy butchers" in circus parlance).

While the circus was a magical and transporting experience for audiences, substantial logistics and coordination were required behind the scenes. Advance advertising crews traveled days and weeks ahead of the circus, putting up posters to let people know the show was soon coming to their area. The show's procurement men would be at the next day's venue, arranging for the delivery of fresh necessities like sides of beef, pies, produce, and coffee. The cookhouse tent was always first off the train in the wee hours to get dozens of eggs frying for busy canvas crews. The staff would throw a flag up to signal that chefs were slinging plates. Behind the scenes in the backlot, a whole temporary city would spring up to support the circus and its myriad performers. This included spaces for professionals from barbers to smiths and farriers, changing rooms and wardrobe, and everything necessary for animal care and feeding.

A major circus typically performed two shows a day, one in the early afternoon and one come evening. A late-morning parade down the town's main thoroughfare happened first to stir up excitement for the endeavor. By the time the evening show's crowd left the tent, much of the show had already been packed up in careful reverse order and loaded onto flatcars to head down the road. On July 12, 1873, *Frank Leslie's Illustrated Newspaper* reported that "A circus, in its management during the traveling season, is not unlike that of an army. The manager holds a council of war with his lieutenants, the contracting agent, press agent, treasurer, equestrian zoological and museum directors, veterinary surgeon, masters of canvas, stables, costumers, transportation, etc. Maps are studied, gazetteers consulted, experiences related, systems of organization suggested; and most careful deliberations prolong the frequent councils, so that no error of judgment may occur to lessen the prospective profits of the adopted line of march."[28]

The biggest shows in the American circus, themselves the size of small armies, emerged during the latter part of the nineteenth century. The resurrected Sells Brothers went on the road in 1871, and P. T.

Barnum agreed to put his name on Dan Costello and W. C. Coup's show that same year, debuting as "P. T. Barnum's Museum, Menagerie, and Circus." The long-running John Robinson Circus took to the rails in 1881. The five Ringling Brothers of Baraboo, Wisconsin, debuted in 1882. By the early 1900s, nearly a hundred shows toured the country, and almost forty were large and flush enough to travel by rail.[29] Dozens of smaller shows competed for audience dollars, filling in gaps in the giants' schedule or sticking to frontier territory.

When the circus became big business, its owners became big businessmen. This was a fact that these men (and they were all men) were all too happy to advertise. Advertisements touted shows' massive expenditures as reason to buy a ticket—if the show could afford a $30,000 chariot, after all, it *must* be good![30] Full-color posters celebrated the show founders' brands and largess, but marketing messages also emphasized that these men came from modest backgrounds. Adam Forepaugh, the Ringling Brothers, P. T. Barnum—these men were millionaire industrialists in an increasingly globalized economy, functionally little different from the Rockefellers, Astors, Vanderbilts, or any of the other so-called "robber barons" of the era. But everyday ticket buyers liked the idea that these particular tycoons were like themselves. Circus barons were working men, and their image often reflected a middle- or working-class idea of what a rich man might be. In an effort to trumpet these men as relatable to everyday ticket buyers, ads reminded attendees that they, too, had come from humble origins. These millionaires had started out as a Philadelphia butcher, the Wisconsin sons of a harness maker, and an ordinary Connecticut Yankee. Not only with lavish spectacle or grand showmanship was circus selling the American Dream in action.

Fundamentally, circus is not just a place and a tent, but it is also a phenomenon and an experience. It's the sort of thing that Michel Foucault famously termed a heterotopia, a place in which "all the other real sites that can be found within the culture, are simultaneously represented, contested, and inverted."[31] Through its acts and structures, the circus both stood outside social norms and glorified them, reflecting mainstream American attitudes on race, culture, conflict, gender politics, and class. When the circus arrived in town, white men and women would parade down Main Street in lavish costumes, riding atop handsome horses and gilded wagons. Nonwhite and disabled performers were presented within carefully circumscribed roles: With limited exception, performers of color were either segregated into spaces like sideshow bands or presented as racialized curiosities. Moving the circus from town to town through the season required a massive labor pool and very often leveraged poor or Black workers out of sight of spectators. Micah Childress described how "by placing African Americans in the lowest subdivisions of labor within the general laborer pool, shows ensured that they had the cheapest labor possible."[32] Women (most of them white) had greater access to opportunity within the shows and were generally exempted from circus labor but faced persistent criticism that their career choice was unfeminine and a threat to the social order. This was either because they were choosing the surely dissolute circus over home and family or, later on, because their independence suggested alignment with the cause of women's rights.

Circus has always been an institution in constant dialogue with its time and circumstance. People go to the circus to put their daily lives aside for a short time, but they cannot really forget everything about that life even as they sit under the canvas big top. How businesses work, what audiences find funny, what will sell tickets: These are all informed by the prevailing social tides. And in the long nineteenth century, those tides ran high and fast thanks to immersive engagement with industry, technology, American national ego, structural racism, and mass media. Circus reflected all of this in the period from 1840 to 1870, when it grew from its small-scale roots to become a uniquely American behemoth.

GRAND SPECTACLE

Nowhere was the distinctively American excess of the golden age circus more evident than in the late nineteenth-century grand spectacle or "spec." A spec act was a lavish production number at the beginning or end of a circus show, typically involving a cast of thousands and a dizzying mix of sets, animals, dancing girls, and action scenes. Lasting as long as a modern action movie and often containing just as many thrills, the goal of the production was to overwhelm the audience with splendor. The Barnum & Bailey production of "Nero and the Destruction of Rome" took place on a stage five hundred feet wide and engaged more than a thousand players to reenact chariot races and gladiatorial combat.[33] Adam Forepaugh allegedly paid $10,000 in prize money to secure the "handsomest woman in the world" to lead "Lalla Rookh's Departure From Delhi" in 1881.[34] (The beauty contest was rigged, but he still spent more than $200,000 on the pageant—more than six million dollars today.)

These spectacles brought historical events to life as entertainment for the whole family. At a time when America was testing its strength and reach as a world power, the circus invited audiences to applaud archetypal stories of white imperial power. Shows placed America in the classical lineage of authority and splendor. They elevated Orientalist luxury in "Lalla Rookh," classical antiquity in "Nero," and a live battle between British and Sudanese troops in "Mahdi or for the Victoria Cross." American mythmaking was an important part of what the circus did, too. Barnum & Bailey's "Columbus and the Discovery of America" and Adam Forepaugh's production of "The American Revolution" both celebrated a morally pure, triumphant America.[35]

Culture authors like Raymond F. Betts and Kurt Andersen have rightly pointed out that American society has always been entranced by fame and make-believe; in his book *Fantasyland*, Andersen writes: "Once people commit to that approach, the world turns inside out, and no cause-and-effect connection is fixed. The credible becomes incredible and the incredible credible."[36] This is the native language of the circus. Circus is a fundamentally visual, reality-breaking art, both behind the scenes and in the ring. It only benefits from tall tales and inflated expectations, it caters to a skittish attention span, and its audience needs no specific language, social class, or level of education to have a good time. This makes circus a rare environment in which performers can challenge prevailing norms. Women who performed in the circus in the nineteenth century were navigating not only a male-driven industry but their own set of social strictures, both inside and outside the ring.

CHAPTER 3

Womanhood, Real and True

Nineteenth-century social structures were largely based on narrow biological concepts of sex and gender, and therefore defined ideal femininity as passive, virtuous, and based within the home. It is safe to say that this was not true universally: No one person or group of people, after all, is ever one thing. Some women were privileged elites, some had to work, some chose independence or activism, and others were limited by their race, class, or station. What matters, though, is that nineteenth-century media and social institutions cooperated to publicize not only a gentle, obedient femininity but the idea that everyone was going along with it.

Circus women could not help but offer an example to the contrary. They traveled, earned their own income, chose to marry and not to marry, and engaged in physical careers that put their bodies and skills on display to the public. They were outsiders in this era of delicate mainstream femininity.

SEPARATE SPHERES

According to the World Health Organization, gender "includes norms, behaviours and roles associated with being a woman, man, girl or boy, as well as relationships with each other. As a social construct, gender varies from society to society and can change over time."[1] In the twenty-first century, it is now more widely accepted that gender is a flexible concept distinct from assigned biological sex. It is not only inaccurate but potentially harmful to use overly reductive categories like the gender binary when considering an infinitely variable human physical and cultural experience. Nonetheless, in the long nineteenth century, white middle- and upper-class Western society loudly adhered to the idea of binary and biologically based gender roles. This had clear social implications.

Nineteenth-century social messaging did more than reinforce the idea of a gender binary between women and men; it attempted to create that division in physical space. Gender studies of the time frequently use the image of "separate spheres" to describe the different environments in which men and women were generally allowed to live, work, and socialize. Driven by biological determinism and reinforced by patriarchy, the concept of separate spheres placed each member of the ideal nineteenth-century household where biology and natural law allegedly would have them. The natural domain of men encompassed careers, political life, public pleasures, and a free-roaming sense of dominion. Women, in turn, were said to be naturally suited for and empowered by an insulated life at home, where they maintained morality, order, and peace for the family. The effect was to flatten concepts of masculinity and femininity, allowing not even a trace of one to infiltrate the other.[2] This system, driven by male needs and social norms, was in reality not so much a question of allocating separate spheres, equal in dignity, as it was a method for centering the needs of men from cradle to grave. Women were inscribed within the circle of the home, looking inward. Feminist theory has always considered "separate spheres" as a misnomer, saying that "men have never had a 'proper sphere,' since their sphere has been the world and all its activities."[3]

Diplomat and philosopher Alexis de Tocqueville praised America for this attitude in the 1830s, writing: "In no country has such constant care been taken as in America to trace two clearly distinct lines of action for the two sexes and to make them keep pace one with the other, but in two pathways which are always different."[4] De Tocqueville considered this a positive good, since in attempting to make men and women equal in work, pleasure, business, and discourse, "both are degraded; and from so preposterous a medley of the works of nature, nothing could ever result but weak men and disorderly women." In a democracy, separate spheres theoretically maintained the integrity of home and state alike, and "white women were perceived as Republican Mothers, responsible for the education of republican sons."[5]

TRUE WOMANHOOD

Western women in the long nineteenth century did not have to look far to find someone telling them how best to live their lives. Women's publications like *Peterson's Magazine*, *La Belle Assemblée*, and *Godey's Lady's Book* interspersed essays and fiction with household tips, advice on fashion and etiquette, and articles about how to achieve a seemingly effortless state of female perfection. Though they were seen broadly, the magazines were aimed at white women in the middle class and above on the logic that the daily newspapers were "too tainted for women who were supposed to provide an Edenic sanctuary for their corrupted working husbands."[6] These publications may not have represented the lives of the bulk of women at the time, but they had broad circulation, the published appearance of authority, and the benefit of social validation. This could easily make it seem like "everyone" was in agreement with norms of behavior, when in fact things were more complicated. Public modeling of ideal womanhood came even from the highest level of society, where Queen Victoria's unending devotion to her husband Albert crystallized the idea of the perfect wife and lady. The queen, in a visual sign of her sentiment and fidelity, commissioned a tiny diamond crown to fit the mourning cap she wore her entire life after his passing.

Women in America have always been publicly expected to achieve a balance among utterly incompatible expectations. Schools of thought may vary, but in the nineteenth century, they generally suggested women should be everything all at once: upright yet sexually dutiful, pretty but not distracting, both competent and quiet, holding up the home but giving all credit to the man in her life (with a man presumed to be the only feasible partner). In these social systems, a woman's domesticity was her virtue and her means to success. "The man bears rule over his wife's person and conduct," noted *The Lady's Amaranth* in 1839, continuing: "She bears rule over his inclinations: he governs by law; and she by persuasion. Nor can her authority ever fail, where it is supported by sweetness of temper, and zeal to make him happy. The empire of a woman is an empire of softness, of address, of complacency; her commands are caresses, her menace are tears."[7]

Perhaps the most well-known concept of feminine ideals from the nineteenth century is "True Womanhood." This aspirational stereotype, assembled from a variety of contemporary women's publications, has been also often called "The Angel in the House" after a truly nauseating poem by writer Coventry Patmore.[8] The cult of True Womanhood asked women in the 1800s to navigate a maddening set of rules and expectations that revolved around four basic virtues: purity, submissiveness, domesticity, and piety.[9]

"Good" women were pure. On the one hand, woman's virginity was regarded as her greatest treasure, necessary to secure a good marriage. But while good men were said to value innocence above all things, they were also apparently its most dedicated adversary, and women were advised to firmly keep male advances at bay. Cautionary tales in magazines and word-of-mouth gossip warned women that one slip of affection or discipline could lead them to poverty, intemperance, or even insanity. After marriage, it was expected that women would be sexual, but dutifully, and without compromising their dignity or godliness. It was a jumble of sexual stereotypes in which women were praised for chastity and feared for uncontrolled sexuality, urged to resist male impulses but, after marriage, gratify them at any time. (As much as people want to think of the nineteenth century as a time of repression, when folks would allegedly put stockings on their piano legs out of prudery, there was as much sex happening then as at any other time in human history.)

The ideal woman was also supposed to appreciate that her value lay in placing her own talents, opinions, wishes, or abilities in service of her husband and family. As justification, women were told they were merely creatures of the heart: inherently different, smaller, and in need of protection from the coarse world. Women were meant to understand that, as one physician claimed, "Woman has a head almost too small for intellect but just big enough for love."[10]

An upright woman's place was in the home, and she was expected to maintain it as a source of unyielding excellence and comfort. A well-kept home was a place to build up compliant daughters, upright sons, and happy husbands who would go forth from the hearth. (Conversely, if she failed in her duty, it was implied that the walk to bars or brothels was very short.) The ideal nineteenth-century woman was therefore expected to serve as homemaker, nurse, cheerleader, arts-and-crafts director, and gentle source of authority within the home. Ladies' magazines and other literature constantly reassured women that the tasks of the home were not only morally uplifting but inevitably more complex and necessary than anyone would have thought. If she needed to relax, that too should set a diligent example; excellent choices for recreation might include any number of productive and pleasing arts, from hair braiding to watercolor paints. One ladies' guide from 1884 offered patterns and instructions for "Berlin work, crochet, drawn-thread work, embroidery, knitting, knotting or macrame, lace, netting, poonah painting, & tatting."[11]

Piety brought all the other virtues together in service to God. Women were expected to cleave to Christianity, to provide a moral example for children, and to support the community. ("Unlike participation in other societies or movements," writes Barbara Welter, "church work would not make her less domestic or submissive."[12]) Motherhood acted as a manifestation and extension of female piety, and it allowed a woman to position herself as the architect of social virtue. She could raise young men to run the nation and well-educated young ladies to carry on the system in an orderly fashion.

REAL WOMEN, MAJESTIC WOMEN

Historical schemes of ideal womanhood generally come to us through media sources: books, pamphlets, advice columns, correspondence. These all have their own context and bias, and, more importantly, just because someone put forth a philosophy of behavior doesn't mean it was followed at all, much less to the letter. "True Womanhood" as it has been explained in scholarship is clear, well structured, and sort of scary. But real life in a diverse society is seldom so tidy. Was every nineteenth-century woman an "angel in the home," piously devoted to motherhood and content to remain blissfully ignorant of public life? Certainly not: Many women could not afford to live such a life, and others simply couldn't think of anything that appealed to them less. To be sure, all these columns and articles capture a common reality of nineteenth-century life for girls and women: They were generally expected to strive for an upright, respectable reputation within their community and social class and prioritize the authority of both individual men and male social institutions. But that doesn't mean we should assume all paths were the same.

There were no doubt women of the era (and men, too) who believed deeply in True Womanhood and its assumption that woman was a wilting flower in need of protection. Some women were indeed frail; others probably pretended to be, when it served their social or personal ends. But then again, there was also a "gymnasium movement" in the nineteenth century in which some women showed enthusiasm for physical activity and its health benefits, directly at odds with the idea of inherent female passivity.[13]

Followed strictly, True Womanhood was idle and fragile, and most women could likely not afford to be either of those things. Perhaps an elite woman with family wealth and an army of servants could celebrate her gentle adherence to social norms. But what about women of lesser means? And furthermore, if work is not considered ladylike, what does that say about the servant staff?

For middle-class women, employment was in fact common and encouraged during the nineteenth century in the form of charity, domestic employment, and salaried work. Work was seen as a moral good, preventing idleness. Moreover, it gave a middle-class woman the means to support her family or to escape entirely if she had chosen a bad spouse. In this case, self-reliance was tolerated not because it was an acceptable end goal but because it was evidence of prudent planning against crisis. Similarly, folks generally did not believe that competence, maturity, reason, and intelligence were alien to women. Women using these traits in ways other than as necessary tools to achieve a good marriage and a moral life, however, was not encouraged. Rather, a competent "Real Woman" was expected to work hard "in the larger context of an extended woman's sphere in which Christian benevolence, responsibility for one's own or extended family, and usefulness to the community are the outlines of a female lifelong duty to God and country."[14]

The commonly discussed public philosophy of acceptable nineteenth-century womanhood excluded whole swaths of the population: You will note that public voices on the matter do not tend to speak much about working and lower-class white women, women of color, or unmarried women and activists. By centering the white, well-to-do experience, the architects of idealized womanhood worked not only to control women but to reinforce white supremacy and racial hierarchy.

INSIDERS AND OUTSIDERS

The question of whether work was ungainly or inappropriate for a woman was not generally asked of women of color or lower-class white women. In the nineteenth-century industrial age, their need to work was explained away in paternalistic, class-based terms. Work for poor, immigrant, or Black women in the 1800s was explained as a corrective moral good: A lower-class woman who worked was unlikely to be a drain upon her family or social aid resources and was too busy to even consider "idleness and its attendant vices and crimes."[15] And of course, enslaved women in the nineteenth century had neither choice nor agency in work. The elite had always been accustomed to maintaining their lifestyle through the labor of lower-class people, but as the middle class became larger and more affluent, they aspired to a similar ease. Both groups, as a result, were content to "dehumanize the workers who made their lifestyle possible."

American women who were part of the nation's westward expansion were also not sitting home with their noses in the latest issue of *Godey's Lady's Book*. These women, many of them queer and women of color, "were neither the martyrs nor Amazons of song and story but hardworking, persistent individuals who, during the heyday of

Victorian domesticity and cross-continental expansion, helped extend women's place from the private home to the national homeland."[16]

The various schools of thought on womanhood united in one thing: They scorned those who did not comply with their rules. A woman who rejected social expectations or made a significant misstep could be shunned by family or friends, dismissed as an unsuitable partner, deprived financially, or exposed to shame and isolation. The scheme of appropriate, innocent femininity not only served to regulate behavior, but it kept women from having the energy and focus to think about or do almost anything else. Women who engaged in activism at the time—many of whom were unmarried—drew harsh criticism from the male establishment for having abandoned their allegedly inherent obligations. As just one example of how this was communicated, a man named Henry F. Harrington wrote in an 1838 issue of *The Ladies' Companion* about Mary Wollstonecraft, Frances Wright, and Harriet Martineau. The women were theorists and activists who had spent the preceding decades writing in support of feminism, abolitionism, and social reform. As a rebuttal to their work to expand the scope of women's rights, he described a child's playroom in which a boy played soldier with a strip of wood while a young girl freely chose her dolls. Why would she have not chosen to be a soldier, too, mused Harrington? Because she was naturally destined for care and motherhood. On this basis, Harrington denied the activists womanhood altogether. In advocating for social and political equality, each of the three demonstrated an unattractive masculine aspect (not to mention, he noted, "all three were unmarried at the period of their most strenuous exertions in the cause"). Harrington went further in his dismissal, concluding that women such as these were no women at all: "Shall these semi-women—these mental hermaphrodites, be admitted to the bar as witnesses in this great cause? No," Harrington said. "They are incompetent; utterly incompetent."[17] By calling these women "mental hermaphrodites," the author decides—and communicates to an everyday female readership—that they deserve neither male power nor female dignity. It was not only a dismissal of the activists but a cautionary tale to women readers.

This exclusionary rhetoric would later extend to suffrage activists.

In a *New York Times* article on the history of the suffrage movement, author Maya Salam writes that "Anti-suffragists already viewed suffragists as abnormal for wanting equal rights, and they pointed to gender-nonconforming suffragists as evidence that the movement was deviant."[18] (That many suffragists were in fact queer only adds to the overall jumble of gender politics.)

Failure to comply with the gender binary and its separate-sphere expectations was consistently cast as a threat to order, civilization, and nature. The religious novel *The Circus Girl and Sunday-School Scholar*, published in 1860, embodies not just the popular understanding about proper womanhood but how transgressive structures like the circus could be seen to undermine it.[19] In the novel, a twelve-year-old girl named Julia shyly happens upon a Sunday school class. Seeing that the girl is emotionally affected by the lesson, the teacher gets Julia to reveal that she is a circus rider who performs as "Señora Lovalo." She says she is embarrassed by her line of work and would prefer to be a good Christian girl but, after the death of her mother, has been pressed into continuing to perform by her father to make ends meet. Julia's sister actually likes her career as a circus performer, so naturally she has a loutish husband and a case of consumption. Julia, lacking a motherly influence, relies on the chaste Sunday school teacher to lead her into plain dresses and clean living. Her sister, having rejected the grace and duty of womanhood, dies from her illness despite making a deathbed confession of faith.

This was a common script in Victorian-era culture, and *Circus Girl* is just one of many melodramatic domestic tragedies threatening women with ruin if they failed to walk the straight and narrow path. In *Circus Girl*, itinerant showfolk are heathens, assailed by stage-door Johnnys and ignorant of salvation. In other similar stories of the era, it might be intemperance, sexual appetite, or ambition that calls down illness, destitution, or even death.

The specifics vary, but the thrust is the same: Women were expected to embrace a soft and unambitious femininity, show deference to their husbands and men in general, maintain the home as a source of order and moral good, and keep their conduct and reputation clean. Not everyone had to be a waifish, unthinking invalid, but the bar was still set unreasonably high: *The Lady's Book* instructed women, in a single issue from January 1835, to keep up on "prevailing fashions," to dress appropriately for the weather lest poor health "reduce the sufferer to the level of a hot-house plant," to educate girls toward "amiability, intelligence, and an absence of affection," to learn hexagonal embroidery, and to be sure that dinner was specifically tailored to the "constitution and digestive powers" of the individual. (At least the magazine had the decency to write that "no error is in this country more common or more dangerous than the neglect of *bread*.")[20] Mothers were advised to "excite in children a detestation of all that is mean, cunning or false." It was a lot to keep in one's head, and no wonder that Virginia Woolf, bone-weary of all the nosy advice, grumbled that "killing the Angel in the House was part of the occupation of the woman writer."[21]

CIRCUS WOMEN

The circuses that operated in the nineteenth century did so within the context of these larger social forces and messages about what was ideal and appropriate behavior for women. And while the circus owners were happy to capitalize on the appeal of attractive performing women, they also had to operate within a society that used institutions like media, family, and the church to spread and enforce ideas of appropriate feminine behavior. Women breaking boundaries (say, flying overhead in very little clothing) could be seen as a threat to social order, and the same newspapers that enabled the circus to advertise itself to a wide audience could be used by community leaders to insist that moral and upstanding citizens must avoid sites of scandal and temptation. Circus women had to thread a difficult needle between provoking excitement in an audience but not going so far as to undermine common social standards for their gender. In that case, visiting a circus would go past harmless titillation to threatening established social order. Social institutions would then need to shun and reject the woman or her behavior, which would threaten the bottom line of the circus.

Media pundits of the nineteenth century were obsessed with figuring out just what sort of woman might join the circus. There was a persistent public belief that because circus women chose independence, self-promotion, and sexy outfits over hearth and home, they were wild, untamed degenerates. And while this was seen as shocking, on the other side of shock lies fascination. Circus women could be very easily dismissed as unruly temptresses, but the very fact of their position outside the prevailing social order also made them extremely exciting and even desirable to everyday audiences. We see this simultaneous revulsion and desire in press accounts where the same public that proclaimed its morals went wild for a good pulp scandal—one 1911 account of a Circassian beauty and snake charmer known as "Morphine Kate" involved not only dramatic snake acts but Kate getting revenge on her abusive husband by dousing him with gasoline from a five-gallon can and lighting a match.[22] An illustration of curvy Kate wrestling a snake takes up the better part of the page.

From the late nineteenth century onward, circus managers worked to dismiss the cruder stereotypes about circus women, which they believed was better for the sake of profitable, family-friendly entertainment.[23] As much as possible, circus women were expected to make it clear that the woman on the poster was just a character, a fiction they performed for the crowd's amusement. The implication was that they wouldn't dream of bringing more subversive aspects of the circus outside the ring bumper.

In 1888, newspapers across the country reprinted a bit of New York City gossip about circus women, supposedly gathered from an anonymous wardrobe woman on "one of the great traveling shows." Most people at the time had a rough idea that circus women were loose and dissolute; they'd have to be, with such a strange career choice and a predilection for wearing provocative tights. But contrary to popular belief, this costumer swore, the ambition and flash was all just a bit for the stage. In real life, she said, "they read, study, paint, play the piano, sew, and some of them keep house, and the majority of them are good and kind, and more than half of them support a mother or helpless sister, or some old aunt or other; and if a stable boy or a ring man gets hurt and his family are in need, they put their hands in their pockets every time and take out all the way from one to ten dollars.

I've Summered and Wintered circus women for fifteen years, and I say they're just like other women, if they don't wear so many clothes."[24]

In a century that mashed up sentimentality, sensationalism, and the virtue of submission in home, relationship, and in public, you can begin to see the bind in which many women found themselves, especially those who chose to perform in public. Women in the developing nineteenth-century circus navigated this public climate and dialogue and, in both their acts and their public personas, performed race, domesticity, ability, and femininity with as much skill and care as any circus act or magic trick.

Among the many loud voices asserting what women should be in the nineteenth century, circus women still managed to be outliers. They were not stationed within the home; they often did not marry; they did body-centered work, performed without apology in the public sphere, and made a living in ways not normally available to others of their sex, race, or class. But because the circus functioned in some ways as a space outside the norm, its denizens were not held to quite the same standards as regular citizens. That, in combination with the fame and publicity associated with their unusual achievements, gave circus women the power to act in ways that posed new questions and set new precedents.

CHAPTER 4

The Queen of Beauty and the Armless Wonder

Lavinia Warren and Ann Leak were two of the "living wonders" who populated dime museums and circuses throughout the United States and around the world in the middle nineteenth century. These two women stood out more than most for a few reasons. Warren, as an adult, stood barely three feet tall, and Ann Leak had been born without arms. But while each of these women made a living performing, their physical difference was only the barest foundation of the attraction. Leak and Warren each enjoyed decades-long careers not as oddities but as perfect performers of the era's most celebrated feminine skills and virtues. Lavinia Warren modeled fashion, luxury, and prosperity on the global stage. Ann Leak performed morality, charity, and modesty for Christian audiences. Each woman was an expert navigator of the new forms of mass media and culture of common experience.

ooooo

Mercy Lavinia Warren Bump was born on Halloween of 1841 in small-town Middleboro, Massachusetts. Warren quickly stood out when, around her first birthday, she all but stopped growing: By the time she was ten years old, Lavinia was about two feet tall and weighed just twenty pounds. Her family treated Warren as they did any of their other seven children. She was expected to attend school and Sunday church services and to help around the house, which she did with the help of a customized stepstool her father built for her. Bold and confident, Warren proclaimed herself an "excellent housekeeper," delighted in riding horseback, and loved to cause trouble. She chuckled that "I went to school like other girls, but being fond of fun and having in common with most children the idea that fun consisted in doing mischief, I fear that my teachers didn't wholly appreciate me from that standpoint."[1] She would race beneath the schoolhouse desks and pinch unsuspecting classmates as the teacher tried to figure out where the yelps and screams were coming from. "I'd dart back to my seat, and when he rose, red and panting from an ineffectual search under the desk," she recalled, "he'd find me demurely poring over my lesson as if I'd never had a thought outside my book." She remembered that the teacher spat in reply between rough breaths, "What does your mother do to punish you? Does she set you on top of the sugar bowl and make you wipe the dishes?" For all her Yankee pluck, Warren was still a young girl concerned with fitting in, and she admitted that "for the time being I was conquered, for any allusion to my abnormal size always caused me great embarrassment, and the helpless man had really no other weapon to turn on me."

When her town decided to split their schoolhouse into an elementary school and an upper division, the town school committee chose sixteen-year-old Warren as its first primary-school teacher. She felt teaching was a "proper and genial vocation" and had every reason to expect it would be her career for life, until a visiting cousin who managed a showboat museum put a bug in Warren's ear about going out West and seeing some of the world. Lavinia, dreaming of "a sail on the beautiful Ohio ... and on the mighty Mississippi, with all the glamor which youth throws about the unknown," could not pass up the opportunity to join in.[2] Showboats were floating theaters in the early 1800s, large multilevel boats that would dock along the Mississippi and Ohio rivers to provide entertainment. The biggest of them could hold thousands of spectators and even host equestrian acts. Displayed as "earth's last and loveliest fairy," Warren sailed on "Colonel" Wood's riverboat, a combination theater, minstrel show, and parade of curiosities, until the incipient Civil War drove Wood to sell his boats and take the company north with some haste.

Word of the "Lilliputian Queen"[3] reached P. T. Barnum, who in 1862 sent one of his agents to her Massachusetts home with orders to offer employment at his American Museum in New York, followed by a European tour. Decades earlier, Barnum had met little person Charles Stratton as a child and turned him into the global star known as General Tom Thumb. Stratton, born in 1838 in Bridgeport, Connecticut, shared a similar childhood story to Warren's; while he was a large baby—about nine pounds at birth—Charles stopped growing around six months of age and by toddlerhood had reached only two feet tall and fifteen pounds. Taking him on as a performer, Barnum embellished a bit for good press: Four-year-old Charlie Stratton became General Tom Thumb, after King Arthur's tiny fairy-tale dragon slayer, and he was billed as eleven years old to make his small size appear all the more remarkable. He first appeared at the American Museum on Thanksgiving 1842, and by 1844 was accompanying Barnum on a grand tour overseas. Stratton was a gifted performer who could sing, dance, perform riotous comedy, and command the fancy of women the world over, to whom he swore he was a general in "Cupid's artillery."[4] Even Queen Victoria adored him, much to the dismay of the British intelligentsia, who wondered aloud why the nation that gave the world Shakespeare was suddenly losing its mind over a tiny Yankee in costume. The painter Benjamin Robert Haydon complained that guests at the Egyptian Hall were flocking to see Tom Thumb rather than his paintings, wailing: "They see my bills, my boards, my caravans and don't read them. Their eyes are open, but their sense is shut! It is an insanity, a rabies, a madness, a furor, a dream. I would not have believed it of the English people."[5]

Barnum warmly received Warren and her family in Bridgeport. After convincing the Bumps that he was not the huckster that rumor made him out to be, Barnum arranged for Lavinia to travel to New York. His own daughters hosted her out of the public eye while the showman made suitable arrangements for her wardrobe and jewelry.

Lavinia Warren met New York society for the first time at the St. Nicholas—the city's first million-dollar hotel—on December 22, 1862.

The St. Nicholas, with its twenty-two-foot ceilings, lavish décor, and seemingly limitless supply of gold paint, was the place to see and be seen in the early 1860s. (A popular joke of the day claimed that "an English comedian declined to put his shoes outside the door to be shined, for fear the management would gild them."[6]) Presenting herself as a graceful and refined Victorian lady, Warren made the rounds to speak with press and dignitaries. She utterly charmed everyone in attendance. The *New York Times* wrote that "Miss Lavinia Warren, a young lady from Middleboro, Mass., is now stopping at the St. Nicholas. So are many other ladies, and if that was all about her, it would hardly be thus chronicled in the *Times*." Warren, though, earned the *Times*'s esteem as being worth the newsprint: "A miniature woman—aye, and the queen of them. Her face is bright and sweet, her eyes brilliant and intelligent, her form faultless, and her manner that of the woman of the world. What more could we desire?"[7] So many people clamored for Lavinia's souvenir photograph that she took out a New Year's Eve advertisement in the *Times* listing the shops at which the image was available for purchase, it being "impossible for her Secretary to answer privately."[8]

Barnum hoped to transfer Warren to his American Museum immediately, but she had no plans to make life quite so easy for him. The day after Christmas, she wrote with a sharp reminder that "I do not intend giving a public exhibition until I have appeared before the Courts of Europe."[9] Negotiations continued behind the scenes while Warren toured in Boston. The deal concluded to her satisfaction in time to debut at the Museum on January 5, 1863. Barnum made hay out of her tough negotiation, advertising that "notwithstanding Miss Lavinia Warren, The Queen of Beauty, refused his offer of one thousand dollars per week, he has been enabled to make such advantageous offers as to induce her to appear at the Museum for a few weeks."[10]

Charles Stratton was not actively performing with Barnum at the time. Though he had assisted the showman in recovery from his 1856 bankruptcy and continued to tour on his own now and again, he also very much enjoyed home life in Bridgeport. Stratton was an active senior Mason and an accomplished sailor who loved to sail his yacht on Long Island Sound. On a visit to the American Museum, he was

Lavinia Warren stands next to a chair.
Image courtesy of the Prints and Photographs Division at the Library of Congress.

taken with Lavinia, though, and pulled his friend aside one day to ask Barnum if he might put in a good word. Barnum replied, "I will not oppose you in your suit, but you must do your own courting. I tell you, however, the Commodore [George Washington Morrison Nutt, a.k.a. "Commodore Nutt," another little person in Barnum's employ] will be jealous of you, and more than that, Miss Warren is no fool, and you will have to proceed very cautiously if you can succeed in winning her affections."[11] He succeeded in a whirlwind courtship, with their wedding hastily planned for February.

Meanwhile, Warren was selling thousands of dollars' worth of tickets every day at the American Museum, and the *New-York Daily Tribune* proclaimed that "the excitement at Barnum's Museum is all along of Miss Lavinia Warren, the compressed beauty."[12] Barnum allegedly offered Charles and Lavinia $15,000 to postpone their wedding so he could wring some more business out of the anticipation. A publicized wedding was one thing, but the couple politely and without hesitation declined the offer to draw things out further. Warren with her characteristic snap noted that "as the General and myself were expecting to marry each other, and not Mr. Barnum," they had no need for his money.[13] Barnum's version of the story was more to the point: He recalled Warren's insistence that he should have offered at least a hundred grand.[14]

The wedding of Charles Stratton and Lavinia Warren on February 10, 1863, was the event of New York society. Two thousand invitations were sent to attend the "Fairy Wedding" ceremony at Broadway's Grace Church, and it still did not meet demand. P. T. Barnum, ever the opportunist, made sure many more could attend a separate reception at the Metropolitan Hotel afterward.

Not everyone was happy about the idea, to be sure: Some people figured that this had to be a publicity stunt at best and that a commercialized wedding shouldn't take place in the church. A writer from the *Brooklyn Daily Eagle* complained that "the fittest place for the exhibition would be the American Museum; and not in a house dedicated to the services of a holy religion."[15] Enthusiasm and curiosity overwhelmed criticism of the wedding as a commercialized sideshow, however. The Fairy Wedding was a sensation, a welcome and lively distraction from Civil War news. The *New York Herald* crowed that it made old Babylon seem like a town fair by comparison: "Here was the carnival of crinoline, the apotheosis of purple and fine linen. Never before was the scarlet lady seen to such advantage. Babylon was a rag fair to it."[16]

The *New-York Illustrated News* described Warren's wedding gown in extensive detail for curious readers, drooling over a gown made "of the richest white satin, with waist pointed in front and behind and laced at the back, low necked with bertha, which were trimmed with point applique. The arm caps also trimmed with the same costly material. The skirt was box-plaited and had one flounce of point applique half a yard in width, trailing in the most graceful manner." Warren's bridal ensemble also included a lace veil, satin slippers with lace rosettes and pearl buckles, and a tiny but impeccably crafted set of white kid gloves with point lace.[17] There was a whole wardrobe planned for the postwedding public relations junket, too: a traveling outfit of lavender poplin and velvet and a gown for meeting Queen Victoria "gotten up regardless of expense." This reception dress, worn for a royal audience, was decorated with satin botanical designs reflecting Warren's worldwide appeal—corn for America, an English rose, French laurel, a shamrock, thistle, and grapes. The designer Ellen Demorest, who made fashion accessible to the masses through her invention of tissue-paper dress patterns, supervised the creation of the trousseau.[18] The General had arranged for $10,000 worth of diamond, emerald, and coral jewelry for his wife. And, because this is apparently what brides have always done to their attendants, the bridesmaid—Lavinia's sister Minnie, also of short stature—wore a "lace puffed dress" at Warren's request.[19]

The wedding ceremony was performed by the Reverend Dr. Willey of Bridgeport.[20] After the ceremony, the party retired to the Metropolitan Hotel, "followed by the immense crowd tumbling over each other to get a glympse of the occupants of the bridal carriage."[21] Thousands of celebrity-crazy New Yorkers filled the streets outside the Metropolitan Hotel as opportunistic concessionaires and pickpockets threaded their way through the throngs. New York police worked to shuttle a line of carriages to entrances and exits as discreetly as possible, and

Barnum welcomed guests inside. The *New York Times* called the whole affair a "breath-expurgating, crinoline-crushing, bunion-pinching mass of conglomerated humanity."[22]

Inside the ballroom at the Metropolitan, the bride and groom stood atop a shiny grand piano to receive congratulations from their guests. Attendants placed the lavish wedding gifts on display for guests to fawn over. It was a small museum of luxury and excess: Tiffany & Co. sent the couple a miniature silver horse and chariot, and the Vanderbilts presented a "coral and gold-set brooch, earrings and studs, of the finest workmanship."[23] The *Times* remarked that, try as you might to talk about anything else in New York that week, the wedding was the only thing on anyone's minds or lips: "Those who did and those who did not attend the wedding of Gen. Thomas Thumb and Queen LAVINIA WARREN composed the population of this great Metropolis yesterday, and thenceforth religious and civil parties sink into comparative insignificance before this one arbitrating query of fate—Did you or did you not see Tom Thumb married?"[24]

Only days after the wedding, the couple was received at the White House by Abraham and Mary Todd Lincoln, whose genuine hospitality and warmth Lavinia Warren recalled fondly. "When Mr. Lincoln stooped his towering form to greet us, there was a peculiarly quizzical expression in his eye which almost made me laugh outright. Knowing his predilection for storytelling, I imagined he was about to utter something of a humorous nature; but he only said, with a genial smile, 'Mrs. Stratton, I wish you much happiness in your union.'" The president and Mrs. Lincoln led the couple to a salon, where they helped Charles and Lavinia to seats beside them on the sofa for conversation. The journalist Grace Greenwood noted that Lincoln had "not the slightest touch of the exaggeration which a lesser man might have been tempted to make use of, for the quiet amusement of on-lookers."

After the wedding, it was back to the American Museum. April newspapers touted the pair appearing for a limited time before heading to Europe in their wedding outfits, with the "rich, rare and elegant bridal presents" along for the show.[25] The Fairy Wedding and its follow-on tours were a chance for the public to join in a festival of luxury, to imagine themselves immersed in high-end travel, fashion, fame, and fortune. Coverage genuinely fawned over the couple but also occasionally made a bit of a winking joke of the whole affair, using their small size as a bit of a punch line to make it seem like the two were "playing at society." Their fame was no joke, though. The wedding, the visit to the White House, and the Strattons' tours over subsequent decades were genuinely popular.

Their actual performances tended to be in the vein of a variety show, with a grab bag of smaller entertainments and a main act that could involve music and dancing, impersonation, theater, comedy sketches, and more. In all of these, Lavinia Warren showcased her talents in the feminine arts and dressed in the manner of an elite lady. The Tom Thumb Company traveled the world, sailing to east and southeastern Asia, Australia, the Middle East, the Mediterranean, and Europe. Over three years in the late 1860s and early 1870s, they traveled more than fifty thousand miles by sea and gave more than 1,400 shows. The fact of travel itself became creative capital as the couple became fond of sharing stories from around the world with audiences who could only imagine such far-flung locales.

Charles Stratton died in 1883 of a stroke at age forty-five. Lavinia's sister Minnie was gone by that point, too, having died in childbirth, and Lavinia Warren was alone and heartbroken. She developed a relationship with Primo Magri, a little person who had at times traveled with the Tom Thumb Company, and they married in 1885. Since Magri claimed to have a legitimate aristocratic title, Lavinia Warren became the Countess Magri. Though Lavinia and Charlie had earned lavishly over the years, they had also spent lavishly, and Magri also had a taste for the high life, so touring took the place of retirement. The pair spent a handful of summers at Coney Island and performed now and again, even appearing in an early 1915 film called *The Lilliputians' Courtship*. Warren died in 1919 and was buried with Charles Stratton in Bridgeport's Mountain Grove Cemetery.

Though she ascended to the heights of fame and privilege, Lavinia Warren remained self-aware and quick-witted. In her autobiography, she humorously recalled a story from her younger years when a woman tutted at her for being too much into fashion and too little into the Lord. In response, Warren quoted Ecclesiastes back at her, urging: "Be not rash with thy mouth and let not thine heart be hasty to utter anything." This was the sort of discourse Ann Leak would have understood.

ooooo

On October 16, 1865, as Lavinia Warren was preparing to join her husband on a rail tour of the United States, the *New-York Tribune* announced the debut of another new and remarkable addition to the program at Barnum's American Museum, which still had hungry public appetites to feed.[26] Barnum promised a "wonderful performance" by Ann Eliza Leak, a woman who "astonishes and entertains" through her fine crochet work, hair braiding, and embroidery, which she could do despite having been born without arms.

Ann Leak was definitely born in Zebulon, a town of some four hundred people in Pike County, Georgia. Whether that happened in 1839, as she sometimes wrote, or in 1841, as the United States Census claims, or at some other time, is less clear.[27] What was clear—immediately so—is that Ann Leak was unique among the family's twelve children. As well as being armless, her right leg was several inches shorter than the left, and as a result Leak did not walk until she was five years old. She did not consider any of this a limitation. Leak wrote in her autobiography that "at quite an early age I commenced using my feet as a child would make use of the hands; piling up blocks, then throwing them down in great glee."[28] Her parents may have at first been consumed by concern for their daughter, but they were soon impressed by the child who learned to crochet and pick up pins from the floor with her feet. Leak plainly made it clear that, piano lessons aside (she gave up when she could not span an octave with her toes), she was up to try nearly anything else. "I have made it a rule that where I cannot do a given thing as well as those with arms and fingers, I abandon its pursuit altogether," she stated, "yet I try to do everything I see others doing, and generally succeed." She was privileged with a good education, entering the local Griffin Female College at eleven years old. Leak pored over books, "*'thumbing'* the leaves as deftly as my mates did with their fingers."

Like Lavinia Warren, Ann Leak was brought up with little practical regard for her disability and was expected to be capable in various womanly skills and arts. By the time Ann left school to supervise her family home in her mother's stead, she could crochet, sew, tie knots, eat with a knife and fork, wind a watch, walk a strong mile, and braid hair, all with her own two feet.

According to her pamphlet memoir, in the early 1860s, Leak traveled with an aunt throughout Georgia and Florida, visiting relatives and friends. She kept herself occupied and financially afloat by acting as a governess and teaching hair braiding to young ladies, a skill which was in high demand after her artful braiding won a twenty-dollar prize at the Macon fair in December 1860. A carriage sent by her uncle carried Ann to his sugar plantation on the Florida–Georgia border, where she ignored even the suggestion of enslavement or a war going on in "our distracted country" and entertained herself with "all the sports and pleasures of plantation-life."

That's one version of the story. This being a story in the world of circus, however, skepticism is advised. Sources that come from under the big tent, so to speak, are often produced more with commercial appeal in mind than strict accuracy. Ann Leak may have been content to master the skills and decorum expected of an upstanding young Southern woman, sitting on a plantation porch while the "feathered songsters of the forest" tweeted overhead, but her narrative elides more complicated family dynamics. The circus promoter George Middleton, in his 1913 memoir, recalls Leak telling darker, sharper stories. Middleton remembered her claiming that "her father was a man who drank a great deal and was very quarrelsome with his friends. Her mother learned of his being in a scrap down in the town, and when she saw him coming home, he had his overcoat thrown over his shoulders without his arms in the sleeves. She claimed this was the reason she was armless."[29] (The idea of so-called "maternal impression" still held water in some corners of nineteenth-century America, drawing on centuries-old superstition that "monstrous" births happen when a woman has a disruptive visual or emotional experience during pregnancy.[30]) Exhausted by twelve children, emotionally broken by her husband's drinking issues, and grieving the loss of sons in the war, Ann's mother Eleanor Leak lived in a general state of despairing overwhelm. To the extent she discussed it, Ann Leak relied on a suitably compassionate gloss, asking, "Is it strange that the spirit of a fond and devoted mother should droop?" Though she had enough respect for her parents' position and her own public image to wrap his condition in the polite euphemism of "feeble health," Leak clearly had private opinions on her father's alcohol abuse, too. It is likely that she helped with managing chores at home, sought employment, and couch-surfed with relatives because she could not count on either parent for stability or support.

Leak opened a small school at home in 1865, teaching eight pupils. Like Lavinia Warren, she likely assumed at first that teaching was the sort of work that would carry her through many years. With its emphasis on equipping children with knowledge and good morals, teaching was generally considered respectable work for women. Ann Leak's school only lasted six months, however, because she quickly realized trying to tame unruly students was not her forte. "Teaching young ideas how to shoot is no play," she recalled in frustration. Since she needed to make a living, and other options were neither easily available nor well paying, show business seemed the best choice. Leak gathered friends and financing, and in the fall of 1865, she left for Barnum's American Museum. She chose Barnum's venue because, plainly, she had no patience for bush-league venues, and the Museum "seemed to be best" in the business.

Two weeks after leaving Georgia on a succession of trains and steamers, Leak arrived, reluctant and seasick, in New York City. She checked into the Metropolitan Hotel, where Lavinia Warren had held her wedding reception, on October 8, 1865. Like Warren, she had a quiet period of preparation for her debut, but where Warren delighted in the rush of the city and the glamour of selecting gowns and jewelry, Leak lamented the city's noise, the grumpy New Yorkers who "stare coldly" as they passed on the street, and the fact that she had to sit for staged promotional photographs, "taken while sitting using my feet; the first time I ever sat for any in that posture."

Ann Leak debuted at Barnum's New Museum on October 16, 1865. The showman's original museum had burned to the ground on July 13 of that year, and Barnum had worked at breakneck speed to get a replacement up and running.[31] Ann Leak's debut was not

Ann Eliza Leak—the armless wonder, 1872, United States.
Photograph by Charles Eisenmann. Image courtesy of the Te Papa Tongarewa Photography Collection at the Museum of New Zealand.

announced with nearly the fanfare of Lavinia Warren's—rather, sandwiched between headlines about Abraham Lincoln's log cabin and "the largest fat woman living," the Museum more quietly advertised "Miss Ann Eliza Leak, born without arms," who "astonishes and entertains by her wonderful performance. Crochets, braids hair, embroiders, etc."

Appearances at venues like Barnum's made for hard workdays, often requiring performers to interact with visitors for twelve hours at a time. This added to Leak's stated ambivalence about her new career. In her journal, she wrote, simply, "Exhibited at Barnum's Museum. I cannot begin to describe the feelings of dread and aversion to it that filled my breast, though friends say I did well." Leak only remained at Barnum's for a few weeks and quickly returned home to Georgia and the comfort of her loved ones.

She nonetheless proceeded to tour throughout the country and was, according to her recollection, at turns successful and fearful. Appearing in Chicago at Colonel Wood's Museum, Leak received ample media coverage, and attendance was good. She was therefore shocked when her agents handed her a check for only ten dollars as her share of profits, along with the assurance that she could trust their math and didn't need to see the books. "*Ten dollars* simply given me as my fair division of the proceeds," she cried. "*Ten dollars*! Can it be *all*?" Leak signed a one-sentence agreement to part ways with her management, "hardly realizing what I was doing," and broke into tears over dinner in her hotel room "at the thought of being left alone among strangers."

The divide in Leak's early career is as plain as the Mason–Dixon line. In the carefully crafted mythology of her biography pamphlet, she remembers people in the South for their generosity. Warm and service-oriented Southern audiences empower her and support her career through seemingly spontaneous acts of charity. By contrast, Yanks are chilly and callous, faceless and commercial. New York gives Leak a fright, and Chicago only reminds her of those shifty managers. As Leak describes her travels home from the American Museum, it is Southern Baptists, Methodists, and Masons who smooth her way with kindness and charity.

Leak regrouped at home and continued to exhibit herself through the 1860s and into the new decade. Leak's appearances leveraged an origin story centered on virtue. She counted on audiences being able to sympathize with a young woman born without the "common avenues of self-help" yet who was called upon to support her family. Leak directed her appeal to good people, playing on their sense of self-regard, and to Masons especially, with their professed mission to act as a social safety net. Her father had been a Mason, and she appealed to members of the community for personal charity. The conversational dance was an exercise in code and decorum: Leak would let slip in that she was from a Masonic family, "having taken the Master's Daughter's Degree," and gentlemen would afford her the appropriate courtesy and respect. Ladies flocked to her on trains and in salons to provide caring companionship. In Southern venues, Leak styled her visitors as "friends" rather than customers and described how "these little reminiscences, casually met with in my wanderings, are like oases in the desert." Appearing in churches, community halls, and homes throughout the South, Leak praised the kindness of "new friends" who helped to arrange her appearances and provided her with generous donations. At one point, she loudly points out that she can "send one hundred and fifty dollars to my parents" and thanks good-hearted people for chipping in to cover her hotel bills.

Leak also sold souvenirs to raise money. She tucked Masonic symbols into the photographs she sold, images in which she sat sober, plain-faced, and holding up a pair of scissors with her left foot. Her demonstrations for the public commonly involved fancy crafting like fine embroidery and crochet, indicating she was raised well and appropriately feminine. At one point, Leak sold paintings and drawings as souvenirs, but eventually she settled on making bookplates or signing autographs on long strips of paper and snipping off portions with a pair of scissors. It was more efficient, and more profitable, too.[32] In these autographs, she very often emphasized industry and the value of hard work: A common note said that "indolence and ease are the rust of the mind."[33] She sold loads of them.

In 1872, she received an engagement proposal from a civil engineer in Philadelphia named W. R. Thomson. She mused to herself: "I like him as a friend but find it difficult to make up my mind to join him in the holy bands of wedlock." She eventually made up her mind, and the pair were married in April 1872. Leak remarked that "I was accompanied by Mrs. Kahn, the mother of the dwarf, and Mrs. Jones, the mother of the bearded child, who acted as witnesses to the solemnization of the marriage." Her father was thrilled she had found a nice guy, but "Mamma was not so easily reconciled, and expressed fears that I would not now love her so well."

By the 1870s, Leak was not only a seasoned professional with bankable appeal but a global star. She joined up with P. T. Barnum for the inaugural seasons of what would become the Greatest Show on Earth and, in 1877, traveled to Australia and New Zealand with the Cooper, Bailey & Co. Circus.[34] Barnum's route book (a sort of yearbook kept by traveling shows) sang her praises:

> *Miss Annie Leak of Georgia, lady born without arms,*
> *Tho' being deprived of them, she's not devoid of charms;*
> *She knits, crochets, writes poetry and prose,*
> *And all this being done by the aid of her toes.*[35]

The main source of information about Leak's life and interior voice is her autobiographical pamphlet, which would have been sold in addition to the autographed souvenirs she offered to patrons. Corroborated by news sources and bits of circus history, it is a rare and valuable case in which we have a woman's life and career related in her own voice. But caveats must apply: Not only was the pamphlet a commercial product and therefore inclined to present the most marketable version of events, but Leak herself had reason to curate a public persona at odds with her private self.

In 1865, Ann Leak claims to have been a timid girl horrified by the prospect of signing autographs and crocheting doilies for paying customers. Only six years later, though, she had built a steady, profitable career in dime museums and circuses around the United States. She was so successful, in fact, that while on the road with "Mr. Barnum" in 1871, she purchased and paid off the mortgage on a Florida home for her parents. As for her feelings toward Barnum himself, she traded her former antipathy for "much pleasure and satisfaction" with touring life on his show. She was by then so seasoned and confident a performer that, after a rough run at a country fair, she simply decided to buy the thing and run it herself: "After mature deliberation I concluded to reduce the show and carry it on at my own expense." Certainly, Leak matured and gained valuable experience on the road. But I would argue that her sharp judgment was there all along. It is clearly shown in how she told the story of her life in public.

Ann Leak was uncommonly clever when it came to managing her public and private personas. Aware of the value of a good story, she played up the idea of her own dramatic growth from a frightened girl into a well-seasoned circus professional. This allowed her to do two important things, painting herself as alternately meek and skilled when necessary. On the one hand, she could legitimize her career choice by saying it was the need to care for her family, not ambition, that led her to the stage. On the other, she could display her skill and wealth to prove that she had been right to do what she did: After all, she had paid for her parents' comfort and married a respectable man. Between her disability and the challenges of her home life, Leak had been encouraged to grow up fast. Beneath the storytelling, it is clear that Leak's pragmatism and keen eye were there all along. Careful not to show too much enthusiasm for her career at first, she led audiences to see her work as an unenviable necessity. The story of the unscrupulous managers who only paid her ten dollars is evidence that she never erred again in letting someone else manage her affairs. Even her moral statements show sharp awareness: At Barnum's New Museum in 1865, despite her stated fear and naiveté at appearing in the city's biggest cavalcade of living wonders, she keenly observed that "Some ladies pretended to faint, perhaps to have a better chance to fall into the gentlemen's arms."

Ann Leak appeared in newspaper coverage through the middle 1890s, touting her remarkable demonstrations at dime museums around the northeastern United States. A clipping from 1894 in the Philadelphia *Times* not only celebrates "Annie Leak Thompson, the armless wonder, who knits, writes and eats with her toes" but mentions newcomer "Houdini, in his mysterious barrel act."[36] An obituary in the *Philadelphia Inquirer* on January 6, 1899, simply reads: "On January 4,

1899, Ann E. Leak, wife of William R. Thomson, aged 59 years. The relatives and friends of the family are invited to attend the funeral service on Saturday afternoon."[37]

ooooo

As the introduction of mass media helped to develop a national popular culture, the scale and nature of fame in America changed. The interactions between media, audiences, and famous figures encouraged a version of fame that involved agency, ego, independence, and free public movement. These things were not only unusual for women in the nineteenth century but were typically considered unfeminine and inappropriate. Leak and Warren therefore had to find ways to properly explain and contextualize their career choices for the public. Aspiring to fame was a nonstarter for a respectable nineteenth-century woman. Graciously agreeing to gratify the public's curiosity for the sake of wholesome amusement, for education, to save the family from poverty? Better. These two women both legitimized themselves by crafting public personas that fit within archetypes of idealized femininity. By cheering for the establishment, each in her own way, they were able to sidestep some of its more difficult strictures.

Though Warren and Leak had distinct lives and careers, they share significant common ground. Each came from a family of modest means and was expected as early as childhood to contribute to running house and home in a typical feminine capacity. In a large family and a rural setting, disability was no reason to be excused from chores. In addition, each family knew that education in typical women's crafts and skills would be necessary for their daughter to operate in mainstream society. Each woman took on teaching work, which was seen as acceptable employment within the bounds of proper feminine behavior. Teachers cared for children and their moral education, so teaching was not only considered virtuous but largely considered part of the "private sphere" in which women were understood to operate.

Warren and Leak both had an association with P. T. Barnum, though in Warren's case it was a far closer relationship. Both Warren and Leak used the evolving mass media to craft personas and narratives and promote themselves, ensuring success and longevity in their careers. It's important to note that both were genuine talents; in an economy that routinely and quickly disposed of curiosity entertainments in response to audience appetite, neither woman would have had a lengthy career if she were simply a physical oddity. But as white women with the privilege and support of institutions like the Barnum empire and Masonic communities, Warren and Leak had a certain guaranteed status and appeal. The newspaper economy additionally fueled the engines of Warren's and Leak's fame.

Lavinia Warren and Charles Stratton used the press cleverly throughout their careers, and not just with the traditional Barnumesque strategy of sowing as many articles around an event as possible. In the early days of photography, they present one of the earliest cases of manipulating images to suit popular demand. Lavinia and Charlie posed in their wedding finery for repeat wedding portraits all around the world as they traveled, and in one of the most famous instances of public relations spin, they often staged photos with borrowed babies wherever they were performing. The couple did not have children, but people liked the story and the idea that the Strattons were complying with the expectations of family and motherhood.

Ann Leak loved the media, too, as much as she portrayed herself as a reluctant performer—in fact, that reluctance itself was a persona she used in press to her own benefit. Leak depended on local news coverage in every city and town she visited, and she eagerly cited her best reviews when compiling the autobiographical pamphlets she sold at her appearances. The approving opinions of third-party male writers legitimized Leak's narrative and gave it the stamp of journalistic approval.

What does an audience want, need, and get from a performer they go to see? As protoinfluencers, each woman had her own answer to that question, performing for her audience without seeming to present anything other than her authentic self. Lavinia Warren provided starry-eyed patrons with parasocial access to luxury, royalty, and the good life. Her appearances were a rare chance for people to see sumptuous, bespoke designer styles in person. Barnum would routinely talk about the number of costume changes Warren might make during an event or the price of her "beautiful and costly" dresses. (The *New York Sun* priced her debut gowns in 1862 at $2,000 each, which would be approximately $50,000 today.[38]) For the public, looking at Lavinia Warren in her fashionable, hyperfeminine attire was an exercise in aspirational luxury, like watching a fashion show or looking at an Instagram feed.

Warren's figure was a miniaturized version of the era's feminine ideal—"A form that Queens might envy" as one paper described—and the press went wild for her.[39] Her elaborate gowns, many of which survive in images if not in actual fabric, demonstrate how carefully Warren dressed on-trend and in pieces with complicated, careful construction. She was said to have received her white ermine cape as a gift from Queen Victoria—a gift from the Queen of England to the "Queen of Beauty."

Lavinia and her sister Minnie Warren, also of short stature, were known as fashion plates, and paper dolls of each woman's likeness were a popular commercial product at the time. The performance of femininity was both an asset and a drawback for women with unusual bodies: Yes, on the one hand, they were able to sell these objects of fashionable fun for children and adults who delighted in changing the doll's many grand outfits, but on the other hand, representations like these made literal "dolls" of little people. Lavinia and Minnie were often made to seem childlike during their careers, with spectators and guests wrongly assuming that their small size meant that they were somehow less able or less intelligent than typically sized adults.

Ann Leak had a different approach, connecting audiences with a sense of their own charity and piety. In crafting her public narrative and interacting with patrons, Leak relied on biblical archetypes of justice, suffering, redemption, and generosity. She was careful to portray herself always as a dutiful daughter, humble woman, and faithful Christian. "Imagine my own and a mother's feelings when it was decided that I must leave the society of my friends, and cast myself upon the sympathies and charities of a world, often cold and unfeeling," Ann proclaimed in her autobiography, recalling her leaving home to become an entertainer. "But, 'I know in whom is my trust,'" she wrote, quoting Paul's letter to Timothy. Leak was careful always to signal respectability in her words, her image, and her products: After all, why would a good girl exhibit herself in dime museums and circuses? Her piety allowed her to appeal to patrons for charity, to ask that crowds in every town and city support her with fees, resources, and connections as a signal of their own virtue. "I deem no apology necessary in appearing before you as a suppliant of your bounty and favor," she wrote. "And, first of all, I beg you not to regard me as an ordinary show character, or travelling mendicant." Saintly Ann Leak assured audiences of two things: They should be glad not to be in her place, and they could pay to feel even better about it.

Both women successfully performed versions of feminine virtue in front of paying audiences for decades. Ann Leak and Lavinia Warren managed the feat of presenting themselves as good women first and public figures second. Each was charming, gifted, and shrewd, creating a career path at a time when disabled women had limited options. At the time, a woman choosing to exhibit herself in public for fame and money would have received straightforward criticism: too much ego, too little care for home and family. By winning over audiences with their upright public personas, Warren and Leak shielded themselves from such opposition.

Even in her time of need, Warren acted the role of nobility, and in a time of relative personal comfort, Ann Leak still appealed to charity. Lavinia Warren and Ann Leak had very different public personalities but used them to similar end and purpose: Each displayed virtues that proper white women were meant to aspire to. Each became successful by performing femininity onstage.

CHAPTER 5

Women Take Flight

The first women to perform on the flying trapeze took flight in the late 1860s, not quite a decade after the French performer Jules Léotard pioneered the act.[1] By the time the circus entered its "golden age" only a few decades later, it was no longer unusual to see women present aerial acrobatics. In fact, as circus exploded in popularity in America, circus owners sought women performers specifically to combine gymnastic skill with their gendered appeal "as models of domestic womanliness, and as objects of titillation."[2] Crowds raced to see beautiful women dozens of feet overhead, leaping and flying gracefully on trapeze, tightrope, poles, ropes, and other nerve-wracking apparatuses. Under the big top, athletic women launched and caught each other on flying trapezes, bobbled fashionable parasols on a highwire promenade, and even hung from thin lines by their teeth, like spangled pendulums.

It was dazzling, beautiful, and thrilling to see. But the nineteenth-century circus, like life outside the tent, tended to hold these women in a bind. Nineteenth-century American society generally worked to minimize women's social power through a "separate spheres" ideology and patriarchal structures that kept women away from money, opportunity, autonomy, and the ability to be heard. Circus women challenged that status quo. They made an independent living, traveled, showed off their bodies, and generally called attention to themselves. What was society to do with them?

Society responded by holding these performers, especially aerialists, to impossibly hyperfeminine standards. Being a "good" circus woman required, all at once and in the right degree, both ambition and modesty, sex appeal and decorum, strength and reserve. Some audiences, having seen the illustration of a lady poised calmly midair on the colorful circus posters, perhaps wanted to be uplifted by a performance of beauty and grace. No small number of men walked down the midway in hopes of catching a long look at her long legs. Her muscularity and training had to be good enough to keep "The Greatest Show on Earth" worthy of its name. Any error could be bad for publicity or worse, life- or career-ending. But neither should she show too much sweat or effort or compromise her feminine softness. And since old ideas about circuses and morality held on in assumptions and whispers, circus women were still expected to guard their respectability lest they risk looking like a floozy or a degenerate. Fashion was a minefield, too—was a woman to wear snug leotards and tiny skirts, modest dress, corsets, or the latest in street fashions? It was impossible to do all at once.

The circus worked to build its image as clean, respectable family entertainment in the decades after the Civil War. This was in large part made possible through new, massive publicity machinery. For the first time, shows employed dedicated press agents to be sure that their news coverage was plentiful, flowery, and favorable. Some of these men, like Richard "Tody" Hamilton, became famous in their own right. This first generation of public relations architects, bold and well funded, loved playful, hyperbolic language and were not above manufacturing spectacle or manipulating news to suit their purposes.

From the middle 1800s onward, publicists worked especially hard to convince audiences that the onstage persona of a circus woman was just that: a character, played for entertainment by a lady who otherwise gladly complied with social expectations. To assure audiences that the show was respectable, promoters held up the performance of beauty and domesticity while de-emphasizing sexuality and subversiveness. This duality helped keep the family-friendly image of the circus intact and held its larger transgressive potential in check.

To achieve that family-friendly image, circus and society alike held aerialists to conflicting standards of womanhood, athleticism, and showmanship. So many well-trained women aerialists tried to find the impossible balance, performing death-defying, athletic acts in show after show with perfect hair and not a ruffle out of place.[3] Part of the appeal of aerial acts was that these women were manifestly both capable and attractive. Owners and media personnel used the burgeoning American media to tell stories about these women and to build an idealized character persona: a beautiful woman, brave and intrepid, able to do somersaults in a corset and still commit herself to being a perfect wife in the off-season. Audiences cheered for her.

Conforming to feminine expectation paid off in terms of marketability, but it was maddeningly difficult. More to the point, historic sources tell us what the public relations men didn't dare to admit: Nobody was that perfect. Two pairs of aerialists demonstrate the heights to which circus women soared and the obstacles they faced in doing so. The human cannonball Zazel, the leaping Lulu, and the aerial Austin Sisters all help us understand that, as far as press and public were concerned, there were many ways to be a woman: It's just that most of them were somehow wrong.

ooooo

For the most part, historians agree that the first true human cannonball act was performed by the aerialist Rossa Matilda Richter. In this entertainment, an aerialist is fired from an oversized spring-loaded cannon. Emerging in a dramatic puff of smoke, the performer flies across the performance space in a tremendous arc and lands in a net an equally impressive distance away. Because circus cannons propel the performer at great speed, the aerialist needs precise awareness of how to exit the barrel with proper velocity and posture. The flier also needs to land at the exact spot where a safety net or air bag has been placed, which can be even more complicated if the act is done outdoors where wind and weather are in play. Though the idea of a human cannonball can seem cartoonish, within circus it is known as a particularly dangerous act.

Richter had trained from a young age and was a talented aerial trapeze flier. In cooperation with a polymath circus artist and inventor known as The Great Farini (real name William Leonard Hunt), Richter chose the stage name "Zazel" and debuted in 1877 as a teenage human cannonball at the Royal Aquarium in London. Spectators in England loved her, but terrified lawmakers worried she was destined to become a bloody wreck in public and proposed regulation against such dangerous stunts. In response, Zazel simply headed to the United States and was there met with great enthusiasm and acclaim. In The Greatest Show on Earth in 1880, she was celebrated for flying seventy-five feet across the arena from the mouth of a cannon, and she soon became the unquestioned emblem of this act. Surviving photographs show her sitting calmly on the barrel of her cannon in a ruched satin bodysuit, and starry-eyed reviewers deemed her a "palpable hit!" (The same coverage jokingly suggested to male readers that a cannon barrel might be a good place to tamp down one's mother-in-law.)

But even as Zazel was celebrated for her "hard and well-directed training," there were constant questions and comments about her fitness, her look, and her ability to correctly and fully perform womanhood.[4] *The Era* commented that "with regard to the general fitness of a woman for the work of an acrobat, there may be differences of opinion, just as there are differences of opinion about her fitness for the work of a doctor."[5] Another British paper claimed that "Zazel appears to be a muscular young man made up to slightly resemble a young woman."[6] It was unimaginable that Zazel could really be a woman: A good woman, an attractive woman, would not perform in such a way.

Some commentators dressed up their opposition as concern, wailing: "Can nothing be done to stop the inevitable progress to destruction of poor Zazel?" Aerial acts like the cannon, trapeze, and high dive, insisted a *Vanity Fair* columnist, were too strenuous and risky for a woman. "Her back must be made of cast-iron or india-rubber to stand such a concussion. As certain as fate she will do this feat once too often, and, if she alights on her head instead of her back, instantaneous death must ensue."[7] Even P. T. Barnum, who hired Zazel in the United States and loved her act, had something to say about her appearance. Writing from the Murray Hill Hotel in 1889, Barnum advised: "My wife says she will give Zazel a bouquet if she will wear

"Miss Zazel" sitting atop her cannon.
Image courtesy of the Tibbals Learning Center and Circus Museum at the John and Mable Ringling Museum of Art.

a *white* costume when up on the wire. Really she cannot be seen up there in dark dress + her act is *too good* to be lost."[8]

News outlets were keen to point out that Zazel may not have shown an appropriate feminine concern for her physical well-being, but she could nonetheless be redeemed into proper womanhood. She was, after all, as good at homemaking as she was explaining how to fall in a net properly. One writer, mentioning that the human cannonball and her husband "live very happily together," was sure to catalog that Zazel "does all her own cooking and housework" when at home, "makes all her own dresses and costumes both for on the stage and off it, and in fact is a thoroughly practical little lady and a good and affectionate mother to her husband's little children. For the rest she is beautiful off the stage as well as on it."[9] In order to preserve and prolong her career, Zazel had to perform both her aerials and her femininity with equal aplomb.

ooooo

There were different standards in play for The Great Farini's adopted son, Sam Farini, even as he undertook similar aerial work in the years before Zazel's debut. Sam, whose real name was Samuel Wasgatt,[10] started his career at less than ten years old under the name "El Niño Farini." He was presented as Farini's son and captivated audiences by dangling from the trapeze with only his head on the bar, playing a drum. After a brief period during which the boy took no new bookings, in 1870 Farini reemerged with a new protégé under his wing: a lissome teenage girl with long blond hair known as Lulu. Lulu made her debut in Paris in 1870 to rapturous applause, soaring into the air from a spring-loaded pedestal of Farini's design that propelled her more than twenty feet into the air from a standing start. (Farini would later refine this design to create the human cannonball act for Zazel.) After a barnstorming European tour during which quiet Lulu delighted audiences and rejected all suitors, Farini brought "Lulu's Leap" to New York in 1873. The act was again a smash hit. Lulu claimed that, at Niblo's Garden that year, "My salary there was $1,000 a week."[11]

Lulu dangling effortlessly from a trapeze by her neck.
Image courtesy of the National Portrait Gallery in London.

Before long, though, audiences and reporters started to wonder about Lulu's identity. Some coverage simply snarked that the gig was up, since Lulu had grown a now unavoidably visible mustache, while a Washington paper reported on a rare accident in 1876 and gasped that the "attending physician discovered that Lulu is a man!"[12] Lulu was, of course, Sam Wasgatt.

Lulu retired in the late 1870s, claiming that it wasn't due to any controversy but rather was a matter of circus having run its natural course. Sam Wasgatt cut his hair, married, and in 1877 had a baby daughter, figuring at that point "it would be better to live in a house than in our trunks."[13] Wasgatt trained as a painter and photographer, and in 1885, he traveled with Farini on an expedition to the Kalahari, where he took some of the earliest photographs of southern Africa.[14] An account of the voyage describes a "splendid athletic fellow" of thirty years, having traded "the catapult and the cannon, the net and the trapeze, for the photographic camera." As for his soaring female persona? "That fallacy was exploded long ago. The fair Lulu with the blond locks thirty-two inches long, Lulu the daring—the graceful, the effeminate, Lady Lulu has changed terribly since last you saw him."[15] Lulu Farini earned fame and adulation because she was a model of femininity: young and innocent, graceful, uncommonly pretty, quiet, and chaste enough to send the boys away.

When Sam Wasgatt put Lulu aside, moreover, there was no judgment or social consequence. As a red-blooded American man (Wasgatt was from Maine and ultimately settled in P. T. Barnum's hometown of Bridgeport, Connecticut), if anything, he gained in social standing. Lulu demonstrated for society that, going by nineteenth-century standards of proper behavior, the best woman for the job could in fact be a man, one who performed femininity without dissent. Zazel, coming into Farini's universe as Lulu departed it, was not so lucky. The same British paper that speculated about her gender also compared her unfavorably to her predecessor: Zazel was "not so nice a performer as Lulu."[16] With neither superlative beauty nor a male alter ego to fall back on, Zazel had to prove hyperfemininity in a less poetic way: by assuring audiences that she could cook and sew as well as fly.

ooooo

Aimee and Rose Austin also navigated the crush of gendered expectation placed on circus aerialists. Aimee was born in England in 1870 as Ada Amy Peck. She first appears in show advertisements at nine years old, making her performance debut alongside Rose Austin in a sister act on the flying trapeze.[17] Seventeen-year-old Rose was also English. Her husband Robert G. Austin—"R. G." for short—was a former member of The Austin and Hess Troupe of performing roller skaters and had gone into the management side of the business to promote his wife's work.[18]

The Austin Sisters were talented and successful enough that, by the middle 1880s, R. G. brought them to the United States and signed with W. W. Cole's traveling circus.[19] Though they were consistently billed as a sister act and spent nearly all their personal and professional time together, it is unlikely the women were related; press claimed Rose and R. G. had adopted young Aimee after seeing her skill in a rink. Presumably Aimee joined the act as a talented apprentice and took Austin's surname since a sister act was snappier in print, not to mention more socially acceptable. The circus had a history of remaking anonymous young talent with a suitably marketable new identity, and moreover, circus women who came from established show families were understood to have better reason to make an otherwise dodgy career choice.[20]

Rose and Aimee performed as a trapeze duo. Aimee was the flier, the one to attract oohs and aahs from the crowd below as she flipped, flew, and tumbled in midair. Rose, freely described as "muscular," did the "heavy work" of catching aerial Aimee in the Austin Sisters' act. Both roles are essential: While it's the flier who typically gets the credit for showmanship in any trapeze duo, the catcher must master timing, friction, and centripetal force while hanging upside down on a moving bar.

The trapeze act was certainly thrilling, but teenaged Aimee soon raised the stakes by adding in a new routine, one that would soon give her the nickname "The Human Fly."

A particularly vivid account of her act is given in Connecticut news from 1885. On the evening of November 24, sodden audience members hurried out of a downpour into the lobby of Bunnell's Museum on Crown Street in New Haven, Connecticut.[21] George Bunnell was a veteran of the New Museum in New York (in which P. T. Barnum himself was a silent partner) and was well-versed in the sort of curiosity entertainment that kept dime museums humming, from trained cats to demonstrations where a man ate shards of glass and lived to tell the tale.

For this Thanksgiving week, patrons were promised not only the usual host of novelties but a headline act by Mademoiselle Aimee Austin herself. After the Austin Sisters performed their usual program on the flying trapeze, Aimee then climbed gracefully from the bar to a polished slab of marble suspended thirty feet over the show floor. Placing her feet carefully on the underside of the slab, she slowly and carefully walked across its length upside down, like a graceful teenage mantis. Or, at least, that was what was supposed to happen: When Aimee turned to begin her ceiling walk, her footing wobbled. The audience rose to their feet, gasping in horror as Aimee "dropped like a shot" to the net below. A reviewer swore that Aimee "lay like one dead for nearly three minutes" in the netting, tears welling in her eyes. Then, at last, the young acrobat rose, and the audience, whose hearts were once again beating, watched her speak in hushed tones with her manager. The two were evidently arguing about whether the show must, in fact, go on. A local prosecutor and two doctors in the audience rushed to the stage, arguing with the gentleman that "it was cruel to make the girl repeat the act, as she must be suffering a nervous shock from the fall, and it was imperiling her life to make her repeat the set." For a young woman to perform a dangerous act was cruelty, whereas the same feat done by a man would have been lionized. Her manager waved the men off, grumbling about nonsense as Aimee remounted the aerial rig. She then flawlessly accomplished an upside-down stroll back and forth across the slick marble to thunderous applause for her bravery and grace.

When Aimee toured to Chicago a few short weeks later, the reviewers were ready, and this time one of them figured out the real trick of her act. Noting that since "the vaudeville patron is so phlegmatic nowadays," it was advisable for performers "to thrill him a little to insure his full appreciation. So the human fly is wont to purposely detach her feet from the board and drop with a fine shriek into the net, which has never yet betrayed her confidence. When the spectators have recovered from the horror of the moment the fly repeats her attempt with a show of desperate courage, and of course succeeds amid a bedlam of plaudits."[22] In other words, Aimee knew the audience was prepared to underestimate her as a scared girl, and she was playing them all.

Aimee broke out of the mold of the typical female aerialist, developing a niche with the "human fly" act and its antipodean walk. The human fly act itself was not a new creation, though Austin was credited with bringing it to the United States and raising it to new heights of popularity. Originating in Europe, one of the act's first practitioners was a man known only as Sanchez, who accomplished the feat with special shoes made to fit into grooves in the ceiling panel. Another well-known performer was Hervio Nano, the "Gnome Fly," a climber whose legs were eighteen and twenty-four inches in length, respectively, and whose real name was Harvey Leach.[23] By the later nineteenth century, female human flies predominated: Aimee was joined by the likes of Miss Silvia the "Skandenavian Ceiling Walker," Anna Merkel the Human Fly, and the enigmatic Mademoiselles Speltarina, D'Antrello, Alma, and Zerate.[24]

Women were drawn to and succeeded at the act for many reasons. The women who were performing aerial acts were already fluent in skills needed for the human fly performance, and physically smaller performers had an easier time working with the required technology. To accomplish what looked like a carefree, unassisted walk upside-down across a marble ceiling tile, Aimee employed specialized shoes fitted with rubber suction cups. As she sat primly in the trapeze, bobbing her legs back and forth above the audience, she would set upon a spot to place her feet, securing a vacuum seal. Leaving the trapeze, she would then invert herself, taking short steps across the polished twenty-four-foot slab in front of her.[25] The shoes were equipped with rubber disks, four and a half inches in diameter and fastened to the sole by a metal stud. A wire loop extended under the top of the shoe, held under tension by a spring so that when Aimee pushed down on the ball of her foot, the suction would release, and she could take a new step. *Scientific American*, assessing the apparatus, calculated that given the surface area of the rubber and the vacuum provided, the apparatus could likely support 240 pounds. Aimee was said to weigh 125.[26]

Performing throughout the Midwest in 1889, papers rhapsodized about Aimee's ability to walk with ease and speed upside down high above the crowd, at all turns demonstrating what was expected of a female performer: talent, yes, but also a "bright little body" and a "rather fascinating personality."[27] She let her long hair fall straight down in a two-foot blond cone to emphasize the literal gravity of the situation, and she wore a sleeveless leotard and ruched shorts trimmed in bits of rickrack, her posture perfect. If not for the upside-down part, she appeared as if she were about to curtsy at any moment.[28] Austin herself remarked that "To me walking with head down is a genuine pleasure. But although it pleases me it may not be found so pleasant by the rest of the world."[29]

Risk was everywhere a human fly looked. If the board was unfamiliar or uneven, if she was disoriented or became faint, she would fall earthward in a split second. The board itself was important to Austin's act going well, too. At one point, *Variety* magazine lamented that "baggage smashers lived up to the title and Aimee Austin had to hustle a new board for her act."[30] Even with a safety net, she could injure herself or others. In 1885, Aimee finished her act with a fall to the net below. A roustabout on the show made the mistake of walking under the net just as she dropped, and "the sag in the net permitted her to hit him, knocking him cold, correspondent reporting 'she nearly drove his head through his body.'"[31] All of this was done not only with seamless grace, but "an amount of rapidity that fairly takes away the breath of the spectator."[32]

Aimee courted danger and projected a hardier version of femininity than most social structures considered proper. Her partner Rose collided with different expectations of womanhood.

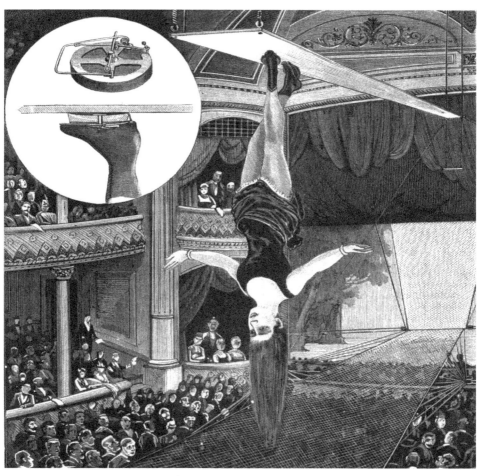

Aimee Austin mid-act as the Human Fly.
Scientific American, July 5, 1890. Image courtesy of HathiTrust.

The Austin Sisters were a successful working act. They were successful enough, in fact, that R. G. Austin was able to buy a house in fashionable Bath Beach, Brooklyn, where he could pass the summer hosting parties where Aimee stood arm in arm with Rose on the grand front stairs, welcoming fifty guests past Chinese lanterns at twilight for a wine-and-fireworks dinner.[33] Not only was there the house in Bath Beach, but "they have built two more, so that their neighbors had come to believe them well to do, as trapeze people go."

Yet in the summer of 1892, Rose Austin went missing. An actress friend of hers had injured herself during a performance, and Rose announced she was going to visit. Rose was seen boarding the Bensonhurst ferry on Monday, August 22, but no one saw her for days after. In a panic, R. G. Austin searched everywhere he thought likely and, on August 24, asked the police to issue an alarm. The *New York Sun* shouted in a headline on Thursday, August 25: "WHERE IS ROSE AUSTIN?"[34] The article was accompanied by an illustration of Rose wrapped in a fur collar with a bow at her chin, her stylish brown hair in an updo and bangs. Notices described her as a "rather pretty brunette of about 35," prone to slip into her English accent when talking quickly, and with an "uncommonly shapely figure" when in her trapeze finery. By Thursday afternoon, the locals were circulating a rumor that her body had washed up on Bath Beach.

Various explanations were put forward in the media. The *New York Times* claimed that Rose had epilepsy.[35] R. G. Austin was heard to corroborate this, saying that his wife was likely to wander during one of her "fits." At another turn, Rose was said to "undergo medical treatment almost constantly because of her exertions on the trapeze," which purported to answer any open questions even though Aimee Austin had no such apparent medical needs. Some accounts portray R. G. as a distraught husband wracked with grief, while others say that he "took matters very philosophically," leading some folks to believe the whole thing was a Barnumesque advertising stunt.[36] It was not the first time Rose had disappeared. Two years prior, "Pretty Rose Austin" had gone missing during the Austin Sisters' run at Koster & Bial's venue in Manhattan and returned after a few days. R. G. opted not to mention this to the police, but newspapers eagerly recalled the fact.[37]

Salivating at the whiff of scandal, reporters interviewed the Austins' neighbors, who described the loud arguments that were allegedly a common event in the performers' home. On one occasion in 1892, it was said, "Austin dragged his wife by the hair from her carriage into the house and beat and choked her. She begged of him simply let her alone, and said that she would give him money if he would let her live peaceably. He retorted that she was constantly drunk." Neighbors had heard "angry voices" from the Austins' cottage on Sunday morning before her disappearance and said that Rose had been heard shrieking, "I can't stand it any longer. I'll go away, for I'd rather die myself than be murdered by a brute like you." R. G. shouted after her: "I'll have another woman here as soon as you get out."[38]

In the end, Rose returned home as mysteriously as she had left, arriving in Brooklyn around 8:30 Thursday evening. She was accompanied home by a brother and "Charles A[l]lers, a liquor dealer hailing from the eastern district of the city."[39] Rose had a black eye and no idea where her coat had gone, but she was otherwise fine.[40] Attended at home by a doctor, Rose would only say that "she was taken sick on the Twenty-third street ferry."[41]

The press had long suggested, sometimes outright, that Rose struggled with alcohol abuse. Trade papers occasionally mentioned that Rose was "indisposed" for a particular performance or that she had "fainted," and R. G. Austin was known to send sharp letters to the editor in response to any suggestion that his wife was anything less than a diligent performer and a perfect lady.[42] He gave epilepsy or fatigue as occasional excuses or simple bad luck: In 1891, a notice in the *New York Clipper* informed readers that Rose "had the misfortune to lose a satchel containing a large sum of money and most of her jewels during her recent trip abroad." As a result, "Mrs. Austin is now resting betimes at her husband's pretty villa at Bath Beach."[43] This all could have been true, a convenient cover for personal habits that did not align with expectations of a married woman or evidence that Rose indeed had an alcohol problem, perhaps in response to persistent domestic abuse and violence. All of these are both possible and difficult to confirm upon the historical record. Publicized impropriety of any sort, though, was not what R. G. Austin wanted. It would suggest to the public not only Rose's moral failure but that he could not control the women in his household.

The Austin family discord was back in the news in the spring of 1893, when the New York papers eagerly printed an item from the police blotter: Two women out drinking with their boyfriends at half past two in the morning attracted "more than ordinary attention" when they were recognized as Rose and Aimee, then playing shows at Huber and Gebhardt's Casino.[44] Police said they found the Human Fly "lying on the pavement and waving her feet, apparently in an attempt to perform her famous ceiling-walking act without a ceiling." The woman identified as Rose, though she was having trouble standing upright, explained the situation to police. One of the women's male companions had observed a passerby getting too familiar with Aimee and pulled a revolver. Full of jealousy and gin, he fired the gun. No one was hurt, but Aimee screamed and fainted. The women gave their names to police as Aimee Peck and Mrs. Francis B. Smith. All were charged with public intoxication, and Diedrich Allers, "a hotel keeper of the eastern district" and brother of Charles, the liquor dealer Rose had returned with after her 1892 disappearance, paid bail.

R. G. Austin was on the matter in the next day's *Brooklyn Daily Eagle*, writing curtly: "Will you please contradict the report that appeared in your paper to-day, in reference to the Austin sisters being arrested for intoxication. I can most positively assert and prove that my wife, one of the Austin sisters, known as Rose Austin, was at home in Bath Beach at the time stated. Kindly give this the same prominence that you did the report mentioned."[45] R. G. Austin apparently felt no need to defend Aimee in the press.

The sister act split a matter of weeks later. Aimee had had enough of R. G. and Rose, and at twenty-three years old, she felt independent enough to do something about it. She took out an ad in the *New York Clipper*, the showbiz paper of record. She wrote, simply:

> To Whom It May Concern
> That I, Aimee Austin,
> Known as the "Human Fly,"
> have dissolved partnership with my sister, ROSE

AUSTIN, and all contracts made by R. G. Austin I hereby cancel, and notify all managers to take notice of same.
May 8, 1893. AIMEE AUSTIN. Address, care of CLIPPER office.[46]

Rose found a new partner, Minnie Silbon, and the pair continued to perform as the Austin Sisters under R. G.'s management. Aimee also continued working, still using the Austin surname under which she had become world famous as the "Human Fly." Without the financial security, name, and backing of R. G. Austin, though, she had to work harder. She and a partner were observed practicing at the 47th Regiment Armory in Brooklyn ahead of the 1894 circus season, using the facility in the daytime when it was not needed for drills. The women hung trapeze rigs and rings from the high ceilings, practicing with aerial coaches in their "skin tights and loose-fitting waists" to the shock of passersby and the military brass, who considered the whole thing more than a little indecent.[47]

Aimee Austin was still performing as a trapeze artist and human fly consistently by the turn of the century, spending the 1902 season as a headline act with the Ringling Brothers circus.[48] In 1904, a Vancouver house excitedly informed patrons that it had ripped out seats to make room for Aimee's act, "one of the most attractive acts ever seen in a vaudeville house." And though her road was harder as an independent performer,[49] she was at least free of Rose and R. G.'s drama. The industry paper *Billboard* reported Aimee Austin's death from bladder cancer in January 1907 at just shy of thirty-seven years old.[50] *Billboard* warmly recounted that she "was well and favorably known among professional people and she leaves a host of friends to share her husband's sorrow."

The end of Rose's story is more difficult to trace. The *Brooklyn Daily Eagle* reported in May 1899 that R. G. Austin brought Rose into court on charges of being a "habitual drunkard" and "failure to look out for her two daughters." The case had allegedly been brought to the attention of child services.[51] The 1900 US census has her still living in Brooklyn with R. G. and two children listed. By that time, her nineteen-year-old eldest had eloped.[52] (The census also notes that

Rose's two daughters were the only ones to survive of five children born during her circus career, another possible reason for her lifelong despair.) An obituary printed in October 1928 in San Bernardino, California, mentions the passing of "Mrs. Rose E. Austin, 69, a native of London, England." She was survived by a daughter, Emily E. Silverton; Rose's younger daughter was named Emeline. As far as the 1920 census was concerned, Rose Elizabeth Austin was a housewife, and her husband Robert George Austin worked as an electrician in southern California; the circus is nowhere to be found in these notes, but both their birth dates line up with what we know of the performing Austins. The obituary claims that Rose, a devotee of Christian Science, had lived in California for forty-seven years: perhaps an error, perhaps an effort to hide her circus past behind a quiet, unremarkable feminine story.[53] Even more provocative, Emily Silverton's death certificate lists her mother's surname as Peck, the same as Aimee's at birth. Were Rose and Aimee sisters after all? Had Rose raised a child of then-unmarried Aimee for the sake of feminine propriety? There are too many questions and not enough sources to answer them.

But even the gaps in the historical record suggest that, through challenges and successes alike, Aimee and Rose Austin, like Zazel and Lulu before them, constantly had to manage their public perception and how well they met the standards of acceptable femininity. Aimee's human fly act was of a piece with a nineteenth-century culture that eagerly policed gender and propriety. Society expected that the girl on the flying trapeze—or in the cannon or on the ceiling—would deliver a suitably alluring display. All the training and skill that went into an aerial act was meant to disappear behind the spectacle, turning the act into a performance of artless femininity: Spectators' stomachs went all aflutter at the prospect of a lovely young woman in flight or taking a dangerous stroll far above their heads. To foster the illusion, these aerialists were expected to comply with a long list of often contradictory expectations. Aimee had to pretend to fall to reassure audiences that female strength was uncertain. Zazel had to emphasize her domesticity, and Lulu, beauty and chastity. All of them had to be pretty and graceful in public at all times or suffer censure in the press: Even after the show ended, the performance of femininity had to go on.

After all, young, lovely girls with ambition are a renewable resource, and performers understood that, for all but the greatest stars of the circus, their time in the spotlight was likely fragile and fleeting. Having literally flown close to the sun, society expected that these women would inevitably return to earth and to the private sphere where they belonged. Yet their actual, more complicated lives nonetheless persisted in the historical record, evidence—along with the vigor and independent spirit in their performances—to challenge popular ideas about what women owed society.

CHAPTER 6

Invisible Girls and Electric Women

On the evening of September 18, 1883, fourteen-year-old Lulu Hurst could not for the life of her manage to fall asleep. Part of it was excitement: Lulu had an older cousin named Lora Wimberly visiting her home near Cedartown, Georgia, and she looked up to Lora with fawning admiration—so smart, pretty, and a good artist, too. The rest of her insomnia was due to the rumble and crack of a nasty thunderstorm outside, which had rolled in just as the girls got into bed together for the night. The storm was rough and noisy, Hurst recalled, mentioning that she sat in the dark "much in fear on account of it." The girls had, despite thunder and sleepover giddiness, nearly managed to nod off when a "quick, muffled, popping sound" startled them from their bed. They searched the bedroom for "big, horny bugs, snakes, etc.," but finding nothing, resolved to go back to sleep. No sooner had Lulu and Lora lay down than the same noise, "peculiar, harrowing, muffled," began again, this time around the bed itself. Hurst called for her parents.[1]

The household searched the room, turned out the girls' bedding, and found nothing. The noise continued. "Every one in the house now became alarmed," said Hurst. "A conference was held and it was decided, on the suggestion of my mother, that the sounds were caused by electricity. On this night the atmosphere was surcharged with electricity on account of the severe storm, and all agreed that there could be no solution but that." Hurst's father, a normally unflappable Confederate veteran, became "completely demoralized." The neighbors were called in to help investigate. Someone suggested that the group start asking questions of this mystic force, whatever it may be. It tapped patterns in response.

Another friend suggested that all present place their hands on a piece of furniture to gather their energies in the mode of then-popular spiritualist séances. Since there was no table nearby, the group all grabbed hold of a chair, which suddenly started to jerk and dance around the room as if possessed. Hurst mused: "The question now came up, was this force associated with any particular person? Was there any one present who controlled this peculiar influence? It was found, upon investigation, that it followed me."

No matter what inanimate object Lulu Hurst held, from that moment on—a chair, a cane, an umbrella—no one could touch it without being tossed aside like a rag doll. With furniture dancing at the slightest touch, and hickory nuts from the tree outside allegedly whizzing into the house at will, Hurst and her family concluded that Lulu had been infused with an unknown electrical energy by the storm. For her part, Hurst alternately referred to this energy reverently as "The Great Unknown," her "Power," or, like a Victorian-era Jedi, simply "The Force." Making a show of it was not on her mind—this would not be a lady's natural choice, of course—"but hundreds of people came to our home," Hurst explained. "They urged us to go before the public."

Magic is a discipline with a complicated history. For centuries, humans have placed religion, science, and entertainment in dialogue with each other to try and understand whether the supernatural is real and whether it is within human grasp. By the nineteenth century, people in the Western world had largely traded centuries of panic and superstition for an understanding that magical entertainment could make for a fun night out. Even after elemental fear had been traded for the idea of sleight of hand, though, ideas about the unknown or disruptive potential of magic remained culturally entrenched. This was particularly true for women. When men performed magic acts onstage, it was typically seen as evidence of skill, dexterity, and dominion. For women, the element of threat remained. Popular stereotypes suggested that women might, whether intentionally or unwittingly, bring forth witchcraft from some dark, impenetrable, and uncontrollable place. As a result, women were historically rare in magical entertainment, appearing at first only seldom or in the role of a lovely assistant.

Lulu Hurst, the "electric woman," emerged from magic's nameless shadows. Relying on some old beliefs about witchcraft and evolving ones about science and possibility, she used her otherworldly powers to defy social frameworks and seize a personal narrative. Hurst redirected the energy of men who would knock her off her feet, onstage and off. In so doing, she made way for headliners to come.

A few weeks after the introduction of cosmic forces into his hearth and home, Lulu Hurst's father was persuaded to put aside his Baptist opposition to public exhibition. Fourteen-year-old Lulu soon began to demonstrate her claimed supernatural abilities before paying public audiences, first locally in Georgia and then in increasingly larger venues over the next few months. In her performance, Hurst would invite volunteers to join her onstage. She stood plainly, in a long dark dress, and extended her arms to hold a pole of some sort—first, a cane; later, a billiard cue—horizontally at chest level. She rested the pole gently in the crook of her thumbs, palms outward in a loose, open grip. When the male volunteer stood opposite her, she urged him: *Push. I'll even lift one foot to help you out.* But when he tried, it was as though the teenage girl was sunk into concrete. No one could move her so much as an inch. Umbrellas in her hands flew to pieces. Hurst would guide three men to sit in a chair with a cane-woven seat—one gentleman seated, another on top of his lap, and a third on the shoulders of the second. Hurst would simply place her open palms on the back of the chair and lift five hundred pounds of man-weight off the ground. She pushed burly men aside without breaking a sweat, blithely running her hands through her dark bangs and laughing. Volunteers and audiences were confounded by her command of unseen forces and bought tickets by the fistful.

The origin story of spiritualism in America is usually roughly traced to Maggie and Kate Fox, teenage sisters from the so-called

"Burned-Over District" in upstate New York (the name refers to the "flames" of religious revival associated with the Second Great Awakening in America). The girls claimed to be able to communicate with spirits through mysterious taps on the walls and tables of their home. An infatuated public proclaimed the Foxes to be genuine spirit mediums. Spiritualism became very popular very quickly, and against a wave of true believers, the Fox sisters became essentially irrelevant to the movement they'd started. (In the end, they admitted they had faked the spirits' raps and bonks by carefully cracking their knuckles or dropping an apple or two under the table.) Historians estimate that as many as nine to eleven million Americans embraced spiritualism by the 1870s, seeking spiritual comfort amid the deep losses of epidemic cholera, enslavement, and the Civil War.[2]

As spiritualism grew and took hold, women took on a strong and prominent role in the movement. Spiritualist seekers and mediums were fairly well split between men and women, but if you mentioned a spirit medium in polite conversation, people most likely imagined a woman. It was an easy fit given the era's ideas of sex and gender, which thought of the feminine essence as inherently weak and unstable in comparison to a man's natural tendency toward intellect and dominion. The very things that made women allegedly unfit for public life at this time—their supposed delicacy, passivity, and generally impressionable nature—were fantastic traits for someone who hoped to channel powers from the great beyond: There was no strong skill or personality to get in the way. (To the extent that male mediums operated, skeptics were all too happy to criticize them as "addle-headed feminine men."[3])

It was here, in leading séances, that women were able to perform a role not typically available to them elsewhere in society. Spiritualist illusion had its critics and believers, but speaking broadly, it allowed women to engage in public life within an image of acceptable femininity. Because spiritualism rejected hierarchy and looked to the beyond as a way to bridge past traumas and future progress, it was a niche in which abolitionists, women's rights activists, and Black women like the authors Harriet Jacobs and Harriet Wilson were able to gain limited but significant traction.[4] Within spiritualism, women could further dialogue on any number of topics the "spirits" wished to entertain, even if those topics were not normally thought appropriate for women. Channeling allowed women to resist political and cultural ideas of womanhood, center themselves and their abilities, make a living, and demand attention. Spiritualism's cultural dominance was so strong that, for a time, it seemed like every preacher, scientist, public intellectual, and everyday person had an opinion one way or the other on séances, spirit photography, and quasi-religious publications like the spiritualist journal *Banner of Light*. Nor was the practice easily dismissed as something only embraced by the lunatic fringe: Mary Todd Lincoln regularly consulted mediums, hoping to communicate with her son Willie after his death from typhoid fever. Mark Twain described a medium's work in an 1867 short story entitled "Among the Spirits."[5]

Women were also culturally understood to be particularly receptive to spirit voices or unknown forces because of a historical association with witchcraft. When Reginald Scot wrote the first English-language text on witchcraft in 1584, entitled *The Discoverie of Witchcraft*, he had a limited, practical purpose in mind. By writing a detailed exposé of how fairground conjurors, performers, and alchemists accomplished what seemed to the untrained eye like natural or ceremonial magic, he hoped to debunk popular hysteria around witchcraft.[6] Scot argued that belief in magic was un-Christian and that witch panics tended to result in the prosecution of poor, disabled, and elderly women for no good reason. ("My greatest adversaries," wrote Scot, "are yoong ignorance and old custome.") Not everyone agreed: King James VI of Scotland (later James I in England) followed with his antiwitchcraft book *Daemonologie* in 1597, which described magic as "a supernaturall worke, contrived betweene a corporall old woman, and a spirituall divell."[7] Like the king, many folks still wanted to believe that witchcraft was a genuine threat, a means by which uncontrolled and uncontrollable women made the devil manifest in the world. Since practices and beliefs associated with witchcraft have been described and defined by men in Western history, they typically sit at the opposite of what any patriarchal society proclaims as its core values. Individual women who fail to identify with social norms and step too far out of line have historically been easily targeted as witches and subjected to persecution, trial, isolation,

Adelaide Herrmann as Sleeping Beauty.
Theatrical Portrait Photographs (TCS 28). Image courtesy of
Harvard Theatre Collection at Houghton Library, Harvard University.

or even execution as a result.[8] By the nineteenth century, witch panics were largely a thing of the past, and magic was broadly understood as a stage art rather than a thing of otherworldly evil. Even so, magician Adelaide Herrmann, then headlining as "The World's Only Woman Magician," had to reassure a reporter for *Broadway Magazine* in 1899 that "I do not intend to be mystic, and it is equally true that I do not wish to pose as a woman who is in league with the devil."[9]

When the entertainment industry started to formally coalesce in the nineteenth century, the ideal woman in a magic act was one who couldn't be seen at all. Londoners at the turn of the nineteenth century delighted in a mysterious entertainment known as the "Invisible Girl."[10] Visitors to this attraction would encounter a glass-walled casket hung by four chains on the corners from the ceiling of whatever dim, intimate room was then hosting the performance. The bottom of the casket and its head- and footboards were solid wood, but the rest was clear glass. Spectators could see through the case fully and even walk around it to see that nothing was secretly connected. A horn like the bell on a phonograph emerged from one end of the casket, and audience members were encouraged to speak questions into the horn. A disembodied feminine voice spoke answers in reply. Inevitably, the Invisible Girl could answer questions in great detail, as though she were right there with the crowd. As for the Girl herself, she was said to be "a daughter of French peasants, and being of such a retiring nature and disposition, she was always kept in a glass casket to make sure she never came to any harm."[11] Though patrons were told the naked eye could not see her, the Invisible Girl was manifestly capable of speech. Audiences were enthralled.

Building on a long history of mysterious entertainments and machines known as automata, the Invisible Girl operated on a simple conceit: The entertainment worked because the speaking-horn funneled sound toward a hidden pipe in the wall behind the casket. A woman sitting in the next room watched the whole proceeding through a camouflaged peephole in the stage wall. She spoke her answers into the pipe, which made them sound suitably muffled and ethereal.[12] Though audiences by and large enjoyed the illusion, there were critics. One writer, in the *Morning Post* of January 26, 1804, sniffed at the futility of such an entertainment: "Talk of half-a-crown to see one Invisible Girl! Why 500 Invisible Girls may be seen on Wednesday at the Pantheon, who will answer questions, sing in several languages, and dance reels all night—for only half-a-guinea!"[13]

The Invisible Girl and her *Post* critic tapped into the idea of women as faceless playthings. So did the Mysterious Lady, a magic act of the 1840s. Like her invisible counterpart, this Lady seemed to be every woman and no specific one all at once. As spectators filed in, she sat in a wooden chair with her back facing the crowd, hands in her lap. She wore a long, dark dress with a modest ruffle to the sleeve and a lace collar. Her hair was rolled at the nape of the neck and tied with a small bow. To her left, a spray of flowers stood in a small Grecian vase. The Lady gave the impression of no particular age and no special fashion. She could be anyone (or their mother), and, indeed, this was the point. As she sat, a gentleman appeared to begin the evening's entertainment. This man would walk through the theater and ask a question here, pick up an object there. He might borrow a patron's watch and ask the Mysterious Lady to tell the precise time, instruct her to describe the fine details of a patron's outfit, or have someone draw an undisclosed card from a deck. She would, without moving a muscle, respond to every query with unfailing precision.

The act, a two-person "second sight" act first seen in the United States between 1841 and 1843, was a sensation on both sides of the Atlantic.[14] One correspondent described it thusly: "The lady sits with her back to the company, and proves that she has a perfect knowledge of every circumstance which takes place behind her, without a possibility of its being reflected, or communicated to her by any collusion, at least hitherto not detected. She can name the spots upon dice, cards, &c., held at a considerable distance from her, where she could have no possible chance of seeing them in the ordinary way. Whisper in the lowest breath imaginable, and she will repeat your words with unerring accuracy. It is a truly wonderful performance."[15] The *Lancaster Examiner* turned to poetry: "Most wonderful Lady! we cannot divine / The silence displayed in that magic of thine!"[16] Queen Victoria took in a performance in London in 1845.

Few people realized that the act depended on carefully coded communication between the lady and her compatriot in the house.[17] The Mysterious Lady was talented, and popular, and even spawned copycat acts that reached for her mysterious mantle, but despite her fame, history did not record her name or what she looked like.

Part of why women have not historically been common in magic is because, socially, the idea of a woman deceiving a male audience has been considered unappealing, if not wholly unacceptable. When institutions and processes of power are dominated by men, the idea of a woman showing power or mocking the prevailing idea of control is truly dangerous. A woman magician presents the idea that men in the audience will have to respond to her performance by admitting that they do not know how she did it, cannot explain it, or perhaps simply are not as sovereign as they claim to be. Magic acts depend on the performer's ability to be accepted for their transgression against social and scientific norms, to be seen as a commanding presence. (And, practically speaking, it helps if the magician can wear clothing with pockets.)

News clippings and playbills assure us some magic women existed. "Frau Professor" Caroline Bernhardt was renowned as a court performer for Austrian and Prussian nobility in the late 1830s.[18] Women who were talented and lucky enough to headline performances were usually able to do so because of their male relatives' name recognition: Madame Wood, for example, was the daughter of the French conjuror Monsieur Adrian, and Lizzie Anderson demonstrated séance techniques for audiences who fondly recalled her father John Henry Anderson, the so-called "Great Wizard of the North."[19] In an 1881 book of more than three hundred pages on the history of magic, entertainment historian Thomas Frost was unable to mention a single woman in the industry who was not a headliner's wife, daughter, or assistant.

So it is unusual and notable that women had a significant role in performing supernatural tricks onstage in the latter half of the nineteenth century and that audiences were open to women in those roles. One of the most notable examples was Lulu Hurst, who earned a snappy nickname: The Georgia Wonder. In fourteen-year-old Hurst's case, that stormy sleepover was a transformative moment—a literal superhero origin story in which electricity imbued her with an elemental force.

Her fame grew due to rave reviews in the local Georgia press. Hurst and her parents, along with manager Paul Atkinson (whom Hurst would later marry[20]) headed north, playing increasingly large theaters and drawing dignitaries and scientists along the way. Hurst remained confident in her power, even as she assured any spectator or scientist that she had no idea from whence it came. According to rumor, she once mystically jump-started her own train after it stalled due to engine trouble. After her run in Washington, DC, Hurst claimed: "Begging pardon of the reader for the grandiloquent style of the above statements, I desire to say in an humbler and simpler vein that the 'Power' conquered Washington."

Curious locals and learned men continued to engage with Lulu Hurst at every stop on her tour for two years straight. Dignitaries, politicians, athletes, and scientists tried to figure her out, sometimes coming to the theater to be tossed around in person, other times asking for private laboratory demonstrations. The famous bodybuilder and strongman Eugen Sandow, who could break chains across his own chest, tried to lift her and couldn't.[21] Astonished onlookers attending her shows shook their heads at how this tall teenage girl, giggling as she sipped lemonade in the wings, could pull this all off. There were certainly doubts and debunkers along the way—*Scientific American* suspected a combination of strength and suggestibility was at play and concluded that "It will probably be found that Miss Hurst's exhibitions are only another phase of the hypnotic phenomena."[22] Even so, houses continued to fill with eager audiences.

By the time Hurst arrived in New York City in the summer of 1884, she was a bona fide star. Atkinson had arranged for her to play twelve nights at Wallack's Theatre, an upscale venue at Broadway and 30th Street that seated twelve hundred people and boasted new construction with an ornate proscenium stage.[23] Underneath the hall's copper and brass chandelier, Lulu Hurst astounded New Yorkers for the better part of two weeks. She held an afternoon preview performance for thirty gentlemen of the press on July 6, 1884, before opening to the public on July 8. At the outset, the *New York Times* only offered a cautious description of the sensation, describing Hurst as "a powerfully built country girl" in a black outfit and sizable gold chain, "about 5 feet 10 inches in height, with black hair worn loosely over her shoulders, dark eyes, and a full, round, fresh looking face, not expressive of any great intelligence, however."[24]

The reviews would change dramatically before long. On the tenth of July, members of one of New York's many "athletic clubs" decided to try their luck before the Georgia Wonder. Twenty burly men in rubber-soled gym shoes volunteered to "either tire out or 'expose'" the phenomenon. With a hundred "less muscular but equally enthusiastic" club men in the front rows to cheer them on, these athletes one by one tried to engage with Hurst in her various tests. The *Times* reviewer described the men as "children in her hands" and reported

Lulu Hurst's cane act.
Image courtesy of the Hargrett Rare Book and Manuscript Library at the University of Georgia Libraries.

that "the athletes retired from the stage after the performance covered with perspiration and confusion. The Georgia girl, who had tossed them about like so many jackstraws, was perfectly cool and not in the least tired." Hangers-on after the show asked Hurst questions in an effort to understand how a teenage girl, fiddling with her bangs, had just whomped a pack of athletes:

> **Q.** Don't you feel tired?
> **A.** Oh, no; not at all.
> **Q.** Do you exert your will power?
> **A.** I don't know what power I exert.
> **Q.** Does it tire you more to have three men to deal with than one?
> **A.** Oh, no; I don't notice the difference. Sometimes it is easier for me to move a strong, heavy man than a small man. To-night, if you noticed, I pushed around some of your strongest club men with only one hand.
> **Q.** What do you stroke your hair for?
> **A.** For fun, I guess. It's only a habit.
> **Q.** Do you retain your clearness of mind in the struggle?
> **A.** Oh, yes, I never forget myself or lose sight of a movement.[25]

The correspondent closed with a single question, asking Hurst, "Don't you feel frightened?" She replied succinctly, "What at—you?"

Scientists and skeptics continued to observe and examine Hurst throughout her tour. Some claimed she had an "extraordinary and occult power," while others openly proposed that tricks of strength and application were at work.[26] However, no hypothesis could dull the demand. The *New-York Evangelist* confirmed that "as much as five dollars is paid for a ticket, and Wallack's Theatre is nightly crowded."[27] Hurst was such a sensation that she commissioned $2,000 worth of dresses (over $50,000 today), so she could wear a different outfit every evening.[28] On July 19, 1884, her final night in New York, she had come far from being a quiet teenage girl in a generic black dress and delighted audiences in a gown of "snowy white."

The famous *Frank Leslie's Illustrated Newspaper* got to the nut of what confounded folks so much about the Georgia Wonder; all of New York, in its own way, was trying to form an opinion as to how "this rosy, giggling and seemingly unsophisticated country girl contrives to out-wrestle athletes, outwit scientists and outstrip trained actresses in that practical drawing power which attracts the shy and elusive dollar to the box office."[29]

Scientists were not the only skeptics. Onstage in Atlanta in January of 1884, she performed her "tests" as usual. Suddenly, the young sister of a local clergyman stood up in the house and shrieked: "Woman shall not rule the world; that is man's province, and woman shall not rule the world!" The woman left her seat and began to rush the stage, muttering "I will not sit down," and "A woman shall not prevail!" Hurst, shaken, left the stage amid cheers and confused shouting. Hurst's manager, Paul Atkinson, addressed the crowd once order was restored, commenting that "It is natural for us to sympathize with each other in misfortune, and we regret exceedingly that this distressing circumstance has occurred. We sincerely hope the lady may soon recover her nerves and be herself again."

So great was Lulu Hurst's fame and appeal that competitors emerged, among them fellow Georgians Annie Abbott and Mattie Lee Price, and even a few Hurst impersonators, whom Lulu dismissed as "parasites." Hurst left New York and toured America coast to coast, covering some twenty thousand miles over two years. She claimed that "the power was just as potent in knocking out 'Mormon elders' as it had been in handling Georgia crackers or New York athletes."

Lulu Hurst's act was indeed potent. She accomplished something men could not understand, and she could beat them using a physicality and level of command that was supposedly unavailable to women. The Great Unknown allowed Lulu Hurst to literally wrestle down the establishment.

But in Knoxville, Tennessee, in 1885, Lulu Hurst abruptly announced to her parents and Paul Atkinson that the Georgia Wonder was done. She would perform no more.

No one heard from Lulu Hurst for years after that. She attended Shorter Female College, a Christian women's university in Georgia, but left her studies to marry Paul Atkinson and start a family. In 1897, with her career years in the rear view, she suddenly decided to write her story. This became a self-published memoir, in which Hurst fully revealed how she had accomplished her magic. Referring to herself as a "weird, supernal meteor" who blazed through popular culture, Hurst promised a story as good as any science fiction: "The inspired fancy and wild imagination of a Jules Verne, Eugene Sue or Victor Hugo would be impotent to conceive a tale so weird and wonderful as this narrative of facts and truths unfolds." But why write, and why more than ten years after disappearing from the public eye?

Hurst claimed she had her reasons for retiring. She was, she said, even at sixteen aware of the way in which her powers were being used to legitimize all manner of spiritualist beliefs: "My phenomena were beginning to be used to prop up all sorts of outlandish and superstitious ideas and notions," wrote Hurst, adding that "This knowledge had oppressed me for a long time." That was her official explanation. It is also extremely likely that, as she acquired both fame and maturity, Hurst realized that the Georgia Wonder could not go on forever. She had a whole life to think of. Spiritualism's grip on American culture was waning, and as the twentieth century approached, long-held ideas of Victorian womanhood were beginning to soften.

Drawing back the curtain on her act, in her own words, continued to give Hurst control over her own story. Where young Lulu Hurst was an innocent country girl, a virtuous channel unaware of her powers, adult Lulu positioned herself as a woman in confident dialogue with culture, science, and reason. Hurst claimed that after leaving the stage, she "determined to apply myself to the study of different branches of knowledge in order to acquire that knowledge necessary to prepare myself for life; also, having in view at all times the acquisition of such knowledge of physics and mechanics as would lead on toward an understanding and explanation of my 'Power.'"

Thinking about muscular exertions and opposing forces, Hurst posed her stated problem in shouting block capitals: "COULD A CHILD FOURTEEN YEARS OF AGE, WITHOUT EXERCISING AN AMOUNT OF CONSCIOUS MUSCULAR POWER OR AGGRESSIVE FORCE AT ALL COMMENSURATE WITH THE UNRECKONED

FORCE OPPOSING HER, BY SOME UNRECOGNIZED LAW OF PHYSICS, MECHANICS OR LEVERAGE, OVERCOME AND ANNIHILATE SUCH UNRECKONED AMOUNT OF MUSCULAR FORCE WHEN OPPOSED TO HER IN CERTAIN SPECIFIED WAYS AND POSITIONS?"

There was an important predicate to keep in mind. Hurst admitted up front, as "Fact No. 1" in her scientific inquiry, that *"Every feat and 'wonder,' so-called, that I ever did was all the result of a little accident."* That first mysterious popping sound at home, produced in the wake of the electrical storm as she tried to sleep next to her cousin—it was really Hurst's hairpin, popping through the lining of her feather pillow. Discovering the accidental noise, young Lulu kept making it to startle her cousin, and then for a laugh, pushed her feet against the footboard of their bed to add eerie creaks and taps to the repertoire. Then the neighbors came over, and they all laid hands on the chair. Here, Lulu claimed to have been confounded past the bounds of her initial joke: "I knew we had our hands on the chair and the people attempted to hold it, while it cut up wild and furious antics. But I noticed this was kept up by the excited people, even after I had taken my hands off the chair. This amazed me greatly. However, in these first experiments I was quick to discover that no one or more of them could hold the chair when my hands were on it in certain positions."

Having studied physics since leaving the stage, Hurst claimed that she awoke in a flash one night in 1895, slapped Paul Atkinson in bed next to her (who asked "what I meant waking him up in that strange, excited way") and proclaimed: "I have found out how that balance test is done. It has just come into my mind like a flash." Essentially, she explained, the chair acted like a giant Ouija board, and any one person's confused pushes threw the others off balance. So, too, with Hurst's tricks with the cane, umbrella, and billiard cue: These feats of seeming strength depended on gentle, reliable counterpressure away from the direction of the "tester's" efforts. Lulu Hurst could lift three men in a dining chair thanks to the application of simple lever and fulcrum principles.

Why reveal her secrets after more than a decade? On the record, Hurst explained that she did not know if the public would even care after so many years, that her process of inquiry naturally took time, and she had no desire to expose her parents and manager, now husband, to suspicions of fraud or complicity. It's quite possible that she and her family knew all along exactly what was going on with this act and were happy to take advantage of the skill and stagecraft of "Laughing Lulu Hurst." Hurst may indeed have figured out these disarming tricks by trial and error based on some early pranks. It's also likely that, as the turn of the century approached, the illusion was simply harder to maintain. Despite Hurst's insistence that no one could figure out her mastery of the Great Unknown, skeptics had regularly proposed solutions during the two years of her nationwide tour. A columnist for *Science* magazine, in 1885, proudly concluded after a laboratory demonstration of Hurst's skill that "An unwise repetition of the performance, however, did away with all its mystery: for, although the performer began with a delicate touch of the staff, the holder soon perceived that she changed the position of her hands every moment, sometimes seizing the staff with a firm grip, and that it never moved in any direction unless her hands were in such a position that she could move it in that direction by ordinary pressure."[30] Late-tour performances in Chicago were reviewed with claims that "Lulu Hurst's Force Waning," and "Some Well-Known Chicagoans Find the Georgia Girl Too Much for Them."[31] These voices growing louder and more frequent may well have been a reason to wrap up the tour on a high note.

A lot changed between Hurst's retirement in 1885 and her book's release in 1897. Radical, independent "New Woman" ideologies had been simmering in the culture for some time, and around 1894, English feminist writers were putting them forth directly in writing. "New Women" stood in stark contrast to the restrictive ideals of Victorian womanhood, encouraging independence in many forms. The movement encouraged greater access to education and political activism, increased agency over home and public life, and practical freedoms like the ability to ride a bicycle or wear pants. It was a period of transition between a restrictive feminine ideal and the introduction of greater independence, and Lulu Hurst was a shrewd navigator of the changing norms. In her teenage years, her mixture of feminine innocence and cultural mysticism allowed her to participate in and implicitly criticize masculine society. By the era of the New Woman, Hurst had developed and embraced her own authority within modern technology and science.

In the end, Hurst concluded that the lesson of her life was simple: "People should learn to never depart from the guidance of reason in all things, and to never abandon in their intellects the truth of the universal rule, both as to time and space, to period and place, of the eternal laws of cause and effect."

When Lulu Hurst began her career in the 1880s, America was wrestling with many deep notions of its own national identity. Institutionally and individually, Americans reckoned with the hurtling Gilded Age advance of science and industry. They navigated Reconstruction and concepts of postwar identity. And there were also lingering spiritualist ideas that raised the possibility of consolation through contact with dear souls beyond. All these threads dealt with questions of things seen and unseen—progress, sovereignty, identity—and where one's belief was best placed. Photographs, telegraphs, electric light all made the world brighter and more immediate—and if these marvels of science and ingenuity were possible, was it so far-fetched that a teenage girl really might be able to harness the unseen forces of the universe? In her early years, Lulu Hurst complied with ideas of femininity by styling herself as merely an obliging conduit for mysterious strength. As years passed and she matured, Lulu Hurst traded that stage myth for the mantle of authority and expertise. As a girl, Lulu Hurst showed a strength she could not fully own. As an adult, she finally claimed it for herself.

CHAPTER 7

Circassian Beauties in the American Sideshow

In the fall of 1864, P. T. Barnum introduced a new wonder to patrons at his American Museum. Appearing alongside the Three Mammoth Fat Girls, the Lilliputian King, the Albino Family, and "Gen. Grant, Jr.," advertisements mentioned a new human curiosity: "A Beautiful Circassian Girl."[1] This was the public's first exposure to an act that would endure through Barnum's era and into the twentieth-century sideshow: the enigmatic, captivating woman known as the Circassian beauty.

A staple of dime museums and traveling shows throughout the nineteenth century, Circassians were women alleged to be from the Caucasus Mountain region and claimed by racist nineteenth-century ideology as an ideal of white beauty. Famous for both their legendary looks and their large, frizzy hairstyles, Circassian beauties required audiences to hold several stereotypes in tension. These women were presented as chaste and respectable, but also billed as former harem slaves. They were supposedly of noble lineage, but appeared as sideshow attractions. And they were represented as the height of white racial "purity" to their predominantly white audiences, yet also as exotic figures whose hairstyle was associated with Black women.

From the middle nineteenth century and well into the twentieth, Circassian women were common circus attractions. The script changed over time, evolving from the original "former harem slave" script to include performances by dancers, "moss-haired women," and snake charmers. Nonetheless, a common current ran through all these exotic acts: They gathered audiences at the connection point between whiteness, conventional femininity, fear, and desire. Circassian beauty acts were a screen onto which crowds could project bias and fantasy.

The idea of Circassian beauty can be traced to Johann Friedrich Blumenbach, a German biologist and racial theorist in the eighteenth and nineteenth centuries. Blumenbach used craniometry—a bunk discipline based on measuring human skulls—to address the question of whether different racial features meant that humanity could be divided into separate species. Blumenbach firmly dismissed this idea, writing that the color of one's skin was "an adventitious and easily changeable thing, and can never constitute a diversity of species."

This is not to say that all humans were equal in esteem according to Blumenbach. Unsurprisingly, he created a hierarchy that considered people of his own race to be humanity's poster children. Assessing and comparing the contours of various human skulls, Blumenbach ultimately arrived at a taxonomy of five racial groups, among which he considered persons from the Black Sea region to be the physical ideal.[2] He coined the term "Caucasian" to describe this group, writing that: "I have taken the name of this variety from Mount Caucasus, both because its neighbourhood, and especially its southern slope, produces the most beautiful race of men, I mean the Georgian; and because all physiological reasons converge to this, that in that region, if anywhere, it seems we ought with the greatest probability to place the autochthones of mankind."

Blumenbach considered this Caucasian population, spread across Europe, Western Asia, and North Africa, to be the "primeval" human race, which had branched into four other categories: Mongolian (Central Asian), American (Native), Malay (Southeast Asian), and Ethiopian (sub-Saharan African). It was, he argued, environmental conditions that had caused a "degeneration" of the fair Caucasian into peoples of color. He also believed that a gradual reversion to white "norms" was possible. To support his assertion that white skin had to be humanity's default starting point, Blumenbach needed little more data than the fact that European ladies who spent their winters indoors exhibited "a brilliant whiteness," while those who "exposed themselves freely to the summer sun and air" quickly ended up with a solid tan. "If then under one and the same climate the mere difference of the annual seasons has such influence in changing the colour of the skin," he reasoned, absurdly, "is there anything surprising in the fact that climates . . . according to their diversity should have the greatest and most permanent influence over national colour."[3] Blumenbach considered his Ethiopian and Mongolian racial categories "extreme varieties," with Native American and Malay, respectively, as "intermediate" classifications between these extremes and the Caucasian ideal.

Blumenbach himself may not have become especially famous, and craniometry (along with phrenology, a loopy sister pseudoscience devoted to divining a person's temperament from the contours of their skull) only had a short period of dubious fame, but the stereotype of idealized Caucasian beauty caught on fast. Circassia, a region of the Caucasus mountains, became ground zero for Western cultural notions of white beauty. Throughout the nineteenth century, books and magazines extolled the virtues of mythic Circassia: fair, buxom women in draped gowns and peasant jewelry; stout, bearded soldiers with daggers at their belts; and a certain warmly simple way of mountain life.[4] A smattering of nineteenth-century "Circassian" branded products promised women they could achieve Circassian beauty in their own home: hair dye to turn light-colored tresses into a "soft, glossy & natural" brown or black, Circassian fabric to achieve the right gauzy look, and various skin products promising "that whiteness, transparency and color so highly prized by all civilized nations." The endorsement of "the elite of our cities, the Opera, [and] the stage" was supposed to be reassuring, but the promise of removing freckles, acne, sunburn, "Moth," and roughness suggests such lotions were little more than a chemical belt sander for the face.[5]

Circassia was more than the rugged, simplistic paradise one might have imagined based on cosmetics ads or travelogues. Circassia was the target of invasion and ethnic cleansing throughout the eighteenth and nineteenth centuries as armies from Russia and Ottoman Turkey encroached by land and sea. The region was invaded during the Russian conquest of the Caucasus and formally placed under Russian control following the end of the Crimean War in 1856. During this period (just before Barnum's Circassian beauty appeared on the scene), the Russian Empire carried out systematic murder and expulsion of the region's predominantly Muslim communities. By the middle 1860s, most of the remaining population had been forcibly evacuated to the Ottoman Empire, where overcrowding, price gouging, and enslavement were enduring risks for Circassian refugees.

There was, concurrently, a Western fascination with melodramatic narratives of white slavery that were popular on both sides of the Atlantic in the mid-nineteenth century. Art and drama explored with breathless horror stories of brute men trafficking in the doom of innocent, blushing virgins (though the reality of human trafficking was far broader, harsher, and less discriminating). In the United States, this manifested in many ways. The sculptor Hiram Powers's *The Greek Slave*, a statue of a nude woman chained at the wrists by Turkish captors, was the first life-size female nude to be publicly shown in America. The statue—a soft female figure carved from white marble—was adopted as an emblem by abolitionists and seen on tour by more than one hundred thousand Americans in the 1840s. Race and slavery were explored in plays like Dion Boucicault's *The Octoroon*, the 1859 story of a young Southern white woman whose marriage plans are thwarted when it is revealed that her mother is one of the plantation's enslaved workers.[6] Despite passing for white, she is put up for sale with the assets of her father's estate. (British audiences got a happy ending, but in American performances, the girl dies by suicide, avoiding even fictional approval of mixed-race marriage.)

It was against this backdrop that, in 1864, P. T. Barnum introduced American Museum patrons to the first "Circassian Beauty." Her face framed in a halo of frizzy hair, this alluring young lady was at first anonymous, then billed as Zalumma Agra, the "Star of the East."[7] (She would eventually appear alongside two other women: Zuruby Hannum, "Pearl of the Sea," and "Orzeta Pacha, The Royal Gem."[8]) Agra appeared at the American Museum in what then counted as suggestive garb: a trimmed, three-quarter-length dress with loose peasant sleeves, and a swath of stocking visible above her mid-calf

One of P. T. Barnum's Circassian Beauty performers, likely Zalumma Agra.
Photograph by Mathew Brady. Image courtesy of the Frederick Hill Meserve Collection at the National Portrait Gallery, Washington, DC.

boots. She occasionally completed the outfit with signals of vague exoticism—a sash of luxurious fabric or a moon-shaped headdress. A biographical pamphlet sold to patrons told the story of Agra's childhood flight from Russian incursion into her native land and how that path somehow brought a woman of supposed royal descent to the sort of New York entertainment venue that also offered pet taxidermy. Agra was said to have been orphaned by invaders as a child and discovered on the streets of Constantinople among masses of refugees by Barnum's right-hand man, John Greenwood, Jr. "Her marvellous beauty and pleasant, intelligent manners at once arrested his attention," declared the unnamed pamphlet author, "while the extraordinary peculiarity of her hair challenged his interest and his admiration."

Greenwood, captivated by the child, hoped to save her from "the beautiful but ignorant *habitat* of a pagan's harem." He negotiated with the girl's friends and Turkish authorities to become her guardian and then secured tutoring and accommodations to help her grow into the "thorough and lavishly educated woman" of eighteen who began entertaining visitors at the American Museum. Audiences were not encouraged to inquire further about details: Agra's promoters insisted that, since she had left the Caucasus as a child, her homeland existed in her mind as "an imperfect and confused dream," and she remembered little of her native language.

As one might expect, the true story was a bit different. Under cover of the interpretive space afforded by imperfect details and confused dreams, Agra's promoters simply created a convenient mythology for her. John Greenwood had indeed gone overseas on a scouting trip in 1864, looking to engage a woman who was rumored to have a horn growing from her forehead. Greenwood found neither her nor anyone else worth exhibiting, and Barnum instructed him via letter to instead look for "a beautiful Circassian girl if you can get one."[9] In his autobiography, Barnum says little about what followed, except that Greenwood disguised himself in Turkish dress to visit the markets in Constantinople, where he saw "a large number of Circassian girls and women."[10] In private correspondence, Barnum was more frank about his willingness to conveniently ignore the evils of the Ottoman slave economy if it got him a guaranteed hit: "If you can also buy a beautiful

Circassian woman," he wrote Greenwood, "do so if you think best; or if you can hire one or two at reasonable prices, do so if you think they are pretty and will pass for Circassian slaves . . . if she is beautiful, then she may take in Paris or in London or probably both. But look out that in Paris they don't try the law and set her free. It must be understood she is free." The Circassian beauty made her debut not long afterward, presented as the result of Greenwood's expedition. An alternative origin story, uncovered by the disability scholar Robert Bogdan in his 1990 book *Freak Show*, offers an explanation that seems far more likely for the sort of Circassian lady who spoke in a perfect American accent and the sort of showman who was not exactly known for his infinite patience: Greenwood came back empty-handed, and the American Museum (not wanting to waste a good story) decided to cast a "Circassian" beauty from the local talent roster.[11]

That the woman in question had distinctive and abundant hair was, as best the historical record can tell us, just an unusual stylistic choice. The look had no foundation in actual Circassian culture; performers were said to wash their hair in beer to achieve it.[12] As the act grew in popularity, though, her style created a stereotype for all subsequent beauties: frizzy hairdos, the larger the better. "The peculiarity of the hair of the Circassian girl, whether native or manufactured," wrote one reporter, "is that it stands out at right angles from her scalp in every direction, much after the manner of the quills upon the fretful porcupine."[13] Whether or not "Circassian" performers were originally from the Black Sea region was generally irrelevant, and in truth the role was a character fiction, played by a succession of women—often lower class immigrant women from locales no more far-flung than Brooklyn. The "Circassian" character had a carefully crafted foreign allure and a particular visual script: voluminous hair that resembled an Afro and exoticized, risqué peasant costumes. Circassian beauties all had names that were suitably strange to American ears, and these usually began with the letter "Z"—Zula Zeleah, Zoe Zobedia, Zuruby Hannum, and Zobeide Luti, to name a few. They appeared in salon-style receptions in which patrons would cycle through the gallery space, observe the women, and perhaps work up the nerve to ask a question.

With limited exception, we do not know the real names of the women who entertained as Circassian beauties. This is unsurprising since silence and anonymity were an important part of the act. The idea was not to celebrate an individual woman for skill, appearance, status, or experience, but to take a woman—any woman—and make a vague myth of her. The three-legged lady, well, there was only one of her. But any one of many pretty, eager women could be made into a Circassian beauty with a little coaching and the right hair and wardrobe. Biographical pamphlets are of little historical use, being little more than promotional yarns, and while primary sources exist about these women, there are none known in which they credibly speak for themselves. This complicates efforts to talk about them in depth and has historically left their stories to be told by men if at all.

The Circassian character was presented as the pinnacle of beauty and evolution. She was an "ideal white woman," yet one whose hair not only signaled exoticism but evoked minstrelsy. We have no idea if Barnum was using the hairstyle part of the act as a deliberate parody of Black people; nevertheless, the choice irretrievably linked Circassian beauties with the racist associations and biases then circulating in American society. This character effectively took the prior cultural fascination with Circassian beauty, which had mostly been used to sell glossy brunette hair dye and flowery stories, and turned it into an obsession with the social construction of race. In circus's evolution, the large textured hairstyles and suggestive wardrobe of Circassian beauties drew on cultural myths about promiscuity, exoticism, and social worthiness, borrowing qualities from other racist stereotypes like the "Jezebel," a lascivious seductress. The author Charles D. Martin describes the Circassian beauty's signature hair as a symbol of racial and cultural conflict: "The ethnic kink supplied a visible bridge between the normalized, exalted whiteness that conferred citizenship and the distinguishing marks of racial difference that facilitated slavery. The emancipated white body still bore the evidence of its dark-bodied captivity."[14] The idea that whiteness, taken to an essentialist extreme, includes signifiers of Blackness is all at once strange, puzzling, and devious.

Circassian women drew on and spoke to a general culture of racial anxiety. In the middle 1860s, the increasingly violent politics of abolition and its detractors added a menacing edge to life in New York, which was conspicuously unfriendly toward President Lincoln and his refusal to make peace with the South. New York mayor Fernando Wood had suggested in 1861 that the city secede from both New York state and the Union, which he called a "venal and corrupt master."[15] That did not happen, but New Yorkers rioted for four days in July 1863 in response to the federal draft, and Confederate press, threatening to burn New York City in response to Union offensives in the South, assured readers that "The men to execute the work are already there."[16] The city remained so staunchly hostile to Lincoln administration policy and abolitionism that Union general Benjamin Butler, nicknamed "The Beast," was posted to the city with thousands of soldiers to ensure peace during the 1864 presidential election. And all manner of then-current arts and "sciences," from phrenology to miscegenation theory, attempted to explain and reinforce the scheme of racial hierarchy that lay at the bottom of the political crisis.[17]

The character of the Circassian woman, supposedly rescued from a life of white sexual servitude, began life anew in the United States in 1865, at the very moment that a nation built on chattel slavery passed the Thirteenth Amendment. The public's guilty fascination with white slavery narratives only boosted her popularity. These characters were a mixtape that suited the then-current mood: enough truth about Circassian slavery to make the story feasible; a racialized visual language that invoked the American political crisis; spicy Orientalist harem tropes of "luxurious and mindless" indulgences among the women and men who "value their women less than their stirrups," which justified white colonialist hierarchy; and a "happy" ending that reinforced Western norms of culture and femininity.[18] The Circassian beauty, saved from the harem, demonstrated acceptable womanhood for paying audiences. She was appealing because she was beautiful; because she rejected foreign debasement in favor of "womanly deportment and social qualities" in America; and because her suggestion of forbidden sexuality gratified secret desires.

In this way, Barnum's American Museum was an arena for acting out social, racial, and gender anxieties through entertainment. This sort of museum, which purported to show the wonders of the world to those who couldn't afford travel, was in fact a highly curated presentation where people and groups could all too easily be fetishized or tokenized.[19] And while Barnum's reputation as an exploitative sideshow huckster is not entirely deserved—he was a reputable employer, paid well, and insisted his employees were "living wonders" rather than freaks—race was undeniably a factor in how he presented performers of color to the paying public. The same P. T. Barnum who spoke before the Connecticut legislature to lobby for Black voting rights in 1865 also relied on lazy stereotypes and exoticism in his paid entertainments.[20] Though he was willing to use his stage to advocate for the temperance movement, race was a more volatile matter of public discourse. Rather than risk alienating paying customers of one belief or another, he tended to simply avoid extreme moral stances onstage where race was involved. While Barnum presented racialized shows—an edited version of *Uncle Tom's Cabin*, for example, or the "What Is It?" attraction with its racist "science"—he was careful to remain in the realm of supposition and suggestion. Any conclusions to be made were left to the audience. All of this centered the white experience and allowed viewers to feel comfortably superior to the humans who were, in their eyes, reduced to "curiosities" on display.

The stereotype of the Circassian beauty continued in sideshows for quite some time. Dime museums and circuses claimed to have the original Zalumma Agra on display for decades, well past the point of possibility—though audiences didn't seem to mind. In the 1880s, when Barnum was enjoying later-life fame as a circus entrepreneur, his Greatest Show on Earth typically included a Circassian woman in its sideshow. One of the most famous Circassian women, Zoe Meleke, offered a promotional biography that simply rehashed Zalumma Agra's old life story.[21]

By this point, it was an open secret that "Circassian" women did not actually come from the Caucasus region. It was arguably never really all that important that they did. As early as 1865, papers suggested that Zuruby Hannum and Zalumma Agra were in fact "Wilhelmina and Katerina," the long-haired daughters of a German barber in Williamsburg, Brooklyn. In 1873, one paper chuckled that the "'Circassian girl,' exhibited by Barnum, is visiting her native village of Olney, Illinois."[22]

Eventually, "Circassian" became known as a character type, a shorthand for women with a distinctive hairstyle performing the exotic, erotic, and odd. By the dawn of the big traveling shows in the 1870s, people no longer readily remembered the stories of war and enslavement in the Caucasus. But since the persona was both versatile and compelling, there was no reason for circus to leave the Circassian beauty behind. Promoters simply came up with a new exotic aspect to advertise. Some performers, like Mademoiselle Ivy, the "Moss-Haired Girl," discarded the Black Sea origin story but emphasized the ample hair alone as a curiosity.[23] Nor did Circassian women need to be white anymore: the Black Circassian performer Zumigo, whose character's name and hairstyle conjured her "Caucasian" predecessors, was billed as an Egyptian, swapping the traditional peasant costume of the Circassian beauty for fancy dresses and fringed leotards.

Many Circassian beauties traded the Black Sea for a nonspecific Eastern exoticism and became snake charmers. Employment notices in the *New York Clipper* in the 1870s and 1880s often featured Circassian snake girls looking for work at a circus or fairground for the season. Millia Zulu, "The Circassian Beauty or Fan Child," exhibited a giant python she could "handle the same as a child would its toys."[24] Zad Zumella sought fairground employment with "her beautiful Anaconda."[25] Zollula Zeita advertised herself as a combination "Circassian Fire-queen, Sword-swallower and Snake-charmer," adding for good measure that she had a "Magnificent Wardrobe."[26] Miss Uno, "Queen Supreme of the Serpent Kingdom," appeared on an 1895 poster for the Adam Forepaugh circus wearing a blue, knee-length fringed tunic with boa constrictors and giant pythons draped over her hair and around her legs, hips, and chest.[27] A Black performer named Lualla entertained London crowds in 1878, with the *Illustrated London News* raving that "'Lualla,' the Abyssinian snake-charmer, is a marvellous mistress of the art, which among Eastern nations has been ascribed to supernatural power, of subduing and reconciling to herself the hated and dreaded race of serpents, long reputed the enemy of mankind."[28]

In addition to the women's exaggerated hairstyles, the snakes served to signal a realm of curiosity and thrill, a danger and foreignness that needed to be tamed by white male authority. Just as the original

Circassians romanticized the near East, these later women, working in a time of active colonialism, drew on the dark glamour of Asia and Africa. Not to mention, a snake charmer suggested woman's original sin, Eve tangled up with the serpent tempter. Circassian performers ably embodied all of this for paying patrons. The appeal was still the same: The Circassian beauty helped audiences draw the line between acceptable femininity and dangerous transgression of proper norms.

One of the most well-known personas to appear in this expanded Circassian character universe was Nala Damajante. On the strength of London performances at the Crystal Palace and Royal Aquarium, circus titan Adam Forepaugh persuaded the "Indian lady snake charmer" to sign on with his circus for the 1883 touring season.[29] Joining the show with "a large importation of reptiles" kept warm in their boxes with blankets and a system of hot water pans, Nala Damajante was announced as "the only Hindoo Snake Charmer in America."[30] A mid-1880s poster from Paris's famous Folies Bergère gives an idea of what audiences came to see. In full color, Damajante holds three thick, ill-tempered snakes at arm's length, their tails curling around each ankle. The snakes hiss open-mouthed, their forked tongues tickling her gold hoop earrings. Damajante herself is the picture of calm amid the writhing mass, her brown skin and distinctive halo of hair set off by the hot pink satin and gold fringe of her harem costume.

A snake act was a surefire hit for a show. Even accounting for the puffery of circus newsprint, sources agreed that snake acts were dangerous, especially when the reptiles were feeling surly or were more active due to warmer ambient temperatures. This translated into gasps and thrills at no small risk to the performer. Her hands were dotted with little V-shaped bite scars. One of Damajante's snakes had nearly dislocated the performer's arm during a performance in Madrid. In Philadelphia on the Forepaugh show in 1883, a ninety-pound python attempted to crush her in its coils: As she lifted the twelve-foot snake from its box, with six already "coiled like a living head-dress over her forehead," the python slid over her shoulder. "It unwound its sinuous length from Damajante's body," wrote one account, "and quickly coiled about the upper part of her chest and throat."[31]

Press rushed to Damajante's agent, the former acrobat and human fly performer John Palmer, to gain access to the woman who nonchalantly used live snakes for jewelry. Because myth was more important than reality, press agents and eager newsmen distributed different versions of Damajante's story to stoke the public interest. In some, she was an Indian mystic who spoke no English, inserting a snake's head into her mouth to prove that she was not afraid of the animals.[32] In other interviews, Damajante answered questions in clear English, explaining, "I think the snakes know me. I have possessed a strange power over them, that I can't account for myself, since girlhood."[33] Yet another account offered, tongue solidly in cheek, that the charmer was actually a saucy Connecticut girl playing the circus for thrills; in this variant, with a twenty-three-foot python coiling around her midriff, Damajante "half closed her eyes, leaned back her head, and said dreamily: 'Tighter, you dude; brace up and take hold of me, can't you?'"[34]

Who was Nala Damajante? Divining the truth is a challenge. Any given nineteenth-century Circassian performer's story was entirely written by men who had an interest in writing whatever version of her story sold best at a given time. Sorting a given individual from her copycats is difficult due to variations in spelling: Depending on what paper you read, Nala's surname was Damajante, Damajanti, Damayanti, or Damazanti. (Imitators performed under intentionally similar titles like Nula Delavanti or Alna Don Junata.) It's also important to remember that although entertainment historians have tended to take at face value that multiple performers with the same name (or close enough to it) are the same person, circus history is too mischievous a discipline for this to be taken at face value. "Nala Damajante" was a versatile and variable alias, the circus has always loved copycat acts as a way to meet demand, and male writers were more interested in documenting the character than reality. There were many Circassian women. There were even many Nala Damajantes.

Who were the women who played this role? One emerges in Germany. Carl Hagenbeck, a well-known promoter and the leading animal dealer in the industry, habitually sent hunters and scouts around the globe to procure live creatures for his many clients. In the 1880s, one of these agents returned to Germany from an expedition to the South Pacific, unloaded his delivery of rare snakes and insects, and introduced his new Polynesian wife. Before long, this woman began to perform in Hagenbeck's own productions as a snake charmer under the stage name Maladamatjaute. A photograph printed in some editions of Hagenbeck's memoir, labeled only as "an Indian snake-charmer" but likely of Maladamatjaute, shows a dark-skinned woman with gold armbands and long natural hair, cradling the head of a large snake in her left hand. Color lithographs made to advertise Hagenbeck's "people shows" during the same period feature the same woman, smiling alongside fat snakes in a belt of coins. In each, she wears a large updo reminiscent of the traditional Circassian beauty.[35]

In America, Nala Damajante was at least two people. A performer identifying herself as "Nala Damajanta, The Original Hindoo Snake-Charmer," placed an ad in the *New York Clipper* in October 1884. She alerted industry players that she was making a career change: "Having severed my connection with John Palmer," the notice stated, "am prepared to fill all contracts made by him for me." Palmer was not pleased. In the following week's edition of the *Clipper*, he huffed that "Nala Damajanta (so called), whom I had engaged for the last three years, has the audacity to advertise that she had severed her connection with me and was ready to fulfill the engagements I had made for MYSELF and ACT." Not only did Palmer threaten to sue her or anyone else who tried to poach his show, but he said he'd already lined up a superior replacement. "I own the Snakes used in the above act," Palmer explained, "which will be used by the Artist I have engaged, who will arrive from Europe this week, and who will surpass the former lady both in costumes and doing the act."[36]

Despite this very clear break-up exchange, when Palmer died in 1896, his two-line obituary in the London papers identified him as the "husband of Nala Damajanti."[37] There may well have been a reconciliation after the spat in the *Clipper*, but more likely, Palmer parted ways with one performer and brought in a replacement to meet continued demand. The first woman may have been Maladamatjaute, come over from Germany, or someone else entirely. French papers in 1887 provide a clue as to just who filled the role and eventually appeared in that famous poster from the Folies Bergère. The French newspaper *Le Gaulois* reported in March of that year on a dispute in which a

"Mrs. Palmer, Snake Charmer."
Image courtesy of the Robert L. Parkinson Library & Research Center at Circus World Museum.

gentleman had filed suit against "Nala-Damajanti, the snake charmer at the Folies-Bergère," for payment of outstanding debts.[38] It turned out to be a case of mistaken identity, but to prove her case, Ms. Damajanti had to "leave behind her picturesque pseudonym, in no way Indian, to identify herself as Emilie Poupon." Poupon testified that she was born in 1861 in France and, in 1881, fell in love with John Palmer while she was governess to a French family in St. Petersburg. At the time of the alleged debt at issue, in 1885, Poupon could demonstrate that she was performing as a snake charmer with P. T. Barnum's circus.[39] Marriage records from England verify that Palmer and Poupon married in 1886.[40]

Even Carl Hagenbeck was willing to admit that the most famous of the Circassian-style snake charmers was actually a white woman from eastern France. In the 1909 German edition of his autobiography, Hagenbeck fondly recalled a "beautiful Provençal woman . . . a girl of extraordinarily slight build, with large, magnificent dark eyes and long, unusually black curls," who had "adopted the melodramatic name of Naladamajante and achieved a kind of fame under that name in America."[41] And as for the stereotypical halo of hair associated with the act, well, apparently even the idiot snakes ("stupiden Schlangen") could see that Nala was wearing a wig all the time. The English edition of the work in 1910 omitted this story entirely, lamenting that snake charming was on its way out as an entertainment.[42]

There were many versions of Nala Damajante, all of them fiction. The name, however spelled, appears to refer to a Sanskrit mythic poem entitled "Nala and Damayanti."[43] It was probably initially chosen because, like the original Circassian beauty's hairstyle, it would seem exotic and foreign to Western audiences. The name—and whether the performer in question was a Pacific Islander, a Brooklyn immigrant, a Black Sea refugee, or a Frenchwoman draped in snakes—mattered less than the performance: one that acted out a racial and cultural identity for the amusement of largely white audiences.[44]

The word "Caucasian" has long been divorced from its origins, but the legacy of the Circassian beauty endures. Ultimately, the many women who performed as Circassian beauties throughout the nineteenth century signaled acceptable femininity to audiences by performing its inversion. Fed by contemporary views of race, entertainment-hungry audiences, and a jarring and beguiling mix of stereotypes, the Circassian beauty attraction has had a lasting impact on how we think about race, class, and gender today. Circassian beauties may seem like a distant relic of the Barnum era, their popularity only hinted at today from the silent stare in a cabinet card or carte-de-visite photograph. But as examples of acts whose masked, anonymous performers reduced lived experiences to racialized stereotypes, they provide a warning that we must still let ourselves hear.

CHAPTER 8

The Remarkable Life of Millie-Christine McKoy, the Two-Headed Nightingale

The Great Forepaugh Show, Circus, Hippodrome, and Menagerie was one of the biggest circus shows of the later nineteenth century, and its namesake Adam Forepaugh was a household name—the "Citizen" to P. T. Barnum's "Autocrat," if you read the gossipy show papers.[1] While Barnum had come up as a showman over decades, Forepaugh was a businessman in the horse and cattle trade. He became a circus owner somewhat by accident when a customer to whom he had sold horses couldn't pay his debts. Forepaugh was a thick-built figure with mutton chops like strips of shag carpeting, and he approached his business with exactly the formidable temperament one might expect from the working-class son of a Philadelphia butcher. So, one imagines Adam Forepaugh was not pleased when, in the summer of 1882, he was handed papers from a federal court in Indiana informing him that he was being sued for libel by a Black woman performer, who demanded $25,000 (on the order of half a million or more today, the equivalent of her annual salary).

At the height of the tented circus in America, rival shows might travel the same or similar routes only a matter of weeks apart from each other from spring through fall, fighting for the same few dollars audiences had to spend on entertainment. Advance teams for each show would head out weeks ahead of the performance, pasting promotional posters on every available building, barn, and store window. Press men did not hesitate to slap their show poster right over a competitor's. Evidence of this practice was seen in 2010 when some residents of Burlington, Vermont, started a home renovation project and discovered a thick stack of giant circus posters glued underneath their siding, including an image of the famed snake charmer Nala Damajante plastered over advertisements for Millie-Christine McKoy, the "Two-Headed Nightingale."[2] Rival circuses also commonly littered each other's travel routes with trash-talking papers known as "rat sheets." These bills had a simple goal: Convince folks that they should spend hard-earned cash on a quality show rather than that other guy's phony trash.

One of Forepaugh's rat sheets disparaged McKoy in favor of his own supposedly superior attraction, claiming: "All good Christian people can but regret that this afflicted object should be hawked over the Country to satisfy the greed of a couple of side show exhibitors," referring to Batcheller & Doris's Inter-Ocean Circus, with which McKoy was then performing.[3] Millie-Christine McKoy was not about to take this sitting down. She had, after all, survived a lot worse than Adam Forepaugh.

We know more about Millie-Christine than many other circus women of the era. Skepticism is still wise where promotional sources are concerned, but her story can begin on some solid facts. She was born in 1851 in Columbus County, North Carolina, where her parents, Jacob and Monemia, were enslaved by a farmer and blacksmith named Jabez McKay. (Millie-Christine and her family used and preferred the spelling "McKoy," which I will use here.) With two bodies joined together at the pelvis, Millie-Christine weighed seventeen pounds at birth, and by all accounts, Monemia's labor and delivery were—aside from the obvious—unremarkable. Though she consisted of two joined bodies with individual names, thoughts, and actions, Millie-Christine grew to understand and refer to herself as a singular collective being; a newspaper account from 1882 said that "Millie-Christine always speaks of herself with either mouth indifferently as 'I,' never saying the plural 'we,' to which she is clearly entitled."[4] Monemia referred to the twins in the same way, calling Millie-Christine "my child."

Word quickly spread about this unusual baby, and she was less than a year old when Jabez McKay contracted with a promoter named John Pervis to exhibit Millie-Christine, legally his property under chattel slavery, as a curiosity in the spring of 1852. From there, Millie-Christine's story became a complicated, terrible drama in which she was handed about, coveted, and displayed like a grand and unusual piece of jewelry.[5]

Human curiosities—that is, people whose anatomy, race, ability, or identity set them apart from the general population—were big business in nineteenth-century entertainment. Even before the so-called "freak show" became an institution, nothing so delighted the public as the opportunity to see individuals whose bodies, skills, or behaviors defied the white Western norm. Sometimes this defiance took the form of flashy performance; sometimes it meant a physical difference like dwarfism or deformity; sometimes it meant the conveniently dramatized exoticism of a foreign race or culture (as with Circassian beauties). In other cases—as with the South African woman Sarah Baartman, shown in England as a curiosity and given vulgar billing as the "Hottentot Venus"—it was, regrettably, "all of the above." Charles Dickens described a typical country fair in *Sketches by Boz*, remarking that "the dwarfs are also objects of great curiosity, and as a dwarf, a giantess, a living skeleton, a wild Indian, 'a young lady of singular beauty, with perfectly white hair and pink eyes,' and two or three other natural curiosities, are usually exhibited together for the small charge of a penny, they attract very numerous audiences."[6]

In 1847, the British humor magazine *Punch* proclaimed that England was in the grip of "Deformito-mania." Under an illustration of theatrical marquees proclaiming "This Is The Ne Plus Ultra of Hideousness," "Hall of Ugliness," and "By Far the Ugliest Biped Is Here," *Punch*'s columnist moaned that "we cannot understand the cause of the now prevailing taste for deformity, which seems to grow by what it feeds upon."[7] Audiences flocked to sensationalized exhibitions of unusual bodies. Many of these shows played up the idea of scientific merit to legitimize their displays of foreign or disabled people, promising educational benefits to gawking, curious audiences. Historical narratives of disability often talk about physical differences as impairments, defects to be overcome or avoided, or occasions for "narcissistic pity or lessons in suffering."[8] Like lurid Google searches made public, curiosity shows allowed visitors to gawk at oddity, to be reassured of their own normalcy and privilege, to be nervous or even turned on by the sight of fellow humans, all with one big social permission slip.

And so theaters, dime museums, circuses, and sideshows in the nineteenth century eagerly featured unusual people for curious visitors in America and England. Many performers in these early sideshows chose to exhibit themselves, happy to take advantage of Victorian-era public demand for the weird and wonderful so they could gain economic independence and community in return. Other performers were not given a choice. This was the hungry environment into which Millie-Christine was born.

John Pervis, having bought Millie-Christine from her enslaved parents' owner, sold her to a would-be showman named Brower. Brower was so eager to exhibit the child that he paid on a promissory note, cosigned by one Joseph Pearson Smith as security for the money. Some initial success showing the twins as a curiosity convinced Brower that local fairground shows were small potatoes compared to what might be possible if he tried his luck in New Orleans. The curiosity trade was common at the time, and the formula must have seemed easy to Brower: Show up in a big city, get a medical doctor to sign off on the legitimacy of your attraction, hold a preview for the eager yipping men of the press, and stand by, ready to take everyone's cash at the ticket booth. But Brower was not just an inexperienced showman; he was also gullible. When an unidentified Texan charmed him with the promise of a fat bankroll, Brower handed the twins over to him without insisting on payment up front. After slowly realizing what he had done, Brower skulked back to North Carolina, red-faced and empty-handed. He informed Smith that he was bankrupt, had no idea of Millie-Christine's whereabouts, and had some new and obvious problems with that promissory note.

Joseph Pearson Smith was now Millie-Christine's owner in the eyes of the law, and her parents were predictably horrified and heartbroken to learn that their daughter's whereabouts were unknown. Smith paid off the debt, hired a private investigator, and got to work finding Millie-Christine.

The private eye chased her for months, always just a few steps behind as he sorted fact from chin-wag through a string of dime museums around the northeastern United States. Because Millie-Christine was a toddler at that point, the exact truth of what happened to her is a murky stew. What we do know is that she was passed from the control of one showman to another, all while being displayed on stages and in salons for affluent people to stare at. One reviewer wrote, "To those who admire any monstrous deviation from ordinary creation, the 'African Twins' will have an extraordinary charm, for here there is something as odd and unprecedented as the most morbid taste could desire."[9]

By 1855, Millie-Christine was on a steamer headed for England, in the hands of "Professor" W. J. L. Millar and William Thompson, two showmen of dubious reputation. The men had invented an origin story for her, meant to pose practical answers to any sticky questions: How was a toddler in this situation? Where had she come from? Could respectable people feel okay about buying tickets to see her? The new backstory explained that Millie-Christine had been born in Africa and sold into slavery in Cuba, where she was allegedly purchased by an American doctor who regarded her as a natural curiosity. After the doctor's passing, Millie-Christine was sold as part of his estate to a gentleman who took her to Philadelphia. Although the 1850 Fugitive Slave Act permitted the arrest of anyone suspected to be fleeing enslavement, even in free states like Pennsylvania, Millar and Thompson were not worried about liability. In their cold appraisal, "the little slaves, 'not being runaway negroes,'" could simply and safely be placed in their own custody.[10] Audiences were assured that profits from ticket sales would help to purchase freedom for Millie-Christine's family. None of it was true.

Millie-Christine, billed as the "United African Twins," drew rave reviews in London and beyond over the next few years, but Millar and Thompson were greedy and didn't trust each other. This caused problems. At one point, Millar absconded with Millie-Christine and fled to Scotland, and Thompson hired street toughs to steal her back.[11] Millar retaliated by starting a search for Millie-Christine's mother, whose claim to custody would trump any showman's. He sent word of the twins' whereabouts to his brother in the United States, along with a request to contact a friend who served as editor of the *Raleigh Register*. This message made its way to Joseph Pearson Smith, who promptly went to Jabez McKay and arranged to purchase Monemia, Jacob, and their other children. After more than a year of negotiations during which letters went back and forth across the Atlantic, Smith reached an agreement with the "Professor" for a three-year performance contract. He and Millie-Christine's mother Monemia sailed for Liverpool in December 1856 to find Millie-Christine. They arrived on New Year's Day and quietly attended one of Millie-Christine's exhibitions. The American consulate had advised them to do this, noting that if the girl recognized her mother in the crowd, "it would be prima facie evidence of the facts" and an asset in court. Monemia was unable to observe quietly, though, and at first glimpse of her daughter, she "uttered a scream of such heart-rending pathos" that the theater rose to its feet. Thompson then attempted to whisk Millie-Christine from the venue but was blocked by a burly Scottish gentleman who advised, "Ye'll nae tak' the bairn ayant the door, maun ye wallop me first."[12]

English courts, which regarded both Millie-Christine and Monemia as free people, returned the child to her mother despite Thompson's protests. According to a Liverpool journalist, he had refused to hand her over, "fancying, probably, that he was still in Georgia or Virginia, and not in England."[13] The *Liverpool Mercury* reported that "the instant that coloured female [Monemia] touched the soil of England she became a free woman, and was entitled to protection, and to all the advantages of the English laws. She now came into court to demand that her children should be restored to her, and [the attorney] could not see upon what pretence they could be detained from her." Thompson, incensed by the court's decision, tried to whip up support from the handful of people milling about the courthouse, offering money to anyone who might help him forcibly take the child. He was unsuccessful.

Even with Thompson out of the picture and Monemia reunited with her daughter, life for Millie-Christine didn't change much. She traveled to different cities and towns with her mother and W. J. L.

Millar, who was by then viewed as the lesser of two evils. At each stop, she was examined by physicians who would gratify their scientific curiosity and proclaim her a bona fide attraction. Then Millar placed Millie-Christine on exhibit with her mother, for the benefit of curious ticket buyers. Millar claimed a particularly slimy high ground, printing in advertisements that he had, at "great trouble and expense," freed Monemia from enslavement, "trusting to be reimbursed for his outlay by the consideration of the public."[14] He continued to claim that any profits from ticket sales would be applied toward the emancipation of Millie-Christine's family in the United States.[15] Freedom, so far as it manifested itself in Monemia's life and her daughter's, was more a marketing asset than a practical reality. Monemia did not want to remain in the United Kingdom, and she did not approve of Millar's increasingly harsh manner. Millie-Christine later recalled that, in addition to threatening Smith and verbally abusing Monemia, Millar "refused to allow us to receive the attention and luxuries which children of tender age require."[16] She asked Smith to help get them back to America, and he agreed. Millar woke one day and found that all three had quietly skipped town, arriving at the Liverpool docks just as the steamer *Atlantic* was due to leave for New York. The group made their way back to North Carolina, where for the first time, five-year-old Millie-Christine would have a semblance of a family life at home.

The Smith family moved to grander quarters in Spartanburg, South Carolina, in 1858. Their new estate consisted of a main house with a piano and seven smaller outbuildings for the Smiths' enslaved workers. (Smith and the law still considered Millie-Christine and her family among these.) Millie-Christine took lessons on the Smiths' new piano, and she soon learned reading and writing, religion, and crafts from Mary Smith. Joseph Pearson Smith was not ready to let go of the idea that Millie-Christine could be a lucrative attraction and planned to take her back on the road again as soon as possible. Millie-Christine's biographer Joanne Martell thinks it was "more than likely" that Mark Twain's account of Mardi Gras that year, in his book *Life on the Mississippi*, mentioned Millie-Christine. Twain's description of the Mistick Krewe of Comus and their 1858 sideshow parade described "all manner of giants, dwarfs, monstrosities, and other diverting grotesquerie—a startling and wonderful sort of show, as it filed solemnly and silently down the street in the light of its smoking and flickering torches."[17]

Smith and the twins went on a steamboat tour of the Mississippi in 1858. They continued to tour the South, though with conflict raging in Missouri and "Bleeding Kansas," Smith was careful to remain in territory in which slavery was the settled law of the land. The mix of showboating and home life in the Carolinas didn't last. As Southern states withdrew from the Union in 1860 and 1861, the entertainment industry south of the Mason-Dixon line largely collapsed. Then Joseph Smith died in 1862, leaving his wife and seven children to settle his affairs. Even though Millie-Christine's career had earned well, Smith had left his family in dire financial straits. In an auction to settle her husband's estate, Mary Smith sold thirteen enslaved people, livestock, and items including furniture and the family carriage. She did not sell Millie-Christine, whom appraisers considered to be worth $25,000.

After the Civil War ended, the Smiths and McKoys were politically and financially on their heels. Teenaged Millie-Christine, though now technically free along with her parents thanks to the Emancipation Proclamation, decided that her future depended on her ability to provide for both families. It's unclear whether Millie-Christine's continued partnership with the Smiths was an act of loyalty or practicality. In a pamphlet autobiography, she described Joseph Smith as a father figure and Mary as a kind guardian who had earned devotion, trust, and "true filial affection."[18] That was certainly possible, since the Smiths had been a large part of her life for many years and had rescued her from a chain of exploitative hucksters. But promotional pamphlets depended on neat storytelling and preferred to avoid uncomfortable complexity. In 2007, the scholar Ellen Samuels uncovered a letter from the McKoys to the Freedmen's Bureau that paints a different story. In this letter, Jacob and Monemia wrote to plead for military assistance in recovering their child from Mary Smith's custody. The McKoys claimed that Smith had not paid them their share of Millie-Christine's profits and had retained custody of their daughter by telling Jacob and Monemia that she was their only hope. They could not truly want Millie-Christine back, Smith had argued, since "the Yankees would kill them to get the children."[19]

Millie-Christine McKoy standing beside a guitar, ca. 1871.
Image courtesy of the Wellcome Collection.

Whatever the truth, fifteen-year-old Millie-Christine chose to go back on tour, with Mrs. Smith and her son Joseph managing routes and ticket sales. It was a way to ensure she made a viable living. Jacob and Monemia spent a short while on tour with their daughter before settling in Welches Creek, North Carolina. Finally freed from enslavement, Millie-Christine toured not as a passive physical curiosity fronted by white male managers but as a unique wonder with her own considerable talents. Millie-Christine managed her own affairs and was paid for her own work. She made much of her own clothing, learned to speak five languages, and was a talented pianist and singer who could use both of her mouths to harmonize. Millie-Christine took considerable pride in her uniqueness and talent, with playbills and posters touting her as "The Two-Headed Lady, the Double-Tongued Nightingale, the Eighth Wonder of the World, the Puzzle of Science, the Despair of Doctors, the Dual Unity."

As she grew into adulthood, Millie-Christine became a tough negotiator with extensive business and entertainment experience. Over her adult career she earned enough money to fulfill her father Jacob's dream of owning the land he had once worked. After many years traveling, she was at ease with all manner of audiences from everyday people to international royalty; Queen Victoria presented Millie-Christine with a pair of diamond hair clips following a performance in 1871.[20] Though her childhood was characterized by enslavement, abduction, and coercion, Millie-Christine was eventually able to assert herself clearly and forcefully against three systems that were keen to dismiss her as a Black disabled woman: the medical establishment, the press, and social expectations of women.

It was typical for human curiosities to undergo medical examination when they arrived to perform in a new city. Promoters would use the testimony of respectable medical men to authenticate their clients in the eyes of the paying public, and the doctors would use this access to poke and prod the performers, often well beyond the bounds of scientific necessity. Women's bodies particularly were probed and pathologized by medical men, too often with a lurid focus on sex. Women of color could expect even less deference or dignity when being examined. Black nudity and so-called anatomical education were a continuing focus at the time in venues ranging from world's fairs and sideshows to the nascent National Geographic Society (founded 1888). The display of Black bodies in this way was ostensibly for scientific and educational reasons, but below the surface it fed a furtive desire for racialized eroticism.[21]

Millie-Christine had been subjected to intrusive medical examinations from her infancy. Doctors posed endless questions, dressing up their own lurid curiosity in scientific guise. Medical men asked: How does she use the restroom? (In Millie-Christine's case, two sets of intestines joined into a single rectum.) Would conjoined women be able to marry? (Logistically, perhaps, but most medical men considered the thought morally distasteful.) How would St. Peter admit such a curiosity into the afterlife? (Consensus: "As they were united by accident," the sisters "will rise again, and will appear with bodies separated, or rent asunder.")[22] The scientist George J. Fisher, in an 1866 book entitled *Diploteratology* (teratology is the study of abnormal development, and the prefix "diplo" means "double"), described a handful of these physical examinations from the medical literature. Among a dreadful set of accounts, one of the most egregious occurred when Millie-Christine was just five years old. The exam included not only a description of the band of tissue connecting the girls but a physical internal examination of their genitals and rectum. One examiner didn't bother to hide his prurient interest, devoting two paragraphs to description of Millie-Christine's genitals but only a single sentence to the mechanics of how she managed to stand and walk on four legs.

Because Millie-Christine was a Black woman with an unusual body, mainstream systems of power saw little need for her consent. When Mrs. Smith brought Millie-Christine to a doctor in Philadelphia to request treatment of an abscess, doctors did far more than the requisite medical evaluation. On one such visit, doctors gave Millie-Christine minor electrical shocks to figure out which stimuli triggered which twin's muscles. One physician took an infamous photo of Millie-Christine in which she appears largely nude, with only a cloth for modesty. Christine, bowed in resignation, looks away from the camera, and Millie stares directly into the lens with an expression that tells you she would burn down the building if she could. The awful reality of this image is that the doctor may well have made medical treatment contingent on her participation. When Millie-Christine decided to continue touring after the end of the Civil War, she made one thing very clear: There would be no more intrusive preshow medical examinations.

This is not the only way in which accounts of Millie-Christine's life, pieced together from incomplete and questionably accurate sources, nevertheless show a marked shift in her agency and control over how she performed and was portrayed. In 1881, the *New York Clipper* advertised a new set of conjoined twins joining the show circuit. Ads touted the "double-headed Bohemian wonder" as the gold standard and dismissed both Millie-Christine and Chang and Eng Bunker (the original so-called "Siamese" Twins) as inferior attractions.[23] This was itself not all that remarkable, since promoters embellished their newest attractions all the time, but the ad called the Two-Headed Nightingale "repulsive in comparison" to this new stunner. Millie-Christine had a very solid sense of her own worth and of her unusual beauty and thought of herself as a wonder of creation. She took out an ad in reply that read:

> I have just read of the wonderful Prodigy advertised by you in THE CLIPPER, and cannot refrain from expressing to you my gratitude, after seeing the good taste (something no one else has ever given you credit for) displayed by you, in speaking of repulsive people, in that you do not mention yourself as one of them, for we of education and refinement, Mr. Uffner, would seriously object to having one classed with us who is so devoid of traits by which a gentleman is characterized as yourself. If people lived to as great an age in these days as some of them did in olden times, OF WHICH I HAVE READ, no doubt you would grow to be a more monstrous monstrosity than you are, but, sir, you would never grow to be a gentleman. —Millie Christine, the Two-Headed Nightingale.[24]

Millie-Christine was no longer willing to ignore the insults of callous promoters or to let newsmen off the hook as harmless.

The circus entrepreneur John Doris approached Millie-Christine ahead of the 1882 season and asked her to join Batcheller & Doris's Great Inter-Ocean Railroad Show. Having recently returned to the United States after a seven-year tour of Europe, Millie-Christine was seriously considering retirement and had no intention of accepting Doris's offer. She insisted on being paid $25,000, plus expenses, to join the circus, figuring the number was so ridiculous as to politely show John Doris the door. Instead, he showed up with a contract for that amount.

Millie-Christine had spent decades traveling around the world and living out of trunks and cases, and the circus offered a certain homey consistency. She would have her own apartment on the Batcheller & Doris train to decorate as she pleased, a community of fellow performers, meals from the cookhouse tent, and a consistent schedule of two shows a day for the duration of the 1882 season, which ran from April to December. Performers had Sundays off. Most notably, she would perform not as a sideshow curiosity or a down-ticket act, but in the main ring, simply as herself. Millie-Christine agreed to this offer and signed on.

By all accounts, this arrangement worked out well for everyone. The Inter-Ocean show was well staffed and reputable, with a delightful array of musicians, aerialists, acrobats, horse acts, clowns, a full menagerie, and the famous human cannonball Zazel. Millie-Christine stayed on with John Doris for two years, singing and dancing on a dance floor laid within the ring.

And then, in May 1882, Adam Forepaugh published his rat sheet, which described Millie-Christine in blistering terms, calling her a "horribly repulsive Negro monstrosity" in a show run by second-rate sideshow men. In addition, Forepaugh's ad claimed that: "The DOUBLE-HEADED DARKEY they advertise so extensively is the same they have carted around the country for years gone by, and exhibited for 10 cents, when they want 50 cents to see the dark-skinned monstrosity. A disgusting sight for ladies and children to gaze upon."[25]

It's unclear why Forepaugh had targeted Millie-Christine with this racist attack. Maybe he had tried unsuccessfully to hire her. It could have been a grudge against Batcheller & Doris, who had recently copied one of Forepaugh's own promotional ideas in offering a $10,000 beauty contest for a woman to star in their big opening act. Or maybe he just believed in hitting the competition as hard as possible as the routes of rival shows overlapped through the season.

In any case, Millie-Christine was not going to let these public insults pass unaddressed. She marched to the law offices of Robertson & Harper on Calhoun Street in Fort Wayne, Indiana. At her request, the lawyers drafted a libel claim and filed it in federal court on June 19, 1882. The complaint requested $25,000 in damages—the value of Millie-Christine's contract—for injury to her "character, reputation and business."[26] The suit claimed that Forepaugh had, with specific and malicious intent, attempted to deprive Millie-Christine of her public following and that his statements were not only false but dangerous. Millie-Christine's "peculiar and strange form" meant that "she is rendered unable to perform manual labor, but by reason of the same facts, the public have been desirous of seeing her and conversing with her, and she has by means of such desire been enabled by exhibiting herself, to obtain a livelihood, and to amass some means by which she hopes to become independent, and beyond the danger of want."[27] These nasty lies, the suit argued, were directly calculated to threaten her ability to make a living.

A marshal showed up to serve Forepaugh with papers during an afternoon performance in July 1882, and according to the papers, he tried to play it cool: "The old gentleman failed to make any demonstration of surprise, but acted rather as if he anticipated the suit."[28] Forepaugh, like many other big circus promoters, regularly had a full slate of litigation, and at first he seemed to think of this as he did any of his other pending disputes. He attempted to settle the suit in December 1882 for a token $200. Millie-Christine responded in the local Fort Wayne news that "she might some time be glad to get $200 for a settlement of a case like this but it was not now."[29] The case would continue for the next two years, even after Millie-Christine moved on from Batcheller & Doris's show. Itinerant showfolk were often hard to pin down, making scheduling and service of process a challenge, but Millie-Christine was extremely patient. Eventually, even the mighty Forepaugh's façade started to crack—the local papers published rumors that he was going to keep Indiana off his circus route that year for fear of legal service. When courts finally convened in December 1884 to rule on the matter, Forepaugh decided to withdraw the case and settle for an undisclosed amount rather than risk a trial.[30] The *Fort Wayne Gazette* summed it up: "The noted case of Millie Christine vs. Adam Forepaugh, which has been on the docket two years, was dismissed at defendant's costs, and it is understood that a basis of settlement was reached by which the Philadelphia circus proprietor gives up a pretty sum."[31]

Millie-Christine could—and did—tolerate a lot in the course of her public exhibition but would not put up with insults to her humanity, education, or uniqueness. She denied doctors access to her body, snapped back at insults in the press, and in public life carried herself as a woman of dignity and education. She worked hard to build a reputation as a woman who controlled her own affairs and who, despite a history of enslavement, exploitation, and invasive examination, was not to be taken advantage of. This required constant effort against significant social obstacles, even for an established headliner like Millie-Christine. Entrenched attitudes about proper femininity were doubly dismissive of Black women.

Consider Anna Olga Albertina Brown, a mixed-race "iron jaw" aerialist who performed as Miss La La in Europe during the 1870s. At the height of her fame in the winter of 1878, Miss La La caught the attention of Edgar Degas. The impressionist made a painting of her dressed in satin shorts with gold trim and dangling fringe and hanging by her teeth below the ceiling dome of bohemian Montmartre's Cirque Fernando. The resulting painting, *Miss La La at the Cirque Fernando*, made its debut to critical acclaim in 1879 at the famous Fourth Impressionist Exhibition in Paris. Miss La La fascinated Degas, along with thousands of Parisian spectators, because of her race, her body, and her unusual talents. In a signature act, Brown hung from a trapeze by her knees while a live cannon dangled from chains she clenched in her teeth. A gifted aerialist on multiple apparatuses, she was also able to pull a 150-pound man up and down on rings while hanging upside down by her knees. The bodybuilder

Edmond Desbonnet admitted that, on meeting her, "I was jealous of her biceps."[32]

In addition to being notably muscular, Miss La La stood tall and straight-faced in most photographs and wore her hair in a short, natural style. Where white circus women were typically praised in language that made them seem lovely, polite, and domestic, Miss La La was made to seem unfeminine. This was true even within her own act, where she was the "black butterfly" to her partner Kaira's white one. A Lyon paper noted in 1885 that "Olga and Kaira's talents are inseparable: Olga represents strength, Kaira, grace and audacity."[33] Advertisements presented Miss La La under a range of racialized stage names, including "The Black Butterfly," "The Black Venus," and "Venus of the Tropics." Where Kaira's proclaimed origin story was a simple story of idyll in a seaside French town, Miss La La's was related in terms of the slave trade: Allegedly, a tribal king named Eké had purchased the shipwrecked girl with gold powder and adopted her under the name Olga. In reality, La La had been born to a Black father and white mother in 1828 in Szczecin, now part of Poland, and had joined the circus at nine years old.

Responses to Degas's painting focused on La La's uncomfortable androgyny and ambiguous race. After celebrating a classical marble nude as "a figure both ruthless and gentle, like the very image of Beauty," art critic Armand Silvestre wrote of La La that she was no mythological "virgin glimpsed through the willows" but rather "a mulatto girl with the shape of an Ephebe [a Greek teenage boy], who has no equal for clinging to hippodrome ceilings with her teeth." The critic described her "frizzy head violently thrown back, her spine stretched out ... spinning slowly at the end of the cable."[34] The description was uncomfortably resonant with lynching.[35] Miss La La was expected to be strong and spectacular as she entertained respectable society, but she was also diminished by audiences and critics because of her failure to represent acceptable ideas of white womanhood.

By contrast, Millie-Christine's typical presentation and performance looked to ideals of nineteenth-century womanhood. She performed in receptions designed to demonstrate conventionally feminine arts such as dance and music, manners, elocution, and social skills.

Miss La La at the Cirque Fernando, 1880.
Image courtesy of the collection of the Zimmerli
Art Museum at Rutgers University.

Millie-Christine sang, told charming stories about meeting royalty, and spoke in many languages. No one could doubt that she was a refined, pleasing Victorian-era woman. Millie-Christine performed stereotypical femininity so well, in fact, that the media began to describe her in the context of white norms. Rather than admit that their stereotypes about Black women might be wrong, audiences and writers sought to distance Millie-Christine from her own Blackness. Illustrations began to smooth her hair and lighten her skin, to emphasize her wondrous talent and comportment. This contrasts dramatically with performances from decades before. As a child, Millie-Christine was often namelessly billed as "The African Twins" or with her last name spelled "Makoi" to seem more exotic and foreign. As an adult, she resisted pressure to continue this tokenism. She insisted on being paid top dollar to perform as herself, without any exaggerated publicity or manufactured identity. Audiences simply read in playbills that she, like any good woman, "is well educated, possessed of splendid conversational powers . . . sings the popular ballads of the day in the most artistic manner," and, of course, "is always gay, cheerful, and happy, of most pleasing appearance."[36]

Millie-Christine died in 1912, at the age of sixty-one. (Millie died of tuberculosis on October 8 that year; by permission of the governor, Christine was permitted large palliative doses of morphine and passed the next day.) She was buried on family land and remained there until 1969, when she was exhumed and reinterred in the Welches Creek community cemetery. Her unusual body was not only a source of pride and wonder but a means to accomplish what most Black Americans could not at the time: economic empowerment, agency, and broad social mobility. In success, she felt a strong sense of obligation: According to a nephew, Millie-Christine used her means not only to resettle her family in North Carolina but to support Black community organizations, schools, and churches with considerable donations. In his words, "She was a talented, generous black woman who was one of the greatest black women of her time. She said that when God made her, he gave her two heads and two brains because her responsibility was so great."[37]

CHAPTER 9

The Splendor and Terror of Bearded Ladies

In the middle nineteenth century, New York's Court of Special Sessions was housed within an imposing complex that covered a full city block in lower Manhattan, commonly known as "The Tombs" for its grim reputation and its Egyptian Revival architecture.[1] Built on a swampy, filled-in pond, the Tombs were a perpetually damp crush of criminal justice activity and hosted everything from police court cases to high-profile executions.

On July 1, 1853, Madame Josephine Clofullia, with P. T. Barnum by her side, climbed the stone steps on Centre Street for her scheduled court date. William Chaar, a visitor to Barnum's American Museum, had filed a false advertising suit against the entertainment icon, claiming that he had "paid the sum of twenty five cents at the door of the American Museum for the purpose of seeing the Bearded Lady," and that "the person who was pointed out to him as the Bearded Lady is, in his opinion, a male and an impostor on the public." Chaar wanted his money back.

Josephine Clofullia made her debut at Barnum's American Museum at the height of summer in 1853, when patrons were eager to take the proprietor up on his promise that the museum was the "coolest spot in New York."[2] Barnum excitedly announced that he had "succeeded, after many fruitless endeavors, in effecting a brief engagement with that extraordinary curiosity, which has created such an overpowering sensation in Europe, the Bearded Lady From Switzerland."[3] Half of the day's playbill was devoted to an engraved portrait of Madame Clofullia in a tiered floor-length gown, a drape of floral pleated lace falling off her shoulders. She stood regally, chin held high to show off her "singular peculiarity," but frankly the beard stood out less than Madame's jewelry. Beneath a substantial tiara, Clofullia wore a necklace, brooch, and a long, decorated belt, each dripping with jewels. Barnum promised she would appear for audiences daily (Sundays excepted), from ten to noon, two to five p.m., and again from seven to ten in the evening. She was extremely popular with visitors—just not, apparently, with William Chaar.

After receiving the complaint at his Museum on Broadway, Barnum notified Clofullia, and the pair set out for Centre Street half a mile away. They were joined by a phalanx of supporting authority, including Clofullia's husband, her father, a police captain of the Second Ward, and a doctor prepared to attest to her biological sex. There is no record of what was going through Clofullia's mind as she walked into the Tombs, passing under the shade of the portico with its giant, papyrus-bud columns. She may have been wearing the handkerchief she often tied around her face in public to deflect attention from her beard. Was she nervous? Irritated? There are no known primary sources in Clofullia's own words, and so it is an exercise in historical quilting and informed guesswork to figure out who the "Bearded Lady From Switzerland" really was.[4]

What we do know from reported accounts is that the bearded lady and her team of supporting gentlemen approached the bench and argued against William Chaar's claim of falsehood in no uncertain terms. The men all declared that Josephine Clofullia was indeed who she claimed to be, exactly the bearded woman Barnum's ads promised. Fortune Clofullia swore under oath that his wife of three years was also a mother, a fact her father corroborated. Barnum, who added that "he pays a large sum of money weekly for her exhibiting," had arranged for medical examination. He produced a certificate signed by three medical doctors attesting to Josephine Clofullia's undeniable status as a "remarkable case of hirsute growth" and "a striking example of organic development for the instruction of the naturalist." The city prison's doctor confirmed he, too, had examined Madame Clofullia "in conjunction with the matron," for decorum's sake, and was "perfectly convinced that, in spite of her beard, she is a woman." Well persuaded, and perhaps eager to disperse the "large crowd of spectators" drawn by the novelty of this particular case, the magistrate ruled in Barnum's favor. No one thought it necessary to ask Madame Clofullia to testify on her own behalf.

P. T. Barnum's American Museum employed a revolving-door cast of extraordinary individuals he considered not freaks but rather "representatives of the wonderful."[5] Patrons strolling through the seven saloons of his museum of curiosities often encountered one of the museum's "living wonders" in person, the performer's unique appearance reflected dimly in the gaslit glass of Barnum's floor-to-ceiling curio cases.[6] Some stayed only for short engagements; others lived for weeks or months at a time in the Museum's apartments, where Barnum provided room and board and where the living room must have been a very interesting place indeed. Madame Josephine Clofullia was the first in a succession of hirsute women Barnum would hire over his decades as a museum owner and circus impresario. By the time of his Greatest Show on Earth, a bearded lady would become a must-have entertainment for any show worth its salt, as much a shorthand for the circus genre as red-striped tents, elephants, or cotton candy.

As entertainers, these women came to prominence during the middle nineteenth century, when many were exhibited as evidence of the wild variety of divine creation. In a time of narrowly defined standards of acceptable womanhood, hairiness on the female body invited social and scientific inquiry into what constituted "real" or "proper" femininity. The lives and accounts of some of the era's most famous performing bearded women show that the answer was complex and highly racialized. White bearded women were allowed the luxury of being a lady notwithstanding their hair, while bearded women of color were more frequently pathologized as "missing links" or evidence of the inferiority of nonwhite races. All of them suffered a loss of autonomy and privacy because of their failure to meet feminine norms.

Excessive hair growth on the human body is generally diagnosed medically as either hypertrichosis, which can occur in any person and over any part of the body, or hirsutism, which happens when people who are assigned female at birth grow hair in areas associated with traditionally male patterns of hair growth, such as the face and chest. Both conditions are common. Hirsute women are mentioned quite often in historical records that date back centuries: Hippocrates is said to have written about a woman who grew a beard after menopause, and the scientists George Gould and Walter Pyle, in their 1897 book *Anomalies and Curiosities of Medicine*, catalogued a list of bearded women from the sixteenth century onward. The men praised the fact that most were largely conventional despite their facial hair, "quite womanly" and "very sweet," and indeed even showing "a strong passion for the male sex."[7]

To speak about a bearded woman is to confront a certain fact up front: Her very existence makes it very hard to accept the concept of a gender binary. A beard, after all, is a fundamental symbol of masculinity, and a certain unkempt hairiness has historically not only been acceptable for men but even signaled credibility. Think Walt Whitman, Martin Van Buren, Gandalf: Their wild whiskers indicate that shaving would have been a waste of time better spent on purposeful work. The gray is a sign not of fading vitality but eminence. A beard traditionally signals status and gravity, social power literally mapped across a man's face. A woman with a robust beard, therefore, has historically been seen as an unwelcome and unnatural intrusion into the masculine sphere. This was not lost on the writer for *Gleason's Pictorial Drawing-Room Companion* who lumped Madame Clofullia in with women's rights activists, describing both as unnatural. "Here is a woman who out-Herods Herod," gasped the writer. "Not content with claiming the right to vote, and laying siege to our nether garments (a la *bloomer*), our beards are actually in jeopardy. Heaven forfend!"[8]

In the latter half of the nineteenth century, scientific theories, heterosexual beauty standards, and the fashion industry encouraged people who identified as women to make themselves as hairless as possible. Reasons to do so could come from evolutionary theory as well as from a system built on the idea of gendered social control. Proponents of the former argued that humans prefer hairless bodies as a matter of instinct and health: Without hair, a person's body is free of parasites and their attendant diseases, can be well cleaned, and both looks and feels good to partners. In the second case, hair removal can be a way to control women in society. Not only does it take time, money, and supplies to regularly remove body hair, but women who choose not to or who do not successfully achieve the proper level of hairlessness can be dismissed as dirty or degenerate.[9]

As hairlessness became more of a social imperative for women in the nineteenth century, their depilation was expected to be done in secret to maintain the idea that soft, smooth womanhood was a state of nature rather than the result of a whole lot of time and effort in the toilette. The writer Kimberly Hamlin notes with some amusement the frustration of nineteenth-century dermatologist George Henry Fox, who really wanted a clear answer to his voyeuristic questions about women's hairiness but was thwarted by the beauty industry at every turn: "Could we but know the secrets of the boudoir," Fox said, "we would be surprised to find out how large a percentage of our female acquaintances resort occasionally if not habitually, to the use of the depilatory, the razor, or the tweezers."[10]

In 1871, Charles Darwin published *The Descent of Man*, which promulgated ideas about sexual selection for certain physical traits.[11] Darwin claimed that evolution had moved humanity to a state of ideal hairlessness, an argument that required some scientific contortion. On the one hand, body hair has advantages for human survival; it keeps us warm and comfortable. On the other, hair can be disquieting, even repellent, reminding us that we are little more than animals who sometimes choose to wear suits. For Darwin's claim to be true, the physical advantages of hair had to be outweighed by the sexual appeal of hairlessness. In other words, in a Darwinian scheme, we are hairless because it's optimally attractive. And if that's the case, women should exhibit not only "superior beauty" in this regard but "superior cleanliness," too. Darwin apparently saw no corresponding evolutionary need to groom his hulking white whiskers.

When Madame Clofullia arrived on the exhibition scene in the middle 1800s, she was unavoidably disruptive to society's ideas of natural womanhood as a soft, smooth, and delicate state. She challenged the idea of a beard as a masculine signifier of strength and status and therefore poked at manhood itself. She complicated sex and gender binaries. People could not look away.

Clofullia was born Josephine Boideschene around 1830 near Lake Geneva in Switzerland.[12] Her pamphlet biography paints a picture of sturdy, upstanding idyll: Her father, Joseph, was "not rich" but well educated and secure; her mother, "always at the head of her competitors" at the best of Swiss boarding schools. Though he had joined the military as required by national custom, her father resigned his commission to spend time at home with his new wife, and the couple welcomed Josephine a respectable eleven months after their marriage. And then the extraordinary began to creep into the picture: Though obviously a new, healthy baby was a joy for the family, "they soon perceived that their child had the body and face covered with a slight down." Family and medical experts alike expected this would pass after infancy, but by her eighth birthday, Josephine's downy fuzz had become a beard "fully two inches in length." At boarding school, young Josephine "excelled particularly in those works adapted to her sex such as embroideries, lace, network and all kinds of needle-work, and thus grew up to the age of fourteen." The family's other three children showed no similar growth of hair, though as for their son, the anonymous biographer sniffs that the boy "is of a feminine appearance, resembles greatly his mother, and now in his eighteenth year, shows no appearance of beard." Doctors urged Mrs. Boideschene to avoid shaving or trimming Josephine's beard, lest it grow back longer and coarser.

Mrs. Boideschene passed away after the birth and sudden death of her fifth child. The family was, for a time, "inconsolable," and resisted all suggestions that Josephine be exhibited publicly. Her father refused these requests as a matter of course until a promoter from Lyon made a one-year offer so attractive he could no longer say no. Objectively, Joseph seemed pleased to be set free from the pressures of a widower's life at home with a house full of children and bills to pay: He sent the other children off to boarding school, leased his home and farm, and went with his daughter to prepare for her debut in Geneva. She met with solid financial success from the start. Since Josephine and her father saw the appeal of a performing lifestyle, Joseph soon took

Madame Josephine Clofullia, P. T. Barnum's "Bearded Lady of Geneva."
Image courtesy of the Missouri Historical Society.

on management duties and planned a posh tour throughout France. It was there that Josephine met Fortune Clofullia, a nineteen-year-old artist of Swiss origin. After a handful of very chastely described dates on which they talked about art, the two fell in love and were engaged to be married.

The Clofullia party projected an aristocratic image. They leveraged the concept of a cultural grand tour in order to telegraph a sense of luxury to audiences, and they engaged with distinguished society and scientific experts to legitimize Josephine's exhibition. In France, they visited Versailles, and Louis-Napoléon Bonaparte was said to have invited Josephine to Tuileries Palace, where he provided her with "princely gifts." London greeted her similarly in 1851, with "all the dignitaries of this immense city" visiting to see such a wonder for themselves. In London, the doctor William Dingle Chowne, one of the founders of the medical school at Charing Cross and its lead physician, devoted a lecture and three articles in *The Lancet* to describing her case.

Madame Clofullia remained in London for two years, entertaining an estimated 800,000 spectators and ultimately starting a family. After losing a daughter in infancy, in December 1852, Clofullia gave birth to a son and named him Albert. The child's face and body were covered in light downy hair, and he would later be described in promotional literature as the "infant Esau" after the notably hairy biblical figure.

In 1853, promoters beckoned Clofullia to America. She stayed for nine months at Barnum's American Museum, where the proprietor was pleased to note that "during that time she was visited and seen by upwards of 3,500,000 persons." P. T. Barnum advertised her as "the only living specimen of this wonderful phenomena in America, if not in the world."[13]

It's easy to read her biography and think that Josephine Clofullia was on easy street, well paid to travel in comfort to Europe's finest destinations in exchange for high-society appearances. However, press coverage and medical records paint a different picture. Because of her beard, Clofullia was deprived of both privacy and bodily autonomy.

At his London lecture, Chowne, a ruddy-faced doctor with curly mutton chops crawling down toward his chin, explained that "a person came to this hospital, requesting to have a testimonial as to the sex of the individual." That person—presumably Clofullia's father—had allegedly sought this validation as she "was under an engagement to marry, but that the masculine appearance of her face produced scruples in the mind of persons who would otherwise have performed the marriage ceremony." (This was a convenient fiction to justify the doctor's purpose; Clofullia was by then not only married but clearly pregnant.) Chowne informed students that he had arrived at the conclusion that the bearded woman was biologically female, his detached clinical language smoothing over the blunt reality of the physical inspection he had conducted. Though hair appeared in a "tolerably broad line" down her back, and in a "masculine distribution" on her lower abdomen, he noted, Clofullia's chest was hairless. Her breasts were "large, fair, and strictly feminine in all respects." Josephine herself commented that Swiss doctors had considered her possibly intersex, with "organs male in their character" inside the abdomen. Chowne dismissed this possibility: "An examination, made in the usual manner, left no doubt of the presence of a uterus."[14]

When she appeared in public, Josephine would fold and tie a handkerchief over her face in the fashion of a mask, shaving only that portion of her cheekbones that would naturally peek out over its upper edges. This was partly to avoid people seeing for free what she'd rather they pay full price for, but in societies that had social distaste for cross-dressing or even actual legislation against its practice, there was another practical reason for this. "In her own village, where she was well known," Chowne wrote, "she had no occasion for the handkerchief, but in a strange place she finds it necessary, lest the police should regard her as a man disguised in woman's apparel."

It was not just the medical community that felt entitled to intimately examine Clofullia's body. The media felt equally obligated. Ahead of her debut with P. T. Barnum in 1853, journalists enjoyed a customary preview engagement. A *New York Post* reporter wrote, "It was our privilege to test the reality of this beard by the decisive experiment, viz., pulling it, and we can testify that it is a genuine out-growth, resembling in silkiness and abundance the imaginary crop which is promised from the use of the various hair invigorators which are in such common request."[15] Josephine Clofullia was advertised as being a perfect lady and performed this role with aplomb: She wore beautiful gowns, spoke in French, sang for museum visitors, and talked about her international travel among society's highest elite. Her audiences admired her ladylike manner and for the most part treated her accordingly. However, because Clofullia was displaying an unusual and unconventional female body, she was expected to quietly surrender some degree of ownership over that body to the skeptical public. The scholar Sean Trainor crisply points out: "It's hard to imagine white American men standing for such transgressions of female honor had Clofullia not worn a beard."[16]

Josephine Clofullia may have been the first bearded woman to make it big in the United States, but she was by no means the only one. In the second half of the nineteenth century, there are historical records of a handful of American bearded women, including Kentuckian Madam DeVere, Madame Viola the "Wide World Wonder," and the alleged Greatest Wonder of the World, Madame Howard, whose pamphlet includes an illustration of her with a full face of hair, floor-length tresses, and a ruffled strapless gown.[17] Though Madame Clofullia was the first bearded woman to work with Barnum, Annie Jones would become the most famous in his employ. Jones first appeared at the American Museum as the "infant female Esau" and later as the "Bearded Girl," standing demurely in pin-curls. As an adult, she had a thick black beard and mustache, favored ribbons and pearls, and often draped her braided calf-length hair over her shoulder.[18]

These bearded women were all white, which meant they could trade in fluffy, coded origin stories that did not require audiences to think all that seriously about their entertainment. Jones's pamphlet biographer, though, happened to ask a more pointed question. How does it happen, he wondered, "that an infant, born of parents fair of complexion and modest and amiable in disposition, should, from the first, be covered with a mass of hair."[19] The implication, of course, was that this was not the sort of thing that should happen to upstanding, moral white families who prized genteel womanhood.

Bearded women were not all "fair of complexion." A little more than a year after Clofullia's New York debut, Julia Pastrana arrived in the United States from Mexico. Appearing in New York at the Gothic

Hall on Broadway, Pastrana was described with lascivious delight by the press. She was not, like Clofullia, a lady who just happened to have whiskers, but rather something "terrifically hideous," with sharp glistening eyes and rough fangs. George O'Dell's *Annals of the New York Stage* describes Pastrana as both chilling and courteous, like a tiger made to speak before paying crowds: "Its voice is harmonious," he relates, "for this semi-human being is perfectly docile, and speaks the Spanish language."[20] The *New York Times* called Pastrana "the most popular Exhibition in New-York," noting that a thousand people had come to see her in only two and a half days and that ladies especially were enchanted by her singing. The *Times* proclaimed that "La Muger Osa"—the Bear Woman—"is the lion of the day."[21]

Julia Pastrana was born in 1834 in indigenous Sinaloa on Mexico's western coast. Born with hypertrichosis and dental deformity, Pastrana attracted showmen's attention early on. Promotional literature stated that Julia's mother had been found raising her remarkable child in the remote mountains. The woman, identified as Mrs. Espinosa, "expressed a great liking for this child" to the ranchero who rescued her and claimed a tribe of so-called "Root-Digger Indians" had kept her from leaving the remote cavern.[22] The allegedly biographical sources about Pastrana are a stew of mythic invention: Some suggest that Pastrana's mother had gotten lost while going into the mountains to bathe; others claim that she feared the influence of spirits or werewolves on the birth of her long-haired daughter and fled for remote terrain. The tribal identity was entirely manufactured to highlight Pastrana's primitive origins with people who "live in caves in a naked state."[23] Discovered by a Mexican explorer, Julia was said to have been taken in by the governor in Sinaloa—whether as a curiosity, a housemaid, or a charity case is unclear. Per the myth, she was baptized, given a Christian name, and taught to cook, wash, iron, and sew. When she was "getting tired of housework," she supposedly decided to leave "for the United States to be exhibited."[24]

Since most of this comes from print materials meant either to promote Pastrana's appearances or bring in more revenue for them, exaggeration should be assumed. Reputable historical sources verify little about her youth but do confirm that, in 1854, Julia Pastrana was accustomed to exhibition as a human curiosity and heading with promoters to America, where they planned a continued career in show business for her. The party arrived in New Orleans on October 28, 1854, on the steamer *Orizaba*, and by December, Pastrana was described by the New York press in superlatives. Attendance at her exhibits was boosted by prominent city surgeon Dr. Alex B. Mott's testimony on December 3 that Pastrana was a half-human wonder: "She is a perfect woman," Mott testified, "a rational creature, endowed with speech which no monster has ever possessed. She is therefore a HYBRID wherein the nature of woman predominates over the brute—the Orang Outang."[25]

Mentioning Pastrana in the same breath as orangutans was neither casual nor accidental. Scientific thought at the time openly questioned whether the great apes were hybrid beings, some sort of unsettling transitional point between apes and man. The orangutan itself was also a creature of public fascination even beyond scientific circles. First publicized in the West in the seventeenth century by European naturalists whose engravings showed two-legged creatures with heavy breasts and shaggy hair, the so-called "man of the forest" immediately provoked vulgar speculation about the relationship between animals and allegedly savage foreign people. This only increased as actual primates were brought to Europe for display in coming centuries.[26] The naturalist Jacob de Bondt was one of many who turned lewd suspicion into published science, claiming the orangutan was the result of Indian women engaging in "detestable" relations with apes and monkeys.[27] Even into the twentieth century, people entertained this notion: The naturalist Odoardo Beccari wrote in a 1904 book that "The Dyaks tell many a tale about women being carried off by orang-utans," and at around the same time, the Congolese man Ota Benga was exhibited at the New York Zoological Gardens.[28] The idea of a creature human enough to use tools and move in immediately familiar ways, yet unable or unwilling to moderate its animal instincts, was both frightening and irresistibly illicit to people during the long nineteenth century.

Popular nineteenth-century attractions eagerly engaged with these tropes, asking: Could humanity be found within the beast—or, ghastlier still, was humanity itself fundamentally beastly? The suggestions were racist and rough and full of forbidden eroticism. Mass media was keen to sell papers by amplifying messages that conflated apes and Black men in the space between humanity and brutality.[29] In the middle 1820s, a popular ballet called *Jocko* romanticized the story of a Brazilian ape who, dashingly danced by the male lead in a furry suit, nobly rescued a child in danger ("jocko" was another name applied to various apes).[30] Edgar Allan Poe told the salacious tale of a murderous orangutan let loose on a beautiful woman in *The Murders in the Rue Morgue*, published in 1841. Robert Louis Stevenson contemplated "the full deformity of that creature that shared with him some of the phenomena of consciousness" in his 1886 novella, *Strange Case of Dr. Jekyll and Mr. Hyde*.[31]

These commonly held social attitudes motivated showmen to double down on racist rhetoric. Because it was both titillating and profitable to make an animal of a woman like Julia Pastrana, she was billed in many such ways. Labels included "'Nondescript,' 'Misnomer,' 'Bear Woman,' 'Baboon Lady,' 'Ape Woman,' 'Hybrid Indian,' 'Extraordinary Lady,' and 'The Ugliest Woman in the World.'"[32] Exhibited to audiences as "the lowest link of humanity and the highest order of brutes," Pastrana appeared in extravagant dress, cosplaying humanity in its many archetypes—in one instance, a red knee-length gown with balloon sleeves; in another, a lace-trimmed sleeveless gown with tiers of pink lace and trailing blue ribbons; yet again, in a dashing sailor's pantsuit.[33] In Germany, she performed in a play written specifically for her, in which a local milkman falls in love with her as a veiled woman and is "cured" of his passions when he finally, after a few slapstick acts, realizes that the veil hides a sizable beard. (Unlike the milkman, the audience has been in on the conceit the whole time.)[34]

Pastrana's public persona was crafted on the idea that she was a primitive being liberated by colonization, Christianity, and culture. Promotional copy sold to curious patrons further dehumanized her, stating that Pastrana was "now four feet six inches high, and weighs one hundred and twelve pounds. She has thick black hair all over her person, except her bosom, hands and feet. Her mouth is elongated, with very thick lips. She has double gums in front, both in the upper and lower jaw—with only one row of front teeth, and those teeth in the back sum of the lower jaw. She is good natured, sociable and accommodating—can speak the English and Spanish Languages—dance, sing, sew, cook, wash and iron—these latter accomplishments having been acquired, of course, since her introduction to civilized life, having been recovered from a state of nature when she was very young."[35] Pastrana was bilingual, socially adept, fluent in the expected set of feminine crafts and trades, could dance a hell of a schottische, and was well traveled. Even so, audiences were still eager to believe a story that she came from a people "very much of the monkey order, very spiteful and hard to govern."[36]

In November 1855, Julia Pastrana married Theodore Lent. Lent was an auctioneer and sometime brothel investor who acted as a staff member on Pastrana's tour along with his brother. Aware of Pastrana's marketability, Lent decided the best way to edge out Pastrana's management was to elope with her in Baltimore.[37] While on the road, Pastrana's Mexican guardian and American promoter awoke one morning to find her gone. After getting warrants against the Lent brothers for kidnapping, they eventually found Pastrana in Theodore Lent's company, as well as a marriage certificate prepared that same day. When questioned, Pastrana stated to a Maryland judge that "she was married and would not give up her husband for anybody."[38] News coverage more coarsely wondered if the bearded woman "belongs to her husband, her guardian, or her lessee."[39] Lent prevailed, and after an American tour, in 1857, he took Pastrana to England and the European continent, where she appeared as a curiosity in salons, circuses, and on the stage.

Accounts from those who saw and knew her describe Pastrana as warm, bright, and devoted to Lent. In return, he was not so much devoted as controlling, and he arguably leveraged her infatuation for his own financial benefit. Judging from Lent's history of shady business dealings and his prior involvement in prostitution, if not trafficking, this was a one-sided love story.[40] By all accounts, Lent carefully controlled his wife's activities, managing her schedule, persuading her to submit to doctors' examinations, and requiring her to stay in her apartment when not performing. As Madame Clofullia had done, she

Julia Pastrana, a bearded woman.
Image courtesy of the Wellcome Collection.

would tie a veil around her face on those occasions she went out in public, perhaps to take in a circus or theater performance with Lent in the evening.[41]

Julia Pastrana and Theodore Lent proceeded onward to Poland and Russia, where she died due to complications of childbirth in 1860. Her son lived just short of three days, and Julia passed on the fifth day. After Pastrana's death, Lent engaged the services of a Russian professor named Sokolov, who had developed a proprietary technique for preserving human bodies. (About his process, he would only say that he injected "decay-arresting mixtures."[42]) Lent sold the bodies of his deceased wife and child to this professor for preservation and then purchased them back when he realized that Pastrana, who was posed with her hands on her hips in a jaunty embroidered dress for all eternity, could still be a profitable curiosity even after her death.

Lent eventually married a second bearded woman, Marie Bartel, for whom he created a fictional identity as Julia's sister "Zenora Pastrana." In the middle 1880s, Lent began to act strangely, manically tearing up banknotes and tossing them into the river in St. Petersburg, among other "irrational things." He died in a Russian asylum.[43]

For decades, the remains of Julia Pastrana and her child wandered, passing from promoters to anatomists and eventually ending up in a hospital basement in Oslo, Norway. More than a century after their deaths, in the 1970s, the two mummified bodies were displayed at a smattering of American carnivals and state fairs alongside an Apollo 16 ride and the "Gay New Orleans Show."[44] Time and damage claimed her son's remains, but in 2013, thanks to the advocacy of artist Laura Anderson Barbata, Pastrana's body was successfully repatriated to Mexico. As a tambora band played music, Julia Pastrana was arrayed in white flowers and buried in Sinaloa.[45]

The tendency to make animalistic spectacle of hairy women would continue well past Julia Pastrana's lifetime; from the 1880s onward, Krao Farini, a Laotian woman with hypertrichosis, was exhibited as the "Missing Link." Krao, who took her surname from her promoter William Hunt—a.k.a. the Great Farini—appeared in various character personas over the years. First, she appeared as a feral child draped in only a loincloth like Kipling's Mowgli. As a young girl, she stood primly in a floral dress with socks and Mary Janes, signaling Western virtue. As an adult, the theme was sexed-up Darwinist evolution, as Krao posed in heeled pumps and held an ostrich-feather fan. The headline read: "Living Proof of the Greatest Theory Ever Propounded."[46]

Bearded women illustrate prevailing social biases, both in the way they were exhibited in their own era and in the way we talk about them today. The beard signified that femininity had somehow gone wrong, so these women had to expend tremendous energy to prove otherwise. In passing judgment on bearded women, society sent a message to all women about compliance with feminine ideals and standards. Men in the medical and scientific establishment felt entitled to inspect and pass judgment on women's bodies, believing they had the right and ability to legitimize them as women or even human. At every turn, women were asked to prove their femininity through physical examination, demonstration of womanly skills and manners, or participation in family life and motherhood. For white women like Madame Clofullia and Annie Jones, that proof of femininity came through performing femininity in fancy salons and gilded dress. Women of color like Krao Farini and Julia Pastrana, however, could only define their femininity by contrast to Western norms: Even in fine form and a lovely dress, they were unable to overcome audience expectations and biases. Mainstream crowds wanted to believe that prehistory still lived on in dark spaces yet to be colonized.

When Madame Clofullia walked into the Tombs on that hot summer day in New York, she was being escorted into a referendum on her femininity. In the proceeding, her appearance was allowed to speak, while she was not. The *New York Tribune* reported that the judge, "deeming that Mr. Barnum had clearly proved his innocence of the charge laid against him, dismissed the complaint, and the parties interested forthwith left the court Room, followed by a large crowd of spectators, whom the novelty of the case had collected."[47] Barnum didn't care whether Josephine Clofullia identified as a woman or not or, for that matter, if anyone else thought of her that way. He had instigated the suit himself: It was good publicity ahead of the Fourth of July weekend.

CHAPTER 10

Ella Zoyara, the "Boy-Girl"

Niblo's Garden was one of the premier entertainment venues in nineteenth-century New York. First opened in the early 1820s at the corner of Broadway and Prince Street—then far enough north of city limits that folks considered getting there a nice country ride—the site was operated as a "pleasure garden" on a former farm and circus ground.[1] Pleasure gardens were popular attractions at the time, the sort of places well-to-do folks might go on an evening or weekend for a pastoral escape from city life. William Niblo, an Irish immigrant who had prospered in the coffeehouse business, owned the lot and outfitted it with everything New Yorkers wanted for a relaxing stroll: ornamental gardens, gently burbling fountains, an ice cream stand, music wafting across the grounds from an open-air saloon, and a 1,200-seat theater for small entertainments.[2] Colored lights glowed warmly across the grounds at night. As Niblo's Garden grew in popularity over the years, the complex expanded. In 1837 *The Ladies' Companion* magazine noted that the venue offered "agreeable and tastefully embellished promenades, brilliant fireworks, occasionally, all the 'rama's'—'pano,' 'dio,' or 'cosmo:'—the best concert singing,—and now and then, conjuring, rope dancing, and, in fact, every description of entertainment."[3]

As New York City continued to grow, so did Niblo's Garden. Niblo launched *The Black Crook*, which theater buffs consider the first modern

American musical. It gave P. T. Barnum his first break in show business with the dreadful 1835 exhibition of the formerly enslaved woman Joice Heth, advertised as George Washington's 161-year-old nursemaid. By the 1860s, the site boasted a 3,000-seat theater considered one of the best houses in the city.

Late in 1859, though, the stage was outfitted to host Cooke's Royal Amphitheatre, a circus company from London. Aerialists anchored swings and ropes to the ornate proscenium arch, the company made space for a Chinese lantern act involving 150 performers, and crews laid down soft matting on the stage in lieu of the traditional sawdust floor so equestrian acts could run at speed and not strafe the audience with wood shavings. The *New York Times* gave Cooke's show a rave review on January 17, 1860, noting lovely costumes, thirty-foot aerial jumps across the stage, the indeed delightful lack of sawdust, and solid horse acts. The last element was an important part of circus entertainment in the nineteenth century: Since people from all walks of life dealt with horses daily, they knew what it took to train and ride with skill. "In New-York, as in every other city of the Union," wrote the *Times* critic, "good circus riding is thoroughly understood and appreciated."[4] The review specifically applauded "Mlle. Ella Zoyara, the principal lady of the company," noting that "the graceful daring of her 'acts' brought down the heartiest applause of the house." The circus brought in "straw houses" for Niblo—sold-out shows, in circus parlance—and Zoyara was consistently praised for her acrobatic riding. Tall, raven-haired, and slender in a seventeen-inch corset and tights, Zoyara rode her horse over a series of gated jumps.[5] Each time the horse approached a jump, Zoyara crouched and leapt, clearing a hoop mounted six feet over the gate and landing evenly on the horse's back just as hooves met the ground again. The *New York Tribune* wrote that she "rivals the best male riders in grace and intrepidity."[6]

Ten days later, the *Tribune* amended its review. "There is a rider attached to the company of equestrians and athletes now performing at Niblo's, called in the bills Mademoiselle Ella Zoyara, whose equine exploits, though they are very surprising in their way, have not caused so much excitement as the doubts entertained as to her sex. Mademoiselle Ella dresses and acts with the grace of a woman, and her face has nothing masculine in its expression; it is, in fact, a most feminine and gentle face. But she has the springy agility of a man, and is taller and straighter than well proportioned women ever are. Disputes nightly arise among the spectators on the subject of the fair equestrian's sex, for fair the so-called Mademoiselle Ella is, whether male or female."[7]

Circus is a fundamentally visual medium. Think of the bold, illustrative type of circus posters and playbills: The words themselves are less important than the visual energy with which they're presented. Audiences watch performances and then relive them in imagination later on. That the circus played games with gender expression was therefore neither unusual nor surprising; it had always done so. Within the dreamy space and time created by the big top, it presented a wide spectrum of gendered characters, evoked by the sort of visual shorthand that read well from the cheap seats: beautiful women and muscular men, a majestic ringmaster in military finery, exotic harem girls and brave lion tamers. The circus also created blends of this visual shorthand, offering clowns in drag, muscular women, men in tights, bearded ladies, and an entire sideshow of individuals who made spectators question the idea of human sameness. This playfulness around gender norms was clear even before the late nineteenth-century era of cultural dominance for the American circus; surviving photographs show Charles Stratton in drag as "Our Mary Ann" in a mid-1800s Barnum production. The animal tamer Jacob Driesbach tended toward photo poses with clear homoerotic appeal, lounging with a big cat in tiny shorts and a strappy harness-style top, in gladiator sandals, or completely nude with only a leopard's head for modesty.[8]

What really shook up the snow globe in the 1860s, though, was Ella Zoyara (born Omar Kingsley), one of the first circus performers to engage in gender play without centering caricature or stereotype in the performance. Nor was Zoyara the sort of performer who kept to the sideshow tent or sought out clinical or scientific validation. She was simply a star.

There is limited surviving information and historical record about Ella Zoyara. We know she emerged in the sawdust rings and theaters of 1850s circus, and we know that Samuel Omar Kingsley died in Mumbai, India (then Bombay), on April 2, 1879, at the age of thirty-nine.[9] Zoyara's real identity, sexual preferences, and attitudes on gender are not documented in the historical record. It is tempting to make inferences, but the surviving sources are limited, and a person's behavior is not alone evidence of identity. Moreover, not every person who rejects the gender binary identifies as queer, and there are problems with projecting modern concepts of gender and sexuality backward onto individuals who lived in times and societies with different understandings of those concepts. Whether Kingsley might have identified in today's world as trans, as nonbinary, as a drag performer, or as something else, we ultimately cannot know. But we can look at contemporary audiences' reactions to female impersonation onstage and at how Zoyara's act challenged social structures based on the gender binary. Throughout this chapter, I will use pronouns that correspond to public presentation, referring to Ella Zoyara as "she" and Omar Kingsley as "he." This largely aligns with how print media referred to the performer at the time, though occasionally gossip columns or too-clever reporters would swap or mix pronouns in a nod to the act's layers.

Ella Zoyara's story reads like a fairy tale, as many circus stories do. Her rise to fame in the 1850s and 1860s was partly thanks to the creation of a good origin story of the kind that public-relations wags were all too happy to whip up, and that often spread through whispered rumors. And since myths and fairy tales serve to help humans explain and make sense of our experiences, Ella Zoyara's backstory was created to explain to a nineteenth-century audience just how and why someone might disregard the bright lines between male and female roles.

Because it was generally written in retrospect from shreds of memory and publicists' desks, Ella's early life story is an exercise in blurry, unverifiable romanticism. In one version of the story, an eight-year-old boy ran away from home in St. Louis, Missouri, in 1848 to join the circus.[10] In another, he grew up in New Orleans as the child of Spanish nobility fallen on hard times, and his mother agreed after much persuasion to let him apprentice with a traveling show.[11] One promoter recalls that his name may have been "Little Sammie." In the New Orleans version, it is said that this young boy was so uncommonly beautiful that, carrying his little tin pail through the market square, "the purchasers at the stalls ceased their merry clash for a moment only to break forth in shrill and soft murmurs and exclamations of surprise. Cakes and sweetmeats were thrust into his hands and pockets, the aunties of Africa vying with ladies in Paris bonnets in their attention and caresses." Whatever his origins, this young boy ends up at the circus, and all the stories converge as the circus manager and horse trainer Spencer Q. Stokes reveals his newest protégé, a strong and beautiful young equestrienne named Ella.

According to a pamphlet biography published in 1866, young Ella went through an intense course of training, demonstrating great talent in the riding ring. And she was not only talented; in accordance with the standards of ideal nineteenth-century womanhood, Ella was charitable, pure, and gentle. Folks said that she "caused every one to love her who came within the magic charm of her gentle disposition; her purity of thought and feeling, and her pity for the poor, came gushing to her heart and prompted the ready alms, accompanied by a few sympathising words, which made her gift doubly welcome. She also proved a loving daughter to Mr. Stokes, whom she looked up to and treated as her very father."[12]

Stokes's influence may have been more than simply paternal. A writer for the *St. Louis Globe-Democrat* in 1884 placed the whole conceit of the act on Stokes's shoulders, suggesting that the trainer saw Ella as a way to help his show stand out in a crowded field of equestrian acts. Consensus holds that, at Stokes's behest, a talented young boy rider became a talented girl rider, and the character was maintained both inside the ring and out of it. One writer maintained that at Stokes's urging, the young boy "never again wore an article of man's apparel till after he was nineteen years old. Stokes, resolved to make the illusion as complete as possible, did not even allow any of his company to know that 'Ella Zoyara' was not a genuine girl."[13]

According to archives maintained by circus historian Stuart Thayer, Ella began to appear publicly in 1850. At about ten years of age, she was alternately billed as Ella Stickney, La Jeune Ella, and Ella Stokes. During this period, she toured with Stokes's show in the American Midwest, performing some of the nation's earliest publicly presented dressage acts.[14] By late April 1852, Stokes felt Ella was meant for a bigger stage and decided to take her to Europe.

In Europe, Ella became a star, bewitching crowds with her graceful, controlled riding style. She made admirers of men and women alike, drawing not only applause but all manner of gifts and favors. In Italy, it was said that "twenty-two ladies stripped off valuable rings from their fair fingers, and sent them with a hastily-written pencilled line or two of love and esteem to the chaste, blushing girl, then standing ankle-deep amid costly boquets [sic] in all the young spring of her budding beauty."[15] Lady riders—*écuyères* in French idiom—were beloved in high society for their skill and for the way they were seen to cosplay the masculinity of equestrian culture and its military roots.[16] Equestriennes had a reputation for being farther up in the hierarchy of the circus, too, which meant it was not uncommon for them to be objects of high-class flirting, a filly for an aristocratic gentleman to tame. For écuyères just as much as everyday ladies, though, virtue required them to rise above the onslaught of male attention. Ella attracted notable admirers during her tour abroad, including King Victor Emmanuel of Italy. Standing all of five foot two and sporting a handlebar mustache like two bananas on his face, the king was smitten and invited the young rider to visit his personal stables, presenting her with a stallion "as a tribute to her great equestrian skill and to her virtue as a lady."[17] Even so, while droves of men "sighed their hearts sore for a chance glance of her beautiful lustrous eyes," Ella was celebrated for having none of it. "The witching Ella was as chaste as beautiful," her biographer assured fans, "and scorned to give her hand where her love had no place to nestle."[18] According to press coverage, no one suspected Ella was anything other than what she appeared. One colleague reminisced, years later, that "his beauty at the time was remarkable. He had a faultless complexion of the purest brunette type, his face never showing the slightest trace of a beard, and his features were perfect and of the most delicate, womanly character, as were also his hands and feet. His hair, of raven blackness, hung in luxuriant masses almost to his waist." The author recalled playing a show in London alongside Ella, "and in that time I never had the slightest suspicion that he was not

Ella Zoyara backstage, riding crop in hand.
Image courtesy of Fred Pfening III.

a girl. It was probably the most successful deception as regards sex ever practiced."[19]

While on tour in Europe in 1858, "Miss Ella" turned eighteen and officially emerged from her apprenticeship to Stokes into free agency. She added the exotic surname "Zoyara" to her character billing, and she signed with circus promoter James M. Nixon to perform with his circus company at Niblo's Garden in New York at the start of 1860.[20] She had experience and star power on her side, and she was ready to return to America.

Niblo's was selling out night after night when the *Tribune* published its exposé. On January 27, 1860, under the headline "A Phenomenon on Horseback," the paper claimed that the celebrated Zoyara's tricks, "though they are very surprising in their way, have not caused so much excitement as the doubts entertained in regard to her sex." Circus owner James Nixon was clearly unbothered by this revelation, as he reproduced the *Tribune*'s pearl-clutching review in a front-page advertisement for the show the next day.[21] By early February, the *New York Clipper* had picked up on the controversy, noting that "We perceive that quite a stir has been caused by the announcement that the person called M'lle. Ella Zoyara, 'equestrienne,' is not a female, but a boy in disguise. What gives some weight to this announcement is the fact that this exposition is advertised in the bills of the circus, without contradiction; thus endorsing, as it were, the truth of the fraud. If this person is a boy, as represented, then a most bare faced imposition has been practiced upon the American public by the management of the concern, and the sooner the public resent the fraud the better."[22] Suddenly, legions of men who had showed up at the stage door with bouquets, making "judies" of themselves, in the *Clipper*'s words, were very confused.[23] A would-be poet composed "Lines to Zoyara" in *Vanity Fair*, musing: "Is't true? what we have read in sundry papers, That you, Miss, are a Master of the capers?" The writer continued:

> How did'st thou learn (a thing on which we dote)
> To suit thine amble to a petticoat?
> Restrain the gait, that nature meant for man,
> To steps diminutive as smallest span?

> Who was the wretch, (O may he e'er be "cussed")
> Reversed Man's law? Man goes upon a "Bust"
> Instead of that (may he ne'er know a spree)
> The swindler "goes" a double Bust on thee!
> Did'st take it quietly, with "nary" tustle
> When first they cramm'd thee in a monstrous bustle?
> Or did'st consent, from beauty's curve to win a line,
> To wear in peace Hermaphroditic crinoline?[24]

Someone suggested that perhaps a committee of "strong-minded women" be called upon to "wait upon Zoyara, and examine the facts of the case," but the rider would have none of it.[25] The *Clipper* jokingly acknowledged the controversy with a snickering mid-February 1860 account of Zoyara's act that switched pronouns with every clause. The piece described a rare accident in the ring by assuring readers that "he is again on hand, however, or at least, on foot, astonishing the spectators by her wonderful command over the horse."[26]

Then, as now, no audience is a monolith, and the playful pronoun swapping suggests that while some men may have been indignant at finding the object of their affection was not as expected, more people were in on and enjoyed what was by then an open secret. It is worth remembering (and scholars often forget) that the nineteenth-century circus and its surrounding whorl of promotional activity were inherently playful. Irony, faux outrage, parody, and competitive shenanigans were all common. Shows acted in dialogue with each other and their audiences in competition for the almighty dollar. Gender play was common among performers. And so, within this context, many of the expressions of outrage over Ella Zoyara were very likely part of the act's unfolding immersive drama.

It's also worth remembering that acts featuring performers who played characters of the opposite gender were not unusual at the time, both inside and outside circus. Well-known actresses like Charlotte Cushman and Adah Isaacs Menken commonly took on "breeches parts" in the nineteenth-century theater, earning praise for how well they performed traditionally male roles.[27] Menken, for her part, had drawn fame not only for performing the part of the prince Mazeppa while riding a real horse onstage in a nude bodystocking but also for having been married half a dozen times and having affairs with the likes of the author Alexandre Dumas.[28]

Thinking of Zoyara as a character persona, we end up asking—albeit in a spirit of curiosity instead of indignation—the same questions as the author of the *Vanity Fair* poem. Who is threatened, humiliated, or upset when someone tests traditionally linked expectations of sex and gender? Zoyara being a cross-gender character explained her athleticism to contemporary crowds. Her performance also complied with the era's prevailing gender norms. After all, Omar Kingsley may have been a man, but Ella Zoyara glorified proper Victorian femininity. She rode an elegant horse in a white gown and tight corset, gesturing gracefully with slender hands and long legs. A flower peeked from the dark curls at her ear. She cleverly and dutifully rejected suitors. The version of the act that was openly known to be gender play did not necessarily leave anyone threatened, humiliated, or upset.

If crowds genuinely believed Zoyara to be a woman, though, and then learned otherwise—if they were not in on the secret from the start—her act was potentially culturally threatening. Considered as a woman, Zoyara proclaimed that femininity need not be fragile: Women could be magnetic and athletic. Outed as a man, she potentially led unaware straight men into homosexual desire and moreover suggested that not every man wanted to be stereotypically masculine. In nineteenth-century culture, swapping genders was more easily excused when the swap did not threaten power dynamics.[29] Actresses like Cushman or Menken had tried to reach beyond the feminine, using gender play to inhabit and aspire to male virtues like courage and valor. So, too, was cross-dressing often excused in the theater when the end goal was humor—there is a long theatrical tradition of men dressing as women for the sake of comedy or satire. It was okay for women to admire male virtue and for men to lampoon meek or humorous femininity. A man seriously aspiring to femininity—not only as an act—was more disruptive. Put another way, the ideal is a woman who men want and women should want to be. Women who dress and behave according to manly norms at least validate the idea that masculinity is powerful, desirable, and authoritative. Men dressing as women, however, challenge ideas of male desirability and dominance. As a result, "the dominant culture reduces the threat of the male cross-dresser by ridiculing him or labeling him a deviant or degenerate."[30]

What did it mean for someone to cross-dress at this time? Modern concepts and language cannot fairly be applied in retrospect. Scholars generally agree "transvestism" was first coined as a term by Magnus Hirschfeld in 1910, and cross-dressing encompasses a broad and complex set of experiences ranging from flexible fashion choices to a thoughtful effort at passing as a person of a particular sex or gender.[31] Zoyara's shock factor, such as it was in 1860, seemed to be in the effort to live as a woman on an everyday basis without any excuses or disclaimers. The famous clown W. F. Wallett recalled of Zoyara that "The exposure must have caused a blush on the faces of many honest females in Great Britain and America, for he had for years dressed with actresses in their rooms, and been received into private families on terms of the greatest intimacy with the ladies, as perfectly unsuspected as Don Juan in the harem. This made the imposition cruel; taking in the public might be pardoned."[32]

For their part, circus promoters were less interested in the specifics of the gender discourse than in the opportunity for fresh ticket sales, and copycat "Ella Zoyara" characters emerged within rival circus companies within weeks. Dan Rice, the nationally renowned "original humorist" of American circus, quickly put a different person on stage under the same name and denounced Cooke's New York Zoyara as a man and an impostor. Rice celebrated his own Ella Zoyara and "her unparalleled Scene of Equitation" in Philadelphia in March of 1860.[33] Rice's efforts were further complicated by the fact that just down the road in Philadelphia, Frank Rivers's show at the Melodeon declared that the "crowning feature" of the show was a dancer lauded as "the original Mlle. ELLA ZOYARA BOYZENARIUS, THE ORIENTAL MYTH, Whose being has entranced the senses of the Old World, and whose fame has so addled the brains of rival managers as to make each of them fancy that they had separately created and were alone able to show this wonderful personage."[34] By spring 1860, there were three separate Zoyaras in major shows around the northeastern United States, and the question of Ella's identity had reached the nineteenth-century equivalent of being ripe for a *Saturday Night Live* parody: George Christy's Minstrels put on a spoof featuring "Mlle. Zo-whar-are-ya, the Oriental Myth, and her beautiful trick horse Zaidee, from the Royal Amphitheatre of the Sandwich Islands."[35] By fall, folks no longer cared about keeping count: *The Era* reported with some eye-rolling that "ANOTHER Ella Zoyara has turned up in California."[36]

Imitators passed out of the spotlight after the initial flurry of Ella-mania, and as for the original Zoyara, any suggestion of indignance soon gave way to a casual, if occasionally mocking, acceptance. In its report on a legal case involving Kingsley, the *New Haven Palladium* succinctly stated that "Ella Zoyara, the boy-girl, has had her circus attached in Brooklyn. Her wife and children are with him."[37] Kingsley had married the equestrienne Sallie Stickney in the fall of 1861 and started a family. They soon departed for points westward.

There were good reasons to hit the road. For people with time and money to spend, shiny new American entertainment was just the thing to "relieve either the drudgery of new industrialised workplaces or the boredom of frontier isolation."[38] Not to mention that, in the wake of the Civil War, there was just more opportunity for a circus to make a good stand in the West than by trying to navigate the physical destruction and cultural tension in the East after the war. Ella Zoyara toured the Pacific coast for two years from 1863 to 1865 and, afterward, using the name Omar Kingsley, formed a partnership with James Cooke and John Wilson to "tour their Great World Circus (substantially Wilson's company) through destinations including Hawaii, Tahiti, Australia, India, China and Europe."[39]

It was at this time, moving into adult life, that Omar Kingsley started to exist more clearly as a distinct identity from the character of Ella Zoyara. The historical record is unclear on when or why the adult Omar Kingsley may have chosen to appear in or out of his stage persona as Ella Zoyara, but there are a few things that may have swayed the decision.

One was risk based. Ella Zoyara may have been welcome on the stage, but Kingsley could no longer rely on the social protection afforded to someone who publicly passed as a young girl. As an adult

Ella Zoyara, a.k.a. Omar Kingsley.
Image courtesy of the Meserve-Kunhardt Collection at the
Beinecke Rare Book and Manuscript Library, Yale University.

owner and performer, Kingsley had to assess the circumstances around a given venue: Was a particular culture or social climate hostile to even the idea of theatrical female impersonation? Reports from the Philippines in 1867 suggest that physical safety was a concern. An amorous member of the Spanish military fell hard for Zoyara in Manila and went backstage to seek an introduction. The officer was rebuffed, and his companions said that it was just as well, since the rider was actually a man. Reports claim that "a party of them went to the dressing-room, seized the subject of dispute as he came from the ring and were about to strip the clothing from him when John Wilson rushed forward and KNOCKED BOTH OF THEM DOWN."[40]

Though the circus and its patrons might have been tolerant of and even delighted by a teenaged boy trying to pass full time as a woman as an element of an act, this did not mean they would offer the same indulgence to an adult man doing this. In the nineteenth century, life outside of the theater was often rigidly critical of anyone who broke norms with their gender expression, and the result could be arrest or violence. In a study of American municipal legislation against cross-dressing, scholar Clare Sears found that, between 1848 and the turn of the century, "thirty-four cities in twenty-one states passed prohibitions against cross-dressing, as did eleven more cities before World War I. Most of these cities, including San Francisco, passed laws that specifically targeted a person 'wearing a dress not belonging to his or her sex' or 'wearing the apparel of the other sex' as part of broader prohibitions against public indecency."[41]

The popular writer and women's rights advocate Sarah Willis Parton, who wrote under the pen name Fanny Fern, explored cross-dressing in 1858 in an essay titled "A Law More Nice than Just." In response to the arrest of a woman for wearing men's clothing—a gesture widely associated with feminist radicalism—Parton wondered, "why this should be an actionable offense is past my finding out." She decided to go for a stroll with her husband, wearing one of his suits, and he, gamely giggling behind her, whispered: "You must not take my arm; you are a fellow." Parton marveled at her newfound freedom, reveling in "no skirts to hold up, or to draggle their wet folds against my ankles; no stifling vail flapping in my face." In the end, she concluded that a woman sitting inside during rainy weeks "till her skin looks like parchment, and her eyes like those of a dead fish" is far less preferable to a solid fresh air walk in a pair of pants. "I've as good a right to preserve the healthy body God gave me as if I were not a woman."[42]

Another consideration for Kingsley was the success of the show. If the financial fortunes of the circus depended on maintaining the illusion of Zoyara's womanhood, at least at first, it was important that she appear when the press and public were paying closest attention. During the Wilson company's tour of Australia in 1867, a legal dispute over the circus's printing costs led to courtroom testimony about the show's part owner and star performer: "Could not say whether he took up his position in the ladies' cabin when travelling or not," testified one witness. "Believe he did not."[43] Owner Cooke confirmed to the court that "Madam Zoyara was a married man, and that he and his wife travelled as sisters, occupying quarters in Ladies' Cabin when on board steamers."[44]

Privacy and presentation were important, because the controversy around Zoyara's identity continued to provide part of the mystique of the act as it arrived in new cities. At first, Ella Zoyara would be billed as a "premiere equestrienne," and before long, some self-congratulatory news outlet would conclude that it alone had outed her, that her true identity was a closely kept secret known only to a select few.[45] At that point in the visit, the drag performance itself began to be celebrated. On tour in China in 1868, press confirmed that "the great Ella Zoyara nightly receives a warm ovation, notwithstanding the doubts as to her sex; indeed, in Hong-Kong she was designated 'He, She, or It!' The impression here is that *she* is a man, which is supported by an occasional display of temper."[46] The bit about temper is certainly true; multiple sources note that Kingsley was a virtuoso of "unparliamentary language" and that people who were accustomed to seeing the rider in woman's clothing were often shocked to see him "come from the canvas one day just after a performance, in male attire, and swearing like a gulf pirate."[47]

By the 1870s, some combination of market demand and personal preference led Omar Kingsley to largely put Ella Zoyara aside in favor of work as a horse trainer and ringmaster. (San Francisco city directories in the middle 1860s already listed Omar Kingsley as "equestrian, Wilson's Circus."[48]) Photographs from the era show him not in the white tights and gauzy Grecian theatrical linens of younger years, but with a bushy mustache, standing casually in a dark tailcoat, patiently training a white horse. Press in 1874 lauded "Mr Omar Kingsley, the ring master," hoping that if he were to have a benefit show, he might favor the audience by riding in character again as "the peerless Zoyara."[49] But by then, Kingsley was content to rely on his reputation as a businessman and trainer. On a visit to Australia, "his marvellous horsemanship attracted less attention than his extraordinary ability to train his equine pals. Under his tuition, the circus horses did almost everything but speak."[50]

Samuel Omar Kingsley died on April 2, 1879, at the age of thirty-nine. He had contracted smallpox while on tour throughout southern Asia with Wilson's Circus. Old recollections from showfolk, collected in the correspondence columns of Australian newspapers, suggest that his second wife remarried a female impersonator on the minstrelsy circuit after Kingsley's passing. The thought is fascinating, though unsubstantiated.[51]

Many unanswered questions weave themselves around and through Ella Zoyara's performances. Were audiences aware of Zoyara's biological sex as they watched her performance—and, perhaps more to the point, did they care?

Another unanswered question is whether Omar Kingsley preferred a feminine gender expression. Some accounts claimed that "he continued to do sewing and fancy work in his spare moments, and when seeking rest and recreation in the privacy of his home would attire himself in a lady's wrapper."[52] This may have been true or could have been a reporter making gossipy speculation. It is equally possible that Spencer Stokes created a drag character during Omar Kingsley's childhood, which Kingsley was willing enough to enact and maintain for paying crowds into young adulthood. Whoever she was—and we ultimately do not know—she was unfailingly alluring and drew admiration and desire from women as well as men. One account of infatuation with Zoyara was published in 1910 in "Mummer Memoirs," a *Sydney Sportsman* column of showbiz memories. A woman wrote in to recall that she and a friend would often wait for the performer's carriage to pull up to the circus entrance, hoping for a glance and calling out to "beautiful Zoyara" to look their way. Of her companion, the writer said: "How she used to laugh in after years when she would say, 'Fancy me thinking I was loving a woman, and it was a married man all the time. I think Kingsley had a magnet; he could draw them all.'"[53]

CHAPTER 11

New Women Join the Circus

By the turn of the twentieth century, American culture was moving toward a more vital, more permissive public sphere for women. Industrialization and Gilded Age business increased the number of women in the workforce. Women with new sensibilities about work, life, and "heterosocial companionship" were increasingly out and about in urban centers looking to live life to the fullest.[1] Women's activism also moved into a new phase, with women seeking socioeconomic power, personal choice, and sexual freedom. This did not proceed unopposed: If anything, with each step toward liberation, women were met with forceful societal resistance. But for the first time, women's voices began to be heard in significant numbers outside the private sphere. This was true for circus as well as in larger society.

The prim "angel in the home" was a dominant character in nineteenth-century literature and discourse, although this is not to say that every woman was or wanted to be one. Male-driven social institutions widely publicized the stereotype, though, for a plain reason: The traditional family served as a foothold and an anchor for men in an American century characterized by war, expansion, industrialization, and massive social change. In this environment, advocates for ideas of proper womanhood had the loudest voice. But after a confining period in which women's maintenance of the home sphere was held up as necessary for the good of society, by the turn of the century, women were able to more openly embrace the idea of participating in public life.

The term "New Woman" arose to describe these newly empowered and often impatient women working to break down the old "separate spheres."[2] New Woman was a confusing term, often applied—particularly by the male establishment—to anything that seemed newly out of step with prior norms for women's behavior. It was an umbrella term for all manner of innovation and dissent, standing in for "all of these contradictory positions and more: suffragist, prohibitionist, clubwoman, college girl, American girl, socialist, capitalist, anarchist, pickpocket, bicyclist, barren spinster, mannish woman, outdoor girl, birth-control advocate, modern girl, eugenicist, flapper, blues woman, lesbian, and vamp."[3] Nor was the label limited to white women: Margaret Murray Washington, the spouse of Booker T., authored a paper on behalf of the "New Negro Woman" in 1895. Pointing out the number of Black Americans, particularly women, who remained socially and economically disadvantaged thirty years after emancipation, Washington advocated for home skills, workforce training, and moral education to help Black families catch up to their white counterparts in profile and prosperity. She urged: "I repeat, we cannot be slow. We are the children of parents who were not the architects of their destiny, and perhaps we should not to-day be censured for having handed down to us a womanhood not equalling in strength that of our Caucasian sisters. But in the years that are to come we will be held responsible if the manhood, the womanhood, of the race is not higher, nobler, and stronger than it is today."[4]

These New Women were strong, willful, openly emotional, perhaps queer, and fond of new and even frivolous trends.[5] The latter was not simply a matter of fun. Where some New Women engaged in pointed political activism, others simply seized the opportunity to live a life with more room for freedom and recreation. In this way, the bicycle became a symbol of progressive womanhood.[6] The introduction of the safety bicycle in the 1880s opened new worlds for women. Because bicycles were affordable, practical, and allowed free movement, and because women cyclists often preferred riding outfits that involved

"Funny Scenes on Bicycles and Roller Skates."
Image courtesy of the Prints and Photographs Division at the Library of Congress.

pants, or "bloomers," bicycles became linked with the women's movement at the turn of the century. An 1897 issue of the British magazine *Cycling: An Illustrated Weekly* featured a woman with butterfly wings cycling on its cover. A column in the magazine described the creature this way: "Its colouring is decidedly gay, its flight somewhat erratic and not very strong. The sex is difficult to determine."[7] The same issue featured a poem entitled "The New Woman to Her Steed," which rhapsodized:

> *My bicycle, my bicycle,*
> *That standest in the lobby*
> *With suspension wheels and springs of steel.*
> *My pet, my only hobby!*

In response, the *Cycling* columnist mocked both the bad poetry and ladies' adoption of cycling as "a series of earthquakes."

Bicycles were no threat to the circus—indeed, as new bicycle models were introduced in the nineteenth century, circus performers figured out how to do tricks on them for cheering crowds on Circus Day. Women rode bicycles on high-wires, ramps, and loops, and one 1900 poster for the Barnum & Bailey show featured a "New Woman" in brown bloomers, a red necktie, and feathered hat riding stridently over a gentleman in a gray checked suit.[8] (Some circus women were also early adopters of automobiles: In 1905, Mademoiselle Mauricia de Tiers would drive a motorcar completely upside down over a loop-the-loop track nicknamed the "Dip of Death."[9])

The banjo was another unlikely but powerful symbol of turn-of-the-century feminism. Manufacturers specifically marketed them to white women, hoping to increase sales by moving the banjo beyond its stereotypical associations with Black musicians and minstrelsy. Banjo manufacturers appealed to women with romance story tropes and swishy marketing, spelling the instrument's name "banjeaux" to make it seem upscale and European. Eventually, having a banjo around was a daring alternative to playing piano in the parlor for New Women. Stereograph photos from the time show women in a variety of lively, socially transgressive, often queer-coded situations with their banjo.

In one image, two women lounge on a furry rug. One rests her head in the other's lap, a banjo across her middle, and her feet resting on a chair to show off knee-length striped socks. Both women are smoking languidly. In another photograph, a banjo is seen to compete with a man hoping for a kiss, and, in yet another, a "New Woman" wearing bloomers and a pageboy cap props one leg up on a chair, commanding the man in her life to finish washing the dishes.[10] P. T. Barnum, who married Nancy Fish, a woman forty years younger than himself, after his first wife passed away, bought his young wife a banjo as a gift. Perhaps it was a way for old Barnum to show he was "with it." These evolving recreations, and the increasing diversity of the amusement business, broadened the scope of what women could do and aspire to. They centered women's experience and encouraged both leisure and independence.

The circus documented this shift, continuing to operate in dialogue with its time and place. This didn't just mean adding banjos, bicycles, cars, and assertive lady riders to the program (though all of these things did happen). As the walls between separate spheres eroded and as more women began to see the circus and more people saw women in the circus, the idea of a performing woman became a bit more normal.[11] In the process—and aided by spreading New Woman ideas—performers gained a larger platform, a greater level of independence, and a measure of increased social acceptability.[12] Performances both represented and challenged the shifts of the New Woman era. On the one hand, circuses were still run by fat-cat male businessmen, and spec acts continued to celebrate classical civilization, American power, and conventional masculinity. But acknowledging the shift into New Womanhood, the 1896 version of the Barnum & Bailey Greatest Show on Earth featured, in its twelfth display, "the new woman supreme in the arena for the first time anywhere." Ads promised a "novel and picturesque exhibition of the assertion of the rights of the twentieth century girl to a place in the circus. A positive usurpation of the ring in which man has no part. Progressive maidens fascinatingly conducting an entire equestrian act in up-to-date costumes." The act managed to both glorify and lampoon New Women at the same time: It showed off women who could capably execute every job they were given but included the act on the same bill as the "very funny capers and frolics of the educated pigs."

Thanks to the groundbreaking women performers of previous generations, there were, for the first time, tropes and patterns for new generations of circus performers to follow. Early nineteenth-century circus women had tested the idea of a given performance, and turn-of-the-century performers could iterate on those ideas. Acts could therefore engage in a more complex social dialogue. First-wave women performers had also experimented with new forms of media, which allowed New Women in the circus to leverage publicity more expertly. They performed with larger, more media-savvy outlets; engaged with technological advances; and took advantage of expanding ideas about women's mobility and independence.

There were still substantial obstacles for women in the circus. For performers outside the white, male, Christian mainstream, marginalization and exploitation were a continuing reality. This was particularly true in sideshow and reflected the continued failure of contemporary society to equitably reckon with class, gender, race, and disability. At the same time, many of these new second-generation acts began to challenge gender norms more openly and purposefully in the ways they designed their performances. Performers more conspicuously explored the idea that femininity could take many physical and performative shapes.

One shape was the strongwoman. Strongmen were already common in culture and entertainment by the start of the twentieth century. Their popularity got a boost from the era's "physical culture" movement, which often equated physical fitness with moral worth and hoped to prevent sedentary working men from sliding into unmanly weakness. When the bodybuilder Eugen Sandow flexed and posed as a Greek statue in front of a velvet curtain at the 1893 Chicago World's Fair, he ignited a cultural obsession with the "imaginary antiquity" of being impeccably swole.[13] A strong male body telegraphed discipline, strength, beauty, and power (and also quietly catered to gay interest). Women's physical norms, though, did not similarly elevate the idea of strength and size. Mainstream culture continued to elevate slender, soft ideas of women's bodies, however: Strongwomen and the "singing strong lady," who could support a piano and accompanist on a tabletop laid across her chest and legs, were listed in George Gould and Walter Pyle's *Anomalies and Curiosities of Medicine* at the turn of the twentieth century.[14]

Gilded Age strongwomen, who joined the circus at a time of expanding feminist ideology, took advantage of colorful advertising media to show that they were just as strong as their male counterparts. Strongwomen challenged popular ideas of female ability and destabilized the white male basis of physical culture, all while showing a culturally nerve-wracking amount of skin and muscle.

Making her vaudeville debut in New York on Christmas Day 1897, strongwoman Laverie Vallee, known professionally as Charmion, astounded and delighted audiences with an unconventional aerial act in which she stripped from a full-skirted outfit down to a leotard and tights. In bringing together strength training, striptease, and an aerial act within a single middle-class entertainment, Charmion was pressing several social hot buttons. For starters, there was the prominence of her body. A woman's body on stage could be received differently depending on the forum: Deliberately artistic or classical performances, such as ballet or Greco-Roman "living statue" displays, could be justified as edifying and tasteful to an upper-class audience. Most displays of women's bodies, though, ran the risk of being scorned as vulgar.

Then there was the social aspect. In one performance, Charmion managed to suggest that women need not wear constrictive, heavy clothing; that they could indeed develop muscular size and strength; and that robust activity might just be a good thing for a woman's health and self-image. Charmion was no ballerina, and she encouraged people to consider that a strong body could still be feminine. Chatting with the audience throughout her performance in a distinctive "chirpy" voice, Charmion used her stage as a platform to suggest that women not only keep active but "have a balanced diet, and remove clothing that would hamper free movement." She advised: "Every woman ought to exercise on getting up in the morning. Take a drink of cold water, then exercise with small dumbbells . . . Be sure to take a little walk each day in the fresh air."[15] She also implied that a muscular body

Portrait of Charmion, strong lady, flexing.
Image courtesy of the Tibbals Learning Center and Circus Museum at the John and Mable Ringling Museum of Art.

could be a desirable one. Thomas Edison sought out Charmion as a film subject, and he did not hesitate to put a whooping box of excited gentlemen aside the stage to cheer on Charmion doing pull-ups on the trapeze in her tight leotard.

Charmion and other performers not only challenged the white male basis of physical culture, but they artfully demonstrated new ideas of female ability. Under the big top, at least, it was clear that not every woman was the same under her ample skirts. Circus strongwomen such as Vulcana, Madame Yucca, and Minerva were more than happy to throw on a leotard or the occasional leather skirt and flex for crowds, or maybe lift a horse. The strongwoman Katie "Sandwina"

Brumbach stood more than six feet tall in her heeled boots and, at a solid 210 pounds, could lift three men onto her shoulders without breaking a sweat. Nicknamed the "Lady Hercules" for the Barnum & Bailey Greatest Show on Earth in 1912, Sandwina in her leotard and flowery headband pitted her strength against a team of horses. In retirement, she and her adoring husband Max ran a saloon at which she would occasionally agree to bend iron bars for the patrons' amusement. In this historic environment, circus women demonstrated a variable spectrum of femininity.

The circus glorified skill and strength, but in the outside world, women, even highly professional New Women, were still constantly restricted, diminished, and judged against an idealized standard of domesticity. Claire Heliot, among the most famous of the new century's lion queens, demonstrates this frustrating dichotomy. (As for the queens themselves, more to come; in best circus tradition, we will save this for fuller discussion until the big finish.) Most men in the lion business depended on shows of strength and intimidation to control big cats, demonstrating dominion over the animal kingdom. In her early 1900s showpiece act, Heliot took a different approach: She invited half a dozen looming lions to table for a formal dinner. Dressed in a long white gown, Heliot turned from one vast rumbling beast to the next before rapt spectators, feeding each one a hunk of horseflesh at the end of a long, elegant fork. As a closing flourish, she coolly offered them "her own pretty head as a delectable morsel for dessert."[16] (The guests respectfully declined.) After dinner, Heliot's lions agreeably performed with a group of boar hounds, doing tricks and pulling the dogs around in a chariot. In an act that seemed to defy both nature and physics, the lions Sascha and Nero padded toward each other from opposite sides of a tightrope, pausing to balance nose-to-nose in the center. At Heliot's quiet command, the pair would turn around, and "like little schoolboys they wheel about and go back to their seats."[17] She typically finished her act by slinging a 350-pound male named Sicchi over her shoulders like a gigantic scarf and triumphantly striding from the ring.[18]

Newspaper headlines described Heliot as "frail but fearless."[19] She was neither, in fact. Where male trainers were lauded for their confidence and command in the face of danger, with Heliot, the press focused on her nurturing side, her white dress, her manifest lack of a husband. Claire Heliot was a stunning talent, but the press constantly minimized her. She became a screen on which the media could project an idealized sort of femininity: the lovely woman who trained wild beasts with pure feminine sentimentality. Sure, she could carry a 350-pound lion on her shoulders as easily and calmly as if it were a sack of bread flour, but wasn't it nice how she wore a white satin evening gown and cooed demurely over the "pets" who shared her boudoir? (As for the lion lifting, author Ellen Velvin claimed Heliot had told her that she started carrying Sicchi when he was young and did so every day as he grew until she grew comfortable carrying as much as five hundred pounds for a short time.)

One article after another went through a litany of how'd-she-do-it questions, believing the game had to be rigged: Were the lions drugged? Tame? Had they been declawed or their great fangs filed down? No: Chloroform would make a lion nothing more than a very untheatrical lump on the sawdust floor; wild animals never fully lose their instincts; removing teeth and claws would doom the animal to deadly infection and would be cruel besides. The truth was, the lions were dangerous, always, because they were lions. Deep down, everyone knew this. Perhaps even deeper down, they might have been ashamed to admit to the dark appeal of a lady lion tamer's act: The idea that her time in the spotlight was not only unnatural but fragile, and if—when?—she slipped up, even the most perfectly executed femininity would not be enough to save her from a wild animal's instinct. The *New York Times* did not mince words, headlining their profile with the question: "Of Which One of Her Fourteen Pets Will She Be the Victim?"[20]

The big top provides a certain cushion against the outside world. Anything too transgressive—such as the vision that, in pushing boundaries, Claire Heliot was risking defying a "natural" destruction—can be explained away as simply for entertainment's sake. At the same time, soaring dreams are possible, too.

The historical record forces us to speculate about early cross-gender performers like Ella Zoyara, but as the idea of separate spheres declined in the early twentieth century, performers who pushed gender boundaries gradually gained space to discuss the motivation behind their work. In the 1920s, the aerialist Barbette used sexy, unapologetic gender play to take the circus's acceptance of gender fluidity into the wider world. The French avant-garde writer Jean Cocteau, who was infatuated with Barbette, adoringly described his friend as "no mere acrobat in women's clothes." No, insisted Cocteau, "He blends a tightrope dancer's skill and perilous performance with the creativity of a poet. An angel, a flower, a bird. We all found him an absolute knockout."[21] In an interview in the September 27, 1969, issue of the *New Yorker*, Barbette, born Vander Clyde in Texas at the turn of the century, recalled that he had been sold on the circus from childhood: "The first time [my mother] took me to the circus in Austin, I knew I'd be a performer. [F]rom then on I'd work in the fields during the cotton-picking season to earn money in order to go to the circus as often as possible. My mother told me I couldn't leave home until I finished high school, and that encouraged me to 'double up'—I was quick in class, and I graduated at fourteen."[22] Clyde joined up with a show as soon as possible.

One of the performers told him that women's clothes, with all the ruffles and feathers swishing to and fro, always made an aerial act look better under the lights. "She asked me if I'd mind dressing as a girl," Clyde recalled. "I didn't, and that's how it began." Adopting the stage name Barbette, Clyde developed a signature aerial act that expertly, beautifully combined the masculine and feminine. Equally adept at trapeze feats and striptease, Barbette took the stage in a short, blond curled wig, ostrich feathers, and pearls. With her dramatic makeup done in the hotly menacing style of a Ziegfeld girl, she was drop-dead gorgeous. At the end of an athletic, graceful aerial act, Barbette would stand at center stage and remove her wig with a flourish, perhaps throwing in a butch flex or two to complete the presentation. Audiences loved it: The William Morris Agency, which at the time also represented Charlie Chaplin and the Marx Brothers, hired Clyde to a $200-a-week contract and sent him to England and then to Paris in the fall of 1923.[23]

Barbette retired from performance after musculoskeletal problems and illness took their toll, but Clyde remained in the business as a coach and trainer. Dressed in sharp suits, he trained acrobats for the Ringling Brothers and Barnum & Bailey shows of the early 1940s and was hired to help Jack Lemmon and Tony Curtis with their drag performances in *Some Like It Hot*. To be sure, Barbette, through her fame, had protections that other historical circus performers did not. And Vander Clyde still retained a level of male privilege: Unlike bearded ladies or other circus women who challenged accepted ideas of feminine presentation, Clyde could fall back on being a successful cis-presenting man in public, and on the idea that Barbette was simply an act, and no threat to social structures.

Looking back, though, Clyde was happy to describe the play between masculine and feminine that specifically interested him in developing Barbette as a character and an act. "I'd always read a lot of Shakespeare, and thinking that those marvellous heroines of his were played by men and boys made me feel that I could turn my specialty into something unique. I wanted an act that would be a thing of beauty—of course, it would have to be a strange beauty."[24]

These twentieth-century circus women—and the examples chosen are just many of the ones possible—were able to think about new ways of being and performing because of the example set by earlier generations. There was still a long way to go. In 1912, circus women held a meeting at which equestrienne Josephine DeMott Robinson, tiger trainer Mabel Stark, aerialist Victoria Codona, and strongwoman Katie "Sandwina" Brumbach gathered with colleagues with the express intention of organizing toward independence and voting rights.[25] More than twenty performers pulled together wooden chairs in the Barnum & Bailey menagerie, sitting in their civilian long skirts and feathered hats. The women had this meeting even though their own show had mocked suffragettes with an act using clowns in drag, and even though the whole affair was likely to be ridiculed as no more than a publicity stunt. Nonetheless, it was more than two dozen women on the same show, standing up for themselves as working women and making plans to fight for their own political destiny. It was a moment many women before them—aerialists, animal trainers, strongwomen, and more—had worked to create. A pair of giraffes casually bobbed their heads in a nearby fenced enclosure as retired bareback rider Robinson addressed the women frankly, making a statement Patty Astley may not have been able to even dream about at the beginning of the long nineteenth century: "You earn salaries. Some of you have property. You have a right to say what shall be done with it."[26]

CONCLUSION

Taming Savage Beasts

Circus women have changed and expanded public perceptions of womanhood. Gender performance has physical, behavioral, and aesthetic aspects, and few things bring all three together like a circus. Performances under the big top are designed to do two jobs: first, to meet the audience where they are, then to take them somewhere else entirely. In the case of gender, performances are grounded in current social norms, yet subvert and transform them in dramatic and exciting ways. If you're open to new ideas about gender, the circus shows them to you presented with sequins and spotlights, making them seem shiny and appealing. If you're opposed, you'll still see the unusual becoming more common over time. Either way, the circus slowly changes the world.

ooooo

Like the circus itself, the lion queen's act emerged from English tradition and came to America during an era of explosive growth. By taking it as a microcosm of American circus development, we can see what circus women have done, how far they have come, and where they still help us to step into the cage with beasts.

At Dublin's Donnybrook Fair[1] in the fall of 1846, the British press noted that the standout entertainer of the outdoor festival was "a certain Mrs. King, who is called the 'Lion Queen.'" Mrs. King would calmly and without a bit of trepidation step into a cage with three huge cats in front of a crowd of paying customers. "She also enters the den of two ferocious hyenas, all of whom are evidently in great dread of her." The account concluded with an acid dismissal, sniffing: "A pleasant time Mr. King must have of it."[2] Mrs. King was not the only lady taming lions at the time: As King went on to perform with George Wombwell's menagerie around the United Kingdom, a "fantastically-dressed lass" known by the name of Madame Pauline de Vere stepped into the ring with fierce beasts as part of the rival Hilton circus. While acknowledging that both "are worth vastly more than the old-song fee which franks the visitor," reporters could not resist taking the women down a peg. Mrs. King was dismissed as a "portly dame" and de Vere as the sort of girl whose "real appellation may be Buggins or Figgins for all that."[3]

Lion queens—as the story of Claire Heliot in the previous chapter shows—engaged with risk in a way that was patently shocking to most people. Even in a traditionally flexible realm like the circus, for a woman to step in the ring with a lion threw any number of social norms out the window. A lion tamer takes on the sort of work where a person invites death over for tea, twelve shows a week, and demands applause in return. And during a nineteenth century marked by strict public ideas about what a woman should properly do, a lion queen not only visibly chose a career over typical expectations of home and family, but she placed her body in jeopardy. A lion queen's performance was a slap in the face to the idea that women were built to find contentment in a quiet, conventional, and domestic life. As far as the public was concerned, a male trainer of exotic animals was usually viewed as an intrepid performer proving skilled dominion over toothy beasts; a woman in that capacity was, frankly, confusing and unnatural. This may have been the reason, beyond simple misogyny, that male critics had dismissed King and de Vere so easily. To these critics, only virile men and flawed women would dare to spend their time taming lions.

Virile men did not lack for examples. Isaac Van Amburgh, the

Madame Claire Heliot, renowned female lion tamer, with one of her dangerous pets at the time she was wowing audiences at the London Hippodrome.
Image courtesy of Illustrated London News Ltd/Mary Evans.

preeminent animal trainer of the 1800s, demonstrated how well he had trained his animals by placing his arm or head into a tiger's mouth, forcing a lion to lick his boots, or calling a group of animals to sit at his side. Standing in a cage crowded with snarling big cats and wearing a Roman gladiator costume, you would not have guessed that Van Amburgh was a native New Yorker who got his start cleaning cages for a small-town menagerie in Westchester County. Nor, from Van Amburgh's theatrical show of magical dominion over the animal kingdom, might you have suspected that his methods largely depended on intimidation; he was known to train his animals with a crowbar.[4]

When the circus came to America and began its period of dramatic growth in the nineteenth century, lion taming was a common element. Lion queens encountered the same eye-rolling dismissal in America that had been common on the old British fairgrounds. A big-cat tamer named Miss Adelina was performing with lions, tigers, and leopards in Norwalk, Connecticut, in 1848 when a heavy wind and rainstorm took down the top of the menagerie pavilion, a mishap known in the circus business as a "blowdown." The canvas sheet fell like pie dough over spectators, animals, and performers, and chaos ensued. As patrons and workers began to crawl out from under the fallen tent into the wet weather, the combination of strangled shouts and roars led folks to believe that the wild animals, in fear and frenzy, had devoured poor Adelina. But when the canvas was cleared and the cats' keeper rushed in to assist, reports claimed that the scene "would defy either poet, painter or sculptor to portray with accuracy." In the center ring stood a lion, rampant; "beneath one of his hind feet lay stretched the dead body of a leopard, and struggling within the invincible grasp of his fore paws were the tiger and surviving leopard. In the opposite end of the cage transfixed as a statue of marble, with dauntless eye and majestic attitude, the same as when she commands the wild beasts to crouch at her feet, stood the Lion Queen Miss Adelina." By way of explanation, the papers reported that, as the canvas started to fall, the tiger and pair of leopards sprang to attack Adelina but "were repulsed by the noble gallantry of the lion who bounded between them and protected her."[5] It was more attractive to suggest Adelina's fragility than to confirm that she was uncommonly calm and skilled under pressure.

If anyone needed proof that women and girls were not naturally frail, they had only to consider young Marie Carroll, daughter of circus rider W. B. "Barney" Carroll. According to circus historian Stuart Thayer, Marie "began going into the cage of the family's pet leopard at the age of six in 1849. She did this for eight seasons."[6] Jacob Driesbach (he of the saucy nude daguerreotype) was comfortable enough sharing the spotlight with his female protégé that, in February of 1848, he handed her the literal reins to his showpiece act: "Miss Cybelle, the Lion Queen," wrote Philadelphia's *Public Ledger*, "intends driving an African Lion, attached to a triumphal car, across a space of fifty feet, which no doubt will prove a grand and exciting spectacle."[7] Of the lion tamer Ellen Chapman, whom he saw perform in July 1847, Charles Dickens wrote in a letter that the "young lady in complete armour" could not only brave lions, tigers, and leopards but "pretends to go to sleep upon the principal lion." "Seriously," wrote Dickens, "she beats Van Amburgh."[8]

Some of the most successful women trainers pioneered and used positive reinforcement techniques. Claire Heliot declined to use torches, noisy pistol fire, crowbars, shoving, or shouting. Instead, she woke at five thirty every morning to train and feed the animals, placing every strip of meat into their jaws herself. It was not the magic of artless femininity that trained lions, but years of consistent, hard work. Heliot insisted that the only trainers who needed to worry about trouble with their lions were those who hit the animals or drank on the job. She had done more than one performance with blood seeping down her white dress, but nonetheless considered lions "the kindest and most intelligent animals in the world" and maintained that "when a lion loves you, you are safe."[9] Nonetheless, she dealt with the constant suspicion that she tamed cats with feminine sentimentality and was only engaged in this lion business because she couldn't snag a husband. "There are those who see through the cheerful front of the little woman wrapped up in her work," one writer mused, "and who wonder if she may be nursing regrets for all time for the reason that she did not know how to master the whim or temper of one mere man."[10] Not to mention that the act itself was a ritualized performance of the feminine: Rather than bluster or crack the whip around her lions, for Pete's sake, Claire Heliot threw them a dinner party with the good dishes.

For the 1890s lion tamer known only as Countess X, a persona of anonymous sexuality was just the thing to captivate audiences. She performed wearing head-to-toe black, and not the sort that a demure woman in mourning might favor. Sometimes she wore tights and opera gloves with a jeweled leotard and bloomers; other times, trim velvet pants, ankle boots, and a tight peplum corset. She chose to wear perhaps the most useful accessory any lion queen before or since had brought into the ring: a black mask. Madame X claimed to be a real countess, performing in disguise to hide her identity. Whether she was indeed a countess or not (probably not), it was the disguise that freed her from having to teeter between decorum and sexualized danger. With her mask in place and a black riding crop in hand, she oozed power and sexuality in public, and she got away with it because there was no real woman to whom any criticism or consequences could stick. Her personality and her speech were refreshingly expansive and unusually physical. When a reporter, granted entry into her dressing room for an interview, asked if he might enter the cage with her, she dropped a corner of her wrap, exposing her naked shoulder and "three long, livid scars showing purple against the white flesh." The Countess pointed to the largest of the five nearby lions and simply explained, "He did it. Do you still want to enter the cage?"[11]

Whatever her real name, Countess X was a skilled professional. She reared her cubs by hand and bottle-fed them every four hours with a mix of milk and mineral water.[12] (Visitors to her pens at the London Aquarium absolutely lost their minds over the cubs, demonstrating that, as far as ticket sales were concerned, cuteness was perhaps even more profitable than danger.[13]) At the Folies Bergère in Paris, reviewers said they had seen many lion tamers, "but none made such a terrifying impression" as the Countess, who "prefers the risks she is currently taking to her brilliant relationships or home life." Reporters were so caught up in the presentation, they did not even care to speculate as to her true état civil.[14] Pleased, the press concluded: "Altogether the performance is a thrilling one, and well worth seeing."[15]

One other way that big-cat acts were a microcosm of the larger

American circus is that they remained predominantly white. Exceptions include Adgie Castillo, a Mexican lion tamer who performed on vaudeville and with major circuses at the turn of the twentieth century, and some unidentified Black women who appear in photographs with menagerie animals.[16] But to the extent women of color appeared within animal acts, they tended to follow the same binary path as did bearded women. Performers either worked to align themselves with white feminine norms of success or ended up in the realm of racialized stereotype. People of color were more likely to be presented as exotic animals' companions than their masters—and, indeed, the ethnological displays of the late nineteenth-century circus were typically presented in close proximity to the menagerie.

Yet in other ways, the circus was evolving. By the early twentieth century, the tiger trainer Mabel Stark would flip ultrafeminine scripts upside down. If Stark was going to perform an identity, it would not involve a chaste white gown like Heliot or sexy capri pants like the Countess. Stark preferred the same outfit as the men wore. She performed with a dozen tigers at once, wearing ornate braided military jackets and short blond curls tight to her head. Military uniforms, with their social connotations of strength, authority, and discipline, allowed trainers like Stark to move past infantilizing ideas of girls and their "pets."[17] Sharing an outfit with the men also gave the circus options: After all, if a top-tier star like Stark had to sit out a show and a male trainer was to substitute for the performance, the audience still had to get what they came for. A surviving photograph of the trainer Louis Roth shows him in his typical military coat and braid but wearing a shoulder-length curly wig and a full face of makeup underneath his cap. By this point, a trainer could entertain audiences as a man pretending to be a woman in a butch uniform: just another circus day.

ooooo

Taken at face value, the historic press, by act or omission, can convince us that performing women were not part of a broader narrative, would never be as strong as the men, or weren't suited for their work. We need to remember by telling their stories—even based on a limited historical record—that this isn't true. Lion taming aside, anything men could do, women often did, too, and better. The wire walker Maria Spelterini repeated Charles Blondin's crossing of Niagara in 1876 to celebrate the American centennial. Like her predecessor, she made the crossing more complex with each attempt, choosing to cross with her hands and ankles bound or with peach baskets on her feet as spectators packed the nearby bridges to catch a glimpse. Recalling Sam Patch, a cliff diver who had a brief period of intense fame, in 1901, a sixty-two-year-old schoolteacher named Annie Edson Taylor embraced the idea of aerial public spectacle as a route to recognition and prosperity. Since no one had yet survived a water-based trip over Niagara Falls, she commissioned an oak barrel of her own design from a local cooper and resolved to go over the side in it or, as Patch had done, die trying. At 4:23 p.m. on October 24, 1901, Taylor flew off the Canadian side of the waterfalls in her barrel, which "shot down the face of the cataract with lightning-like rapidity."[18] Hooked from the river after the 158-foot descent, Taylor emerged from the barrel, wiped at a cut on her scalp, and told reporters that, though she had no intention of repeating her feat, "I am not sorry I took the trip."[19] The *San Francisco Examiner* called her "The Most Daring Woman in America."

History and media remember men like Van Amburgh, Blondin, and Patch as larger-than-life figures in an age of American imperial chest-thumping. The likes of Heliot, Spelterini, and Taylor have been written off as anomalies. Headlines of Spelterini's successful crossing identified her not by name but as "A Female Blondin" and emphasized that her tightrope walk was not the only thing worth looking at, since she performed in "tights of the color nature gives the cuticle of the Caucasian race."[20] Triumphant Annie Edson Taylor was celebrated in the press but not without mention that she was a "quiet, modest, refined and ordinarily sensible" woman who intended to retire and do good "for a woman, be she a true woman, can bless and glorify the lowest grade of humanity."[21] If you believed the press, these women succeeded out of pure luck rather than muscle or will.

But despite the narrative, these women succeeded, and they succeeded through the independence, mobility, and chance to make the impossible possible that the nineteenth-century circus provided. The

Maria Spelterini crossing Niagara Falls and the Niagara Rapids.
Image courtesy of the Miriam and Ira D. Wallach Division of Art Prints and Photographs, Photography Collection, and the Digital Collections, respectively, at the New York Public Library.

women of the nineteenth-century circus provided subversive examples of strength and independence, showing that the female body need not squeeze into a single corseted mold.

To be sure, circus women did not have it easy, nor were they unopposed in their efforts to demonstrate and enjoy physical, emotional, and political freedom. This was doubly true for performers of color, who had to navigate racial bias as well as ideas of proper femininity. Where the likes of Sandwina and Charmion were said to unite strength and beauty, Olga Brown (a.k.a. Miss La La) was exoticized as a "Venus of the Tropics." In addition, even into the twentieth century, circus women often had to project an image of social respectability to legitimize their daring day jobs. Press agents highlighted strongwoman Sandwina's loving marriage, trumpeted the fact that circuses did not tolerate unseemly behavior, and even staged photographs of circus women doing their laundry on the backlot.

Yet the nineteenth-century circus gave so many women the ability to perform in their own weird, wonderful ways. These brave forerunners and their stories come down to us over the years having fought the male-dominated media, restrictive concepts of womanhood, and a noted lack of precedent. The women in this book represent just a few of them, and they are only the beginning. Without them, the world may never have been able to enjoy Princess Nysaki, the Japanese jiujitsu expert employed by the Sells-Floto Circus in the 1920s, or the enigmatic mid-century crocodile hypnotist Koringa in her eerie, green-tinted makeup and leopard dress. Harry Houdini might not have been inclined to rave about sword swallower Edith Clifford and her ability to swallow "a specially constructed razor, with a blade five or six times the usual length, a pair of scissors of unusual size, a saw which is 2½ inches wide at the broadest point, with ugly looking teeth ... and several other items quite unknown to the bill-of-fare of ordinary mortals."[22]

Today, disciplines like drag performance and women's sports are leading the way in showing new paths forward for feminine bodies in the public sphere. The historic circus led in starting this conversation. If today we think it is utterly normal for Pink to fly over the concert stage in aerial silks while singing her latest hit, for *RuPaul's*

Drag Race to headline Halloween at the Big Apple Circus, for Eddie Izzard to run thirty-two marathons in a month while talking about trans rights, or for *The Greatest Showman* to hit number-one movie status in America while featuring a bearded lady in a leading character role, it is in no small part because of historic circus women. Many of these same athletes and performers are publicly disparaged as unattractive or even illegitimate when they fail to fit binary gender norms. Yet the idea, demonstrated by the women in this book, that infinitely variable human bodies have worth and beauty is not only reassuring but radical. Like so many performers today, these women stepped into the cage with literal and cultural beasts. They used their voices and performances to publicize a broad, accommodating concept of gender expression under the circus tent. When we're able to continue that conversation and think about bodies—all of them!—as variable, capable, and worthy, everyone wins. The cotton candy? That's just an added bonus.

ACKNOWLEDGMENTS

A book, like a circus, is a deceptively complex undertaking. From the outside, a circus is all fun and spectacle, but a lot of work goes on backstage to be sure the show can go on as planned. A circus involves behind-the-scenes logistics to build the magic city, performers who dazzle with sequined substance, and an audience to interact with the spectacle in a meaningful way. So, too, with a book, and over the past decade of exploring nineteenth-century circus women, I have accumulated my own crew of tent bosses, jugglers, lion tamers, and cheering fans. Here, at least, I can thank some of those people. This *is* my circus, and these *are* my monkeys.

This book would not have been possible without the support of the librarians, archivists, and museum staff in whose collections these women come to life. Kathy Maher, John Swing, and Adrienne Saint-Pierre at the Barnum Museum freely provided expertise and access to materials, and platformed my Emmy-winning Barnum series *Showman's Shorts*. On multiple trips to Sarasota, Florida, I was welcomed with open arms by curator Jennifer Lemmer Posey and the amazing staff at the Circus Museum at the John and Mable Ringling Museum of Art. The Ringling offered speaking opportunities in support of research on Lavinia Warren and Millie-Christine McKoy, and their commitment to sharing the history and the wonder of the circus is both energizing and contagious. Thank you to Pete Shrake, Jen Cronk, and the Robert L. Parkinson Library & Research Center at Circus World in Baraboo, Wisconsin; to Maureen Brunsdale at Illinois State University's Milner Library, Matt Wittmann at Harvard's Houghton Library, Matt Mason at the Yale Beinecke Rare Book & Manuscript Library, and the staff of the Bridgeport History Center.

Thank you to the staff at the Harry Ransom Center at the University of Texas at Austin, and to Janet Davis for taking time to meet with me when I visited. Thank you to Beth Lander and the staff of the library of the College of Physicians of Philadelphia for generous access to materials about performers who challenged concepts of disability. My fellow board members at the Circus Historical Society have provided encouragement and been generously open to questions. Disability scholars Chris Mounsey and Stan Booth encouraged work on Ann Leak through their VariAbilities conference and its embrace of all body types.

Several kind folks lent me their personal and professional expertise, their suggestions, scholarly conversation, and resources and research materials. No one is more enthusiastic about circus nor more generous with his knowledge than Fred Pfening III, which is why I am a proud, card-carrying "Pfening Pfan." Vanessa Toulmin was kind enough to share resources about her research into Patty Astley. David Carlyon offered thoughts and materials about Dan Rice and Ella Zoyara. Chris Berry helped run down some rogue poster images. Jordan Jefferson is the best legal librarian there is and has never once been annoyed when I have barged into her workday with pressing matters from the nineteenth century. I am grateful to Walt Woodward for guidance on life and history. Developmental editor Jill Rothenberg helped to shepherd this idea through its proposal phase and lent it weight and cohesion. I now owe writing instructor Sue Shapiro lunch. Special thanks to Jeff Greenbaum and Maura Wogan at Frankfurt Kurnit Klein & Selz for their legal know-how.

Different media outlets and editors have been vital to my developing scholarship about the circus. Portions of the chapter on Circassian beauties originally appeared in *The Public Domain Review* on September 16, 2021, in an article entitled "Circassian Beauty in the American Sideshow." Thank you to Adam Green and the *PDR* for the opportunity to build on that work here. Portions of the text on New Women, discussing strongwomen, first appeared in *JSTOR Daily* on August 24, 2022, under the title "The 'Trapeze Disrobing Act.'" Thank you to Catherine Halley and JR Johnson-Roehr for permission to include material.

It has been a pleasure to work with my literary team. I get excited about circus history in a way most people save for stuff like cat memes.

This means that, when I am out in public company, I am prone to mention that, say, I have a great story about performing conjoined twins. Then, suddenly, everyone is not only deeply interested in finding the nearest shrimp tray but feeling the need to check their pockets. But the women I have worked with in bringing this book to fruition instead responded by leaning in and saying: "*Tell me more.*" They understand the improbability and the magic of the circus, and I am grateful to be working with them. Alice Martell is a sharp, witty agent (and she fell in love with those conjoined twins, too). I am grateful to work with Margot Atwell, Jeanne Thornton, and the good folks at the Feminist Press, whose commitment to socially transformative writing is a continuing inspiration. I couldn't imagine a better fit for this work about so many unusual and transgressive women.

Throughout the project I have been sustained by friends and family. This book would not have been possible without support from the high-flying ladies of the Sub Par Circus, with whom I share circus research and invaluable friendship: Kristin Lee, Aíne Norris, Amelia Osterud, and Kat Vecchio; Jenny Leigh DuPuis, Jennifer Lemmer Posey, and Susan O'Shea. Thank you, Natalie Hennessy, for helping with the hard work of building structure, not to mention the harder work of continually encouraging an author with feedback, friendship, and celebrity thirst traps. I look forward to Tuesday mornings because of M. M. De Voe and my Pen Parentis writing group and always enjoy sharing encouragement, accountability, and mutual cheerleading with such a great group of writer-parents. I am grateful for my parents' unfailing support of my wanting to run away and join the circus; also, for dressing me up as a clown that year for Halloween. And, finally, thanks to my husband Chris and daughter Isabel. My writing means they have put up with an itinerant performer in many ways and for many years. They have not only tolerated but encouraged my work, whether that has meant my using paid time off to go research in far-flung places, disappearing on tiny writing retreats to scrape away some quiet, or dragging them along on harebrained circus-themed detours during family vacation. They have provided support, understanding, and even (thanks, kiddo) an early cover design.

Thank you for reading this. As we say in the circus: See you down the road.

NOTES

Introduction. Step Right Up!

1. "Benjamin Jarrat, of Norfolk Glazier," n.d., Tibbals Circus Collection, Circus Museum, The Ringling, object no. Ht8000299; Anthony Carlisle, "An Account of a Family Having Hands and Feet with Supernumerary Fingers and Toes," *Philosophical Transactions of the Royal Society of London* 104 (1814): 94–101.
2. E. E. Cummings, "The Adult, the Artist and the Circus," *Vanity Fair*, October 1925.
3. *Ringling Bros and Barnum & Bailey Combined Shows Route, Personnel and Statistics for the Season of 1952*, 20 (Ringling Brothers and Barnum & Bailey, 1952).
4. "The Great Forepaugh Show," advertisement, *Anderson Democrat* (Indiana), May 2, 1879, p. 3.
5. S. L. Kotar and J. E. Gessler, *The Rise of the American Circus, 1716–1899* (McFarland, 2011). For more on Astley, see Dominique Jando, *Philip Astley & the Horsemen Who Invented the Circus: 1768–1814* (Circopedia, 2018); the online Philip Astley Project; and Steve Ward, *Father of the Modern Circus 'Billy Buttons': The Life & Times of Philip Astley* (Pen and Sword History, 2018).
6. Vanessa Toulmin, "'My Wife to Conclude Performs the Rest'—Patty Astley the First Lady of Circus," *Early Popular Visual Culture* 16, no. 3 (July 3, 2018): 290–300.
7. "Advertisement," *Public Advertiser*, August 19, 1772.
8. See Daniel Wildman, *A Complete Guide for the Management of Bees, Throughout the Year* (London: T. Jones, 1802) and Toulmin, "My Wife to Conclude Performs the Rest," *Early Popular Visual Culture*.
9. Mary Wollstonecraft, *A Vindication of the Rights of Woman*, Penguin Great Ideas (Penguin Books, 2006), 68.
10. Jando, *Philip Astley & the Horsemen*, 36.
11. Toulmin, "My Wife to Conclude Performs the Rest," 1.

12. Janet M. Davis, *The Circus Age: Culture & Society under the American Big Top* (University of North Carolina Press, 2002), 10.
13. "Circus Women, Model Wives," *Philadelphia Inquirer*, May 14, 1905.
14. Ricky Jay, *Celebrations of Curious Characters* (McSweeney's Books, 2011).
15. Greta LaFleur, Masha Raskolnikov, and Anna Kłosowska, eds., *Trans Historical: Gender Plurality Before the Modern* (Cornell University Press, 2021), 4.
16. Audre Lorde, "Age, Race, Class, and Sex: Women Redefining Difference," in *Sister Outsider: Essays and Speeches* (Crossing Press, 1984), 115–16.
17. Chris Mounsey, "Speaking Forwards in History," in *The Variable Body in History*, ed. Chris Mounsey and Stan Booth, Queering Paradigms 6 (Peter Lang, 2016), 3.
18. Rosemarie Garland-Thomson, *Staring: How We Look* (Oxford University Press, 2009), 161, 6.
19. Wendy Rouse, "The Very Queer History of the Suffrage Movement," *National Park Service* (blog), n.d., accessed December 28, 2024. https://www.nps.gov/articles/000/the-very-queer-history-of-the-suffrage-movement.htm.
20. Jean Clair, Galeries nationales du Grand Palais (France), and National Gallery of Canada, eds., *The Great Parade: Portrait of the Artist as Clown* (Yale University Press; National Gallery of Canada, 2004), 350.

Chapter 1. Media and Sources in an Era of Connection

1. See, e.g., Michael Haines, *The Population of the United States, 1790–1920* (National Bureau of Economic Research, 1994). Demography is mathematically driven but somewhat inexact since it has to reckon with gaps in census methodology, changing birth and death rates in an evolving developed nation, the failure to appropriately count Native people or people of color, and how migration flow was assessed. Nonetheless, if anything, the data probably undercounted population and solidly demonstrates growth.
2. Message of President James Monroe at the commencement of the first session of the 18th Congress (The Monroe Doctrine), December 2, 1823; Presidential Messages of the 18th Congress, ca. December 2, 1823–March 3, 1825; Record Group 46; Records of the United States Senate, 1789–1990; National Archives.
3. See, e.g., Julius W. Pratt, "The Origin of 'Manifest Destiny,'" *American Historical Review* 32, no. 4 (1927): 795–798.

4. "Great and terrible things were suddenly asked of the virgin land whose riches seemed as inexhaustible as its dimensions." Arthur King Peters, *Seven Trails West* (Abbeville Publishing Group, 1996), 7.
5. Joe Dobrow, *Pioneers of Promotion: How Press Agents for Buffalo Bill, P. T. Barnum, and the World's Columbian Exposition Created Modern Marketing* (University of Oklahoma Press, 2018), 14.
6. Leonard C. Thomas, *News for All: America's Coming-of-Age with the Press* (Oxford University Press, 1995), 5.
7. M. Claudet, "No. VIII. The Progress and Present State of the Daguerreotype Art," *Transactions of the Society, Instituted at London, for the Encouragement of Arts, Manufactures, and Commerce*, vol. 55 (1843), 89–110.
8. LeRoy Ashby, *With Amusement for All: A History of American Popular Culture since 1830* (University Press of Kentucky, 2012), vii.
9. *The Diaries of William Charles Macready, 1833–1851*, vol. 2 (New York, B. Blom, 1969), 421; quoted in Nigel Cliff, *The Shakespeare Riots: Revenge, Drama, and Death in Nineteenth-Century America* (Random House, 2007). See also Claudia D. Johnson, "That Guilty Third Tier: Prostitution in Nineteenth-Century American Theaters," *American Quarterly* 27, no. 5 (1975): 575–84.
10. My use of the phrase "intimate strangers" here is inspired by Richard Schickel, *Intimate Strangers: The Culture of Celebrity in America* (Ivan R. Dee, 2000).
11. See, e.g., Jon Butler, Grant Wacker, and Randall Herbert Balmer, *Religion in American Life: A Short History*, 2nd ed. (Oxford University Press, 2011).
12. Brenda Wineapple, *Ecstatic Nation: Confidence, Crisis, and Compromise, 1848–1877* (Harper Perennial, 2013), 187.
13. See, e.g., Emily Ogden, *Credulity: A Cultural History of US Mesmerism*, Class 200: New Studies in Religion (University of Chicago Press, 2018) and James Braid, *Magic, Witchcraft, Animal Magnetism, Hypnotism and Electro-Biology: Being a Digest of the Latest Views of the Author on These Subjects* (London: John Churchill, 1852).
14. "Taste for Reading - Its Increase &c.," *State Telegraph*, October 12, 1842.
15. *Barnum, the veteran showman, attributes his success to a persistent, liberal, and judicious use of printer's ink*, trade card, Circus Museum, The Ringling.
16. A. H. Saxon, "P. T. Barnum and the American Museum," *Wilson Quarterly* 13, no. 4 (1989): 130–39.
17. See Richard Adams Locke and J. N. (Joseph Nicolas) Nicollet, *The*

Moon Hoax; or, A Discovery That the Moon Has a Vast Population of Human Beings (New York: W. Gowans, 1859) and Kevin Young, *Bunk: The Rise of Hoaxes, Humbug, Plagiarists, Phonies, Post-Facts, and Fake News* (Graywolf Press, 2018).

18. Neil Harris, *Humbug: The Art of P. T. Barnum*, Phoenix ed. (University of Chicago Press, 1981) and J. E. Hilary Skinner, *After the Storm, or, Jonathan and His Neighbours in 1866* (London: R. Bentley, 1866).
19. Phineas Taylor Barnum, *Humbugs of the World* (London: John Camden Hotten, 1866).
20. Warren I. Susman, *Culture as History: The Transformation of American Society in the Twentieth Century* (Pantheon Books, 1984; repr., Smithsonian Institution Press, 2009), 280.
21. See, e.g., Horatio Alger, Jr., *Ragged Dick and Struggling Upward* (Penguin Books, 1985); Washington Irving, *Diedrich Knickerbocker's History of New-York* (Heritage Press, 1940); and Edward Watts, *Colonizing the Past: Mythmaking and Pre-Columbian Whites in Nineteenth-Century American Writing* (University of Virginia Press, 2020).
22. Amelia Osterud, "The True Life and Adventures of Tattooed Performers: Tattoos, Captivity Narratives and Popular Culture," in *Tattoo Histories: Transcultural Perspectives on the Narratives, Practices, and Representations of Tattooing* (Routledge, 2020).

Chapter 2. Building the Nineteenth-Century Big Top

1. See Huang Minhua, "The 'Hundred Entertainments': China's 2,000-Year-Old Tradition of Acrobatics," *UNESCO Courier* 41, no. 1 (1988); John G. Younger, "Bronze Age Representations of Aegean Bull-Leaping," *American Journal of Archaeology* 80, no. 2 (1976): 125–37; and Plato, *The Republic of Plato*, trans. Benjamin Jowett, 3rd ed. (Oxford: Clarendon Press, 1888), 316.
2. Charles Gates Sturtevant, "Who's Who in the American Circus: Sturtevant's List of Circuses 1880–1889," Circus Historical Society, accessed December 28, 2024, https://classic.circushistory.org/History/Sturtevant.htm.
3. For examples of early modern conjuring texts, see Reginald Scot, *Discoverie of Witchcraft*, ed. Brinsley Nicholson (London: Elliot Stock, 1886) and *Hocus Pocus Junior: The Anatomie of Ledgerdemain, or, The Art of Juggling set forth in his proper colours, fully, plainly, and exactly, so that an ignorant person may thereby learn the full perfection of the same, after a little practice: Unto each Tricke is added the figure, where it is needfull for instruction* (London: T. H. for R. M., 1635). Ricky Jay's *Many Mysteries Unravelled: Or, Conjuring Literature in America, 1786–1874* (American Antiquarian

Society, 1990) goes into the transmission of magic literature into early American society and culture.
4. Ambroise Paré, *On Monsters and Marvels*, trans. Janis L. Pallister (University of Chicago Press, 1982).
5. Clifford L. Snyder, "Setting The Record Straight On Old Bet," *American Heritage*, April 1974.
6. "Van Amburgh's Menagerie," *New York Times*, April 5, 1862.
7. Barbara Benedict, *Curiosity: A Cultural History of Early Modern Inquiry* (University of Chicago Press, 2001), 2.
8. See Charles Coleman Sellers, *Mr. Peale's Museum: Charles Willson Peale and the First Popular Museum of Natural Science and Art* (W. W. Norton, 1980).
9. "Scudder's American Museum," *Evening Post* (New York), May 22, 1812.
10. "Circus," *General Advertiser* (Philadelphia), April 22, 1793.
11. Stuart Thayer, *Annals of the American Circus, 1793–1829* (Rymack, 1976), 238.
12. William L. Slout, *Clowns and Cannons: The American Circus During the Civil War* (Emeritus Enterprise, 2000), x–xi.
13. Slout, *Clowns and Cannons*, 128.
14. E. E. Cummings, "The Adult, the Artist and the Circus."
15. Yale Law School, "Avalon Project - Journals of the Continental Congress - The Articles of Association; October 20, 1774," accessed August 16, 2023, https://avalon.law.yale.edu/18th_century/contcong_10-20-74.asp.
16. See Stuart Thayer, "The Anti-Circus Laws in Connecticut, 1773–1840," *Bandwagon* 20, no. 1 (1976): 18–20, and *A Law for Suppressing of Mountebanks* (1773), quoted in Timothy Green, *Acts and Laws of the State of Connecticut, in America* (Hartford: Hudson and Godwin, 1784), 161.
17. *The Circus Girl and Sunday-School Scholar* (Philadelphia: American Sunday School Union, 1860).
18. Thayer, *Annals of the American Circus*, 194.
19. David Carlyon, "'Soft and Silky Around Her Hips': Nineteenth-Century Circus and Sex," *Journal of American Drama and Theater* 22, no. 2 (2010): 25–48.
20. Andrea Stulman Dennett, *Weird and Wonderful: The Dime Museum in America* (New York University Press, 1997), 5.
21. "The Political Blondin," *Frank Leslie's Budget of Fun*, September 1, 1864.
22. David Carlyon, *Dan Rice: The Most Famous Man You've Never Heard Of* (Public Affairs, 2001), 411.
23. Janet Davis, "The Circus Americanized," in *The American Circus*, ed. Susan Weber, Kenneth L. Ames, and Matthew Wittman (Bard Graduate Center; Yale University Press, 2012), 33–34.

24. Fred Dahlinger, Jr., "A Short Analysis of Steam Calliope History Before 1900," *Bandwagon* 17, no. 6 (1972): 25–27.
25. "P. T. Barnum's Grand Colossal Museum and Menagerie," *Evening Post* (Cleveland, OH), Aug 6, 1852, p. 3.
26. See Matthew Wittmann, *Circus and the City: New York, 1793–2010* (Bard Graduate Center, 2012).
27. Fred Dahlinger, "The American Circus Tent," in *The American Circus*, ed. Susan Webber, Kenneth L. Ames, and Matthew Wittman (Bard Graduate Center; Yale University Press, 2012), 221.
28. "A Night in a Circus," *Frank Leslie's Illustrated Newspaper* 36, no. 928 (1873): 282.
29. Janet M. Davis, *The Circus Age: Culture & Society under the American Big Top* (University of North Carolina Press, 2002), 7.
30. *Forepaugh's Great Aggregation, Museum, Menagerie and Triple Circus*, 1880, trade card, Circus Museum, The Ringling, object no. ht2000400.
31. Michel Foucault and Jay Miskowiec, "Of Other Spaces," *Diacritics* 16, no. 1 (1986): 22–27.
32. Micah Childress, "Life Beyond the Big Top: African American and Female Circusfolk, 1860–1920," *Journal of the Gilded Age and Progressive Era* 15, no. 2 (2016): 176–96.
33. "Booklet: Nero; or The Destruction of Rome," box 12, P. T. Barnum Research Collection, Bridgeport History Center, Connecticut.
34. *Adam Forepaugh: Lalla Rookh's Departure From Delhi*, 1884, lithograph, Tibbals Circus Collection, Circus Museum, The Ringling, object no. ht2004557.
35. See *The Mahdi* (Courier, 1897), lithograph, Tibbals Circus Collection, Circus Museum, The Ringling, object no. ht2000108; *Adam Forepaugh: American Revolution*, 1893, lithograph, Tibbals Circus Collection, Circus Museum, The Ringling, object no. ht2000418; and Barbara Barker, "Imre Kiralfy's Patriotic Spectacles: 'Columbus, and the Discovery of America' (1892–1893) and 'America' (1893)," *Dance Chronicle* 17, no. 2 (1994): 149–78.
36. Raymond F. Betts and Lyz Bly, *A History of Popular Culture: More of Everything, Faster and Brighter*, 2nd ed. (Routledge, 2013); Kurt Andersen, *Fantasyland: How America Went Haywire: A 500-Year History* (Random House, 2017), 7.

Chapter 3. Womanhood, Real and True

1. "Gender and Health," World Health Organization, accessed August 16, 2023, https://www.who.int/health-topics/gender.

2. Cynthia Eagle Russett, *Sexual Science: The Victorian Construction of Womanhood* (Harvard University Press, 1991).
3. Eileen Kraditor, ed., *Up From the Pedestal: Selected Writings in the History of Feminism* (Quadrangle Books, 1968), 9.
4. Alexis de Tocqueville, *Democracy in America*, trans. Henry Reeve (Boston: John Allyn, 1873), 258–59.
5. Helen Lefkowitz Horowitz, *Attitudes toward Sex in Antebellum America: A Brief History with Documents*, The Bedford Series in History and Culture (Bedford/St. Martin's, 2006), 3.
6. Jeffrey A. Auerbach, "What They Read: Mid-Nineteenth Century English Women's Magazines and the Emergence of a Consumer Culture," *Victorian Periodicals Review* 30, no. 2 (1997): 121–40.
7. "Matrimony," *Lady's Amaranth*, June 15, 1839, p. 271.
8. Coventry Patmore, *The Angel in the House*, ed. Henry Morley (London, Paris & Melbourne: Cassell, 1891).
9. Barbara Welter, "The Cult of True Womanhood: 1820–1860," *American Quarterly* 18, no. 2, pt. 1 (1966): 151–74.
10. Welter, "The Cult of True Womanhood," 159–60.
11. *The Young Ladies' Journal Complete Guide to the Work-Table* (London: E. Harrison, 1884).
12. Welter, "The Cult of True Womanhood," 153.
13. Jan Todd, *Physical Culture and the Body Beautiful: Purposive Exercise in the Lives of American Women, 1800–1870* (Mercer University Press, 1998).
14. Frances B. Cogan, *All American Girl: The Ideal of Real Womanhood in Mid-Nineteenth Century America* (University of Georgia Press, 1989), 212.
15. Gerda Lerner, "The Lady and the Mill Girl: Changes in the Status of Women in the Age of Jackson," *American Studies* 10, no. 1 (1969): 5–15, back cover.
16. Winifred Gallagher, *New Women in the Old West: From Settlers to Suffragists, an Untold American Story* (Penguin Press, 2022), xii.
17. Henry F. Harrington, "Female Education," *The Ladies' Companion, a Monthly Magazine; Devoted to Literature and the Fine Arts* (1838).
18. Maya Salam, "What Suffrage Owes to Queer Women," *New York Times*, August 16, 2020, sec. TW, p. 16.
19. *The Circus Girl and Sunday-School Scholar* (Philadelphia: American Sunday School Union, 1860).
20. *The Lady's Book*, vols. 10–11 (Philadelphia: Louis A. Godey, 1835).
21. Elaine Showalter, "Killing the Angel in the House: The Autonomy of Women Writers," *Antioch Review* 50, no. 1/2 (1992): 207–20.
22. Will Branan, "Angus Gaines, the Hoosier Snake Charmer," *Star Press*, September 17, 1911.

23. Peter Stallybrass and Allon White, as related in Robert Clyde Allen, *Horrible Prettiness: Burlesque and American Culture*, Cultural Studies of the United States (University of North Carolina Press, 1991).
24. "Circus Women," *The Shippensburg News*, June 22, 1888.

Chapter 4. The Queen of Beauty and the Armless Wonder

1. Countess M. Lavinia Magri, *The Autobiography of Mrs. Tom Thumb (Some of My Life Experiences)*, ed. A. H. Saxon (Archon Books, 1979). Quotes from Warren and descriptions of her young life are generally drawn from this source.
2. "The Royal Bohemians," *Buffalo Evening Post*, October 20, 1862.
3. See, e.g., "Advertisement," *Cleveland Daily Leader*, July 17, 1860.
4. See A. H. Saxon, *P. T. Barnum: The Legend and the Man* (Columbia University Press, 1989), 126, reproducing a script and referencing collections of the New-York Historical Society.
5. Tom Taylor, ed., *Life of Benjamin Robert Haydon, Historical Painter*, vol. 2 (New York: Harper & Brothers, 1853), 483.
6. Jefferson Williamson, *The American Hotel*, The Leisure Class in America (Arno Press, 1975), 52.
7. "A Small But Precious Parcel," *New York Times*, December 23, 1862.
8. "Advertisement (Lavinia Warren)," *New York Times*, December 31, 1862.
9. "A Prize Beyond Barnum's Reach," *New York Times*, December 27, 1862.
10. "Barnum's American Museum," *New York Times*, January 4, 1863.
11. Phineas Taylor Barnum, *Struggles and Triumphs; or Forty Years' Recollection of P. T. Barnum* (Buffalo: Warren, Johnson, 1872), 587.
12. "Theaters, &c.," *New York Tribune*, January 26, 1863.
13. Magri, *The Autobiography of Mrs. Tom Thumb*, 58.
14. Barnum, *Struggles and Triumphs*, 602.
15. "Marriage a la Barnum," *Brooklyn Daily Eagle*, January 26, 1863, p. 2.
16. "The Tom Thumb Wedding, *New York Daily Herald*, February 11, 1863, p. 1.
17. "The Great Little Wedding," *New-York Illustrated News*, February 21, 1863.
18. Margaret Walsh, "The Democratization of Fashion: The Emergence of the Women's Dress Pattern Industry," *Journal of American History* 66, no. 2 (1979): 299–313.
19. "The Great Lilliputian Wedding," *Brooklyn Daily Eagle*, February 10, 1863.
20. See also Charles Stratton (General Tom Thumb) and Mercy Lavinia Warren Bump (Lavinia Warren), marriage certificate, February 10, 1863, collection of the Barnum Museum, Bridgeport, Connecticut.

21. "The Tom Thumb Wedding," *New York Daily Herald.*
22. "The Loving Lilliputians," *New York Times*, February 11, 1863.
23. *Sketch Of The Life, Personal Appearance, Character And Manners Of Charles S. Stratton, The Man In Miniature, Known As General Tom Thumb, And His Wife, Lavinia Warren Stratton* (Wynkook & Hallenbeck, 1863), box 16, P. T. Barnum Research Collection, Bridgeport History Center, Connecticut.
24. "The Loving Lilliputians," *New York Times.*
25. "Advertisement: Irving Hall," *New York Times*, April 2, 1863.
26. See Eric D. Lehman, *Becoming Tom Thumb: Charles Stratton, P. T. Barnum, and the Dawn of American Celebrity* (Wesleyan University Press, 2013); "Advertisement: Barnum's American Museum (Ann Leak)," *New-York Daily Tribune*, October 16, 1865.
27. Ann Leak, 1860 United States Census. Year: 1860; Census Place: District 1001, Spalding, Georgia; Roll: M653_136; Page: 173. Ann Leak had a December birthday on the twenty-third just before the Christmas holiday. While the 1860 census claims that she was eighteen years old in 1860, suggesting birth in 1841, and while she herself often fudged the date of her birth on autographs to give herself the benefit of youth, she claimed to have been born in 1839 on many early autographs, and a death notice in the *Philadelphia Inquirer* reports her age as fifty-nine at her death in January of 1899.
28. Ann Leak, *The Autobiography of Miss Ann E. Leak, Born without Arms: Containing an Interesting Account of Her Early Life and Subsequent Travels in the United States and Australia* (Melbourne: Azzopardi, Hildreth, 1867). Unless otherwise noted, quotes by Ann Leak in her own words throughout the chapter come from this source.
29. George Middleton, *Circus Memoirs: Reminiscences of George Middleton as Told to and Written by His Wife* (G. Rice and Sons, 1913), 70.
30. J. W. Ballantyne, "Teratogenesis: An Inquiry into the Causes of Monstrosities," *Edinburgh Medical Journal* 42, no. 3 (1896): 240–55; R. J. Lee, "Maternal Impressions," *British Medical Journal* 1, no. 736 (1875): 167–69.
31. See, e.g., the *New-York Tribune* and the *New York Times* editions for October 16, 1865.
32. "Nature's Broad Jests," *Brooklyn Times Union*, April 30, 1892.
33. Robert Bogdan, *Freak Show: Presenting Human Oddities for Amusement and Profit* (University of Chicago Press, 1990), 219.
34. *The Australian Tour of Cooper, Bailey, & Co.'s Great International Allied Shows 1877*, ed. W. G. Crowley (Brisbane: Thorne & Greenwell, 1877).
35. Richard A. Arnold, ed., *Route of P. T. Barnum's Great Traveling*

Exposition and World's Fair through the Principal Cities and Towns in the U.S. Season of 1872 (Chicago: J. S. Thompson, 1872).
36. "Ninth and Arch Museum," *The Times* (Philadelphia), September 25, 1894.
37. "Obituaries - THOMSON," *Philadelphia Inquirer*, January 5, 1899.
38. *Sketch Of The Life, Personal Appearance, Character And Manners Of Charles S. Stratton, The Man In Miniature, Known As General Tom Thumb, And His Wife, Lavinia Warren Stratton* (Wynkook & Hallenbeck, 1863), box 16, P. T. Barnum Research Collection, Bridgeport History Center, Connecticut.
39. "Advertisement: Barnum's American Museum," *New-York Daily Tribune*, January 13, 1863.

Chapter 5. Women Take Flight

1. See "Accident to Mdlle. Azella," *Aris's Birmingham Gazette, etc.*, April 11, 1868, p. 4.
2. Janet M. Davis, *The Circus Age: Culture & Society under the American Big Top* (University of North Carolina Press, 2002), 83.
3. See, e.g., the Ringling Brothers' flying trapeze poster depicting four women in dark ruffled leotards and sashes, their curls perfectly tied in headbands with bows. Another Strobridge poster, this time advertising a spectacle named "Solomon and the Queen of Sheba," shows "hundreds of beautiful dancing girls" in perfect step and matching costume. In 1905, a San Francisco journalist noted that "Long gowns and up-to-date fashions have invaded the circus as well as the stage, and one of the much discussed characteristics of the current ring show is the modish style of dress that prevails in every act where such costuming is possible. Even the dressing of the hair is done in the latest fashion and with great care. Bows, aigrettes and ornamental combs are as much a part of the circus rider's toilet as that of a society woman." "The Passing of the Girl in Tights," *San Francisco Call*, September 3, 1905, p. 3.
4. "Zazel Scrapbook, 1877–1879," scrapbook, Tibbals Collection of Scrapbooks, Circus Museum, The Ringling.
5. "Zazel Scrapbook."
6. "Zazel Scrapbook."
7. "Zazel Scrapbook."
8. "Zazel Scrapbook." Barnum's handwriting is terrible and it's unclear if the date here on the letter is 1880 or 1889, but the point stands.
9. "Zazel Scrapbook."
10. His surname is sometimes also spelled "Wasgate."
11. "Lulu's Girl Life," *Buffalo Times*, January 22, 1884, p. 2.
12. "Untitled," *Evening Star* (DC), September 11, 1876, p. 3.

13. "Lulu's Girl Life," *Buffalo Times*, p. 2.
14. G. A. Farini, *Through the Kalahari Desert: A Journey to Lake N'gami and Back* (London: S. Low, Marston, Searle & Rivington, 1886).
15. "Farini's Discoveries," *Chicago Tribune*, September 12, 1885.
16. "Zazel Scrapbook."
17. "Provincial Theatricals: BOLTON," *The Era*, December 21, 1879.
18. "The Austin and Hess Troupe of Skaters," *The Era* (London), November 25, 1877. The ad notes R. G. Austin skating alongside "Mdlle. Rosalie, the graceful and accomplished Lady Skater," and it is possible this was Rose.
19. See "Cole's Circus," *Kansas City Journal*, April 29, 1884, p. 3; "W. W. Cole's New Colossal Show," *Virginia Free Press*, August 6, 1885, p. 3.
20. "Where Is Rose Austin?," *The Sun*, August 25, 1892: "Aimee Austin is not believed in variety circles to be related to Rose, though the pair have always traveled as sisters. The story goes that Austin and his wife saw Aimee in a London skating rink, and that they adopted her when she was very young." The *New York Evening World* of August 26, 1892, adds: "Aimee, 'the Human Fly,' who is said to be a sister of Austin, and again is said to be not related to either of the couple, denies that she went away with Rose."
21. "Mlle. Aimee Falls," *Morning Journal-Courier* (CT), November 25, 1885.
22. "A Dearth of New Plays," *Chicago Tribune*, December 20, 1885.
23. Ricky Jay, "The Gnome Fly," *Jay's Journal of Anomalies* 3, no. 3 (1997).
24. See "Park Theatre," *Daily American*, February 20, 1885; "Fall of a Ceiling Walker," *Preston Chronicle and Lancashire Advertiser*, September 8, 1877; "Amusements," *Buffalo Evening Telegraph*, April 5, 1884; and "John Robinson's Fifty Cage Menagerie," *Bismarck Weekly Tribune*, September 25, 1885.
25. "Scientific Phenomena," *Dayton Herald*, August 2, 1890.
26. "Walking on the Ceiling Head Down," *Scientific American* 63, no. 1 (1890): 8.
27. "The Human Fly," *Kansas City Times*, January 3, 1889; "M'lle Aimee Austin, The Human Fly," *Dayton Herald*, October 29, 1889.
28. "The Human Fly," *Kansas City Times*.
29. "The Human Fly," *Scranton Gazette*, May 5, 1893.
30. "50 Years Ago," *Variety*, April 24, 1935.
31. "50 Years Ago," *Variety*, June 12, 1935.
32. "The London Music Halls," *The Era* (London), July 17, 1886.
33. "Variety & Minstrel Gossip," *New York Clipper*, July 21, 1888.
34. "Where Is Rose Austin?," *The Sun*, August 25, 1892.
35. "Cannot Find Rose Austin," *New York Times*, August 25, 1892.

36. "Rose Austin Returns," *Brooklyn Daily Eagle*, August 26, 1892.
37. "Rose Austin Still Missing," *New York Evening World*, August 25, 1892.
38. "Rose Austin Home Again," *The World*, August 26, 1892.
39. "Rose Austin Returns," *Brooklyn Daily Eagle*.
40. See "Rose Austin Returns to Her Home," *New York Times*, August 26, 1892; "Rose Austin Home Again," *The World*; and "Forgets Where She Was," *New York Evening World*, August 26, 1892.
41. "Forgets Where She Was," *New York Evening World*.
42. See "Variety, Minstrel & Circus," *New York Clipper*, March 31, 1888; "Two Fall From a Trapeze," *New York Times*, July 12, 1894.
43. "Variety and Minstrelsy," *New York Clipper*, 432.
44. See "He Insulted the Actress," *Brooklyn Daily Eagle*, March 6, 1893, and "Variety Performers Fined," *New York Evening World*, March 6, 1893.
45. "Rose Austin Was Not Arrested," *Brooklyn Daily Eagle*, March 7, 1893.
46. "To Whom It May Concern," *New York Clipper*, May 13, 1893.
47. See "A Free Show," *Brooklyn Citizen*, March 16, 1894, and "Among the Guardsmen," *Brooklyn Daily Eagle*, March 18, 1894.
48. *The Circus Annual: A Route Book of Ringling Brothers World's Greatest Shows Season 1902* (Central Engraving & Publishing, 1902).
49. See "'Human Fly' Sues for Diamond Pin," *Oregon Daily Journal*, July 8, 1904, and "Supreme Court Calendar," *Statesman Journal*, March 23, 1906. The *Statesman Journal* notes: "Cases set for hearing during the first week of April by Clerk Murphy yesterday . . . Tuesday, April 3 - Aimee Austin, respondent, vs. Oscar Vanderbilt, appellant."
50. "DEATHS (Aimee Austin)," *Billboard*, January 19, 1907.
51. "Mrs. Rose Austin in Court," *Brooklyn Daily Eagle*, May 5, 1899.
52. See "Miss Austin Said to Be Married," *Brooklyn Daily Times*, October 13, 1899, p. 6; "United States Census, 1900," Family Search, entry for Robert G Austin and Rose E Austin, 1900, https://www.familysearch.org/ark:/61903/1:1:MSNR-HSR.
53. See "Mrs. Rose E. Austin," *San Bernardino County Sun*, October 22, 1928, p. 11; "United States Census, 1920," Family Search, entry for Robert G Austin and Rose E Austin, 1920, https://www.familysearch.org/ark:/61903/1:1:MHQJ-7SS).

Chapter 6. Invisible Girls and Electric Women

1. *Lulu Hurst (The Georgia Wonder) Writes Her Autobiography* (Rome, Georgia: Lulu Hurst Book Co., 1897). All quotes in Lulu Hurst's words throughout this chapter are taken from her self-published memoir unless otherwise noted.

2. See, e.g., Emma Hardinge, *Modern American Spiritualism: Twenty Years' Record of the Communion between Earth and the World of Spirits* (pub. by author, 1870); and Erin E. Forbes, "Do Black Ghosts Matter?: Harriet Jacobs' Spiritualism," *ESQ: A Journal of Nineteenth-Century American Literature and Culture* 62, no. 3 (2016): 443–79.
3. R. Laurence Moore, "The Spiritualist Medium: A Study of Female Professionalism in Victorian America," *American Quarterly* 27, no. 2 (1975): 200–221.
4. See Forbes, "Do Black Ghosts Matter?"; also Harriet Jacobs, *Incidents in the Life of a Slave Girl* (W. Tweedie, 1862); R. J. Ellis and Henry Louis Gates, "'Grievances at the Treatment She Received': Harriet E. Wilson's Spiritualist Career in Boston, 1868–1900," *American Literary History* 24, no. 2 (2012): 234–64; and Ann Braude, *Radical Spirits: Spiritualism and Women's Rights in Nineteenth-Century America*, 2nd ed. (Indiana University Press, 2001), xv. Braude notes that "every religious worldview must participate in the construction of gender if it is to provide a comprehensive vocabulary of meanings and actions for managing experience and interpreting reality."
5. Mark Twain, *The Celebrated Jumping Frog of Calaveras County,* 3rd ed. (New York: C. H. Webb, 1869).
6. Reginald Scot, *Discoverie of Witchcraft*, ed. Brinsley Nicholson (London: Elliot Stock, 1886).
7. King James I, *Daemonologie* (John Lane; E. P. Dutton, 1924).
8. Christina Larner, *Witchcraft and Religion: The Politics of Popular Belief* (Basil Blackwell, 1984).
9. Margaret Steele, ed., "The World's Only Woman Magician (Broadway Magazine, November 2, 1899)," in Adelaide Herrmann, *Queen of Magic: Memoirs, Published Writings, Collected Ephemera* (Bramble Books, 2012).
10. See Thomas Frost, *Lives of the Conjurors* (London: Tinsley Brothers, 1875).
11. H. S. Chandler, "Miracles of the Past: The Invisible Girl," *Magicana* (September/October 1981), CA Id 22419, Conjuring Arts Library.
12. See John Nevil Maskelyne, *Automata* (Magic Circle Foundation, 1989); "Harry Houdini Scrapbook 08," scrapbook, n.d., Conjuring Arts Library; Steven Connor, "Talking Heads, Automaton Ears," in *Dumbstruck: A Cultural History of Ventriloquism* (Oxford University Press, 2000).
13. "Untitled," *Morning Post*, January 26, 1804.
14. See Edwin A. Dawes, "A Rich Cabinet of Magical Curiosities 421, The 'Mysterious Lady' and the Mystery of Mrs. Matthews," *The Magic Circular*, December 2013. Dawes discusses a few performers who may have borne the mantle of the Mysterious Lady, including Georgianna Eagle and one "Mrs. Matthews."

15. "The Mysterious Lady," clipping, n.d., Magic Collection, Harry Ransom Center, University of Texas at Austin. Note: Clipping is dated March 29, 1845, in pencil annotation.
16. "Wonderful Performance!," *The Lancaster Examiner*, July 26, 1843.
17. Sidney W. Clarke, *The Annals of Conjuring* (The Miracle Factory, 2001), 369.
18. Herrmann Sagemüller, "Sagemüller's Lexikon," electronic resource, n.d., Conjuring Arts Library.
19. See Ricky Jay, ed., *Extraordinary Exhibitions: The Wonderful Remains of an Enormous Head, the Whimsiphusicon, & Death to the Savage Unitarians* (Quantuck Lane Press, 2005); and "Lizzie Anderson," program, February 1846, Magic Collection, Harry Ransom Center, University of Texas at Austin.
20. "Personal Gossip," *Frank Leslie's Illustrated Newspaper*, February 19, 1887.
21. Henry F. Harrington, "Female Education," *The Ladies' Companion, a Monthly Magazine; Devoted to Literature and the Fine Arts*, October 1838; John Angell James, *Female Piety: Or, The Young Woman's Friend and Guide Through Life to Immortality* (New York: Robert Carter & Brothers, 1853).
22. "The Umbrellas and Chairs of Lulu Hurst," *Scientific American* 51, no. 1 (1884).
23. "Wallack's New Theatre," *New York Times*, December 4, 1881.
24. "People Moved at Will," *New York Times*, July 6, 1884.
25. "Children in Her Hands: Twenty Club Athletes Retire Discomfited," *New York Times*, July 10, 1884.
26. "The Umbrellas and Chairs of Lulu Hurst," *Scientific American*.
27. "Scientific and Useful," *New-York Evangelist*, July 24, 1884.
28. "Lulu Hurst's Many Dresses," *New York Times*, July 20, 1884.
29. "Lulu Hurst's Exhibitions," *Frank Leslie's Illustrated Newspaper*, July 26, 1884.
30. S. Newcomb, "The Georgia Wonder-Girl and Her Lessons," *Science* 5 (June 1885): 106–8.
31. "Lulu Hurst's Force Waning," *New York Times*, December 31, 1884; "Lulu Hurst: Some Well-Known Chicagoans Find the Georgia Girl Too Much for Them," *Chicago Tribune*, December 30, 1884.

Chapter 7. Circassian Beauties in the American Sideshow

1. "Amusements," *New York Times*, November 21, 1864.
2. Johann Friedrich Blumenbach, *The Anthropological Treatises of Johann Friedrich Blumenbach* (London: Longman, Green, Longman, Roberts & Green, 1865).

3. Blumenbach, *The Anthropological Treatises*.
4. Mrs. Harvey, *Turkish Harems and Circassian Homes* (London: Hurst & Blackett, 1871).
5. "Trademark Registration by J. J. Mack & Co. for Davidson's Circassian Bloom Brand A Preparation for Beautifying the Skin, Trademark No. 13720," 1886, Prints and Photographs Division, Library of Congress.
6. Andrew Parkin, ed., *Selected Plays of Dion Boucicault* (Catholic University of America Press, 1987).
7. "Biographical Sketch of the Circassian Girl, Zalumma Agra; or, Star of the East," 1868, control no. ltf90014899, General Collections, Library of Congress. The narrative of Agra's life as described in this chapter is taken from this pamphlet.
8. "Advertisements," *New York Daily Herald*, August 4, 1865.
9. Letter from P. T. Barnum to John Greenwood, May 14, 1864, Lost Museum Archive, accessed December 28, 2024, https://lostmuseum.cuny.edu/archive/letter-from-p-t-barnum-to-john-greenwood.
10. Barnum, *Struggles and Triumphs*.
11. Bogdan, *Freak Show*, 234.
12. "Those Circassian Girls," *Democrat and Chronicle* (Rochester, NY), February 9, 1889.
13. "How Circassian Girls Are Made," *Carbondale Leader*, June 16, 1882.
14. Charles D. Martin, *The White African American Body: A Cultural and Literary Exploration* (Rutgers University Press, 2002), 104.
15. John Lockwood and Charles Lockwood, "First South Carolina. Then New York," *New York Times*, January 6, 2011, https://archive.nytimes.com/opinionator.blogs.nytimes.com/2011/01/06/first-south-carolina-then-new-york/.
16. "Spirit of the Press," *New York Times*, October 19, 1864.
17. David Croly, *Miscegenation: The Theory of the Blending of the Races, Applied to the American White Man and Negro* (New York: H. Dexter, Hamilton, 1864).
18. See, e.g., Linda Frost, "The Circassian Beauty and the Circassian Slave: Gender, Imperialism, and American Popular Entertainment," in *Freakery*, ed. Rosemarie Garland-Thomson (New York University Press, 1996) and Don Juan van Halen, *Narrative of Don Juan van Halen's Imprisonment in the Dungeons of the Inquisition at Madrid, and His Escape in 1817 and 1818; to Which Are Added, His Journey to Russia, His Campaign with the Army of the Caucasus, and His Return to Spain in 1821* (London: H. Colburn, 1827).
19. Saxon, "P. T. Barnum and the American Museum."
20. "P. T. Barnum's Speech on 'Negro Suffrage,' May 26, 1865," Lost Museum Archive, accessed December 28, 2024, https://lostmuseum.cuny.edu/archive/p-t-barnums-speech-on-negro-suffrage-may-26-1.

21. For discussion of the Meleke pamphlet, see Linda Frost, *Never One Nation: Freaks, Savages, and Whiteness in U.S. Popular Culture, 1850–1877* (University of Minnesota Press, 2005), and Bogdan, *Freak Show*, 239.
22. "Barnum's Humbugs," *Chicago Evening Post*, December 23, 1865; "Untitled," *Star and Enterprise*, October 21, 1873.
23. George Conklin and Harvey W. Root, *The Ways of the Circus: Being the Memories and Adventures of George Conklin, Tamer of Lions* (Harper & Brothers, 1921).
24. "Powers' National Museum," *New York Clipper*, December 8, 1877.
25. "Zad Zumella, Circassian," *New York Clipper*, September 14, 1872.
26. "Advertisement," *New York Clipper*, January 29, 1887.
27. *Adam Forepaugh: Uno*, 1895, lithograph, Tibbals Circus Collection, Circus Museum, The Ringling, object no. ht2000427.
28. "The Royal Aquarium, Westminster," *Illustrated London News*, January 5, 1878.
29. "Circuses," *New York Clipper*, February 24, 1883.
30. "Playing With Snakes," *South-Western Presbyterian*, June 14, 1883; *Route Book of the Great Forepaugh Show, Circus, Hippodrome and Menagerie Season 1883* (Silbons, 1883).
31. "A Snake Charmer's Tale," *The LaFayette Sun*, September 24, 1884; "Playing With Snakes," *South-Western Presbyterian*.
32. "Nala Damajante. The Lovely and Graceful Hindoo Maiden Who Toys With Anacondas," *Daily Alta California*, January 9, 1884.
33. "Playing With Snakes," *South-Western Presbyterian*.
34. "Untitled," *Puck*, July 2, 1884.
35. Henry John Drewal, *Mami Wata: Arts for Water Spirits in Africa and Its Diasporas* (Fowler Museum at UCLA, 2008); Henry John Drewal, "Beauteous Beast: The Water Deity Mami Wata in Africa," in *The Ashgate Research Companion to Monsters and the Monstrous*, ed. Asa Simon Mittman and Peter Dendle (Routledge, 2012). Drewal documents a fascinating cultural exchange through which posters of Nala Damajante, reprinted over future decades, made their way to Africa and significantly influenced iconography of the deity Mami Wata.
36. "Important Notice to Managers," *New York Clipper*, October 11, 1884.
37. "Obituaries," *The Era*, April 25, 1896.
38. "Chronique Des Tribunaux," *Le Gaulois*, March 17, 1887.
39. Alvaro Betancourt, *Route Book of P. T. Barnum's Greatest Show on Earth and the Great London Circus Since the Consolidation Seasons of 1881, 1882, 1883, 1884, & 1885*.
40. "John Palmer, 29, Marries Mathilde Marie Emilie Poupon, 24, in Walworth, Surrey," #177, April 20, 1886, London Metropolitan Archives, London, England, London Church of England Parish Registers, reference number P92/JN/025.

41. Carl Hagenbeck, *Von Tieren Und Menschen* (Vita deutsches Verlagshaus, 1909).
42. Carl Hagenbeck, *Beasts & Men: Being Experiences for Half a Century among Wild Animals* (Longmans, 1910).
43. Henry Hart Milman, ed., *Nala and Damayanti and Other Poems* (Oxford: D.A. Talboys, 1835).
44. See, e.g., Janell Hobson, *Venus in the Dark: Blackness and Beauty in Popular Culture*, 2nd ed. (Routledge, Taylor & Francis Group, 2018).

Chapter 8. The Remarkable Life of Millie-Christine McKoy, the Two-Headed Nightingale

1. "Circus Kings in Arms," *The Times*, April 11, 1881.
2. Kory W. Rogers, "On the Covers," *Bandwagon* 60, no. 2 (2016): 5.
3. Transcribed from "The Complaint of Millie Christine, Alias Christine Millie," June 19, 1882, National Archives and Records Administration (Chicago), NAID: 192125956 and NAID: 192044942.
4. "The Two Headed Nightingale," *Parsons Weekly Eclipse* (Kansas), September 7, 1882.
5. Millie-Christine's life story is here drawn from sources including Joanne Martell, *Millie-Christine: Fearfully and Wonderfully Made* (John F. Blair, 2000); "The History of the Carolina Twins: Told in 'Their Own Peculiar Way' By 'One of Them'" (Buffalo: Buffalo Courier Printing House, ca. 1800s); "History and Medical Description of the Two-Headed Girl" (Buffalo: Warren, Johnson, 1869); and "Biographical Sketch of Millie Christine, the Carolina Twin" (Hennegen, ca. 1902–1912).
6. Charles Dickens, *Sketches by Boz* (Chapman & Hall, 1913).
7. "The Deformito-Mania," *Punch*, September 4, 1847.
8. Rosemarie Garland-Thomson, "Feminist Disability Studies," *Signs* 30, no. 2 (2005): 1557–87.
9. "The African Twins," *Berrow's Worcester Journal*, September 22, 1855.
10. "The United African Twins," *Liverpool Daily Post*, July 26, 1855.
11. "Abduction of the African Twins," *Leeds Intelligencer and Yorkshire General Advertiser*, August 21, 1855; "Abstraction of the African Twins from Dundee," *Aberdeen Journal and General Advertiser for the North of Scotland*, September 5, 1855.
12. "Biographical Sketch of Millie Christine, the Carolina Twin," 8.
13. "The African Twins," *Liverpool Mercury*, January 12, 1857.
14. "The African Twins," *Caledonian Mercury*, January 21, 1857.
15. "The African Twin Monstrosity," *Leeds Mercury*, January 31, 1857.
16. "History and Medical Description of the Two-Headed Girl," 9.
17. Mark Twain, *Life on the Mississippi* (Boston: James R. Osgood, 1883).
18. "History and Medical Description of the Two-Headed Girl," 9.

19. Ellen Samuels, "Examining Millie and Christine McKoy: Where Enslavement and Enfreakment Meet," *Signs* 37, no. 1 (2011): 53–81.
20. Queen Victoria recorded meeting Millie-Christine in her journals; see RA VIC/MAIN/QVJ 24 June 1871 (Princess Beatrice's copies), retrieved August 14, 2023, proquest.libguides.com/queenvictoria/content.
21. Hobson, *Venus in the Dark*, 118–19.
22. George J. Fisher, *Diploteratology* (Albany: Van Benthuysen's Steam Printing House, 1866).
23. "The Double-Headed Bohemian Wonder," *New York Clipper*, January 15, 1881.
24. "To Mr. Francis M. Uffner," *New York Clipper*, January 22, 1881.
25. See Martell, *Millie-Christine*, 223.
26. "The Complaint of Millie Christine."
27. "The Complaint of Millie Christine."
28. "Forepaugh's Fuss," *Fort Wayne Daily Gazette*, July 9, 1882.
29. "The Two Headed Girl: Begins Another Suit Against Adam Forepaugh for $25,000 — Offer of a Compromise on the Part of Forepaugh Indignantly Rejected," *Fort Wayne Sentinel*, December 14, 1882.
30. "Home News," *Fort Wayne Weekly Sentinel*, July 4, 1883.
31. "United States Court," *Fort Wayne Daily Gazette*, December 10, 1884.
32. Edmond Desbonnet, *Le Rois de La Force* (Libraire Berger-Levrault, 1911). This source was noted by Marilyn R. Brown in "Miss La La's Teeth: Reflections on Degas and 'Race,'" *Art Bulletin* 89, no. 4 (2007): 738–65.
33. "Olga et Kaira," *Lyon S'Amuse*, November 22, 1885.
34. Armand Silvestre, "Le Monde Des Artes," *La Vie Moderne*, April 1, 1879, 52–53.
35. Brown, "Miss La La's Teeth," *Art Bulletin*.
36. "Miss Millie Christine, The Famous Two-Headed Nightingale," folded handbill on yellow paper advertising Millie Christine, the Two-Headed Nightingale, and Harvey's Midges (smallest people in the world: Princess Lottie, Prince Midge, Miss Jennie Worgen and General Tot), appearing at the Piccadilly Hall, London, 17 February 1885, Wellcome Collection.
37. Martell, *Millie-Christine*, 262–63.

Chapter 9. The Splendor and Terror of Bearded Ladies

1. "Doom of the Old Tombs," *New York Times*, July 4, 1896.
2. "American Museum Playbill," July 5, 1852, playbill, THE AS TCS 65 Box 317, Harvard Theatre Collection, Houghton Library, Harvard University.
3. "American Museum Playbill," July 9, 1853, playbill, THE AS TCS 65 Box 317, Harvard Theatre Collection, Houghton Library, Harvard University.

4. Clofullia's entry into the Tombs is described in "A Rich Scene at the Tombs," *New-York Daily Tribune*, July 2, 1853.
5. Philip B. Kunhardt, Jr., Philip B. Kunhardt III, and Peter W. Kunhardt, *P. T. Barnum: America's Greatest Showman* (Knopf, 1995), 39.
6. "Playbill: Barnum's American Museum . . . Living Wonders," 1855, playbill, lateral file 4e, Harry Ransom Center, University of Texas at Austin.
7. George M. Gould and Walter L. Pyle, *Anomalies and Curiosities of Medicine* (London: Rebman, 1897).
8. "The Bearded Lady of Geneva," *Gleason's Pictorial Drawing-Room Companion*, April 23, 1853.
9. Rebecca M. Herzig, *Plucked: A History of Hair Removal* (New York University Press, 2015).
10. Kimberly A. Hamlin, "The 'Case of a Bearded Woman': Hypertrichosis and the Construction of Gender in the Age of Darwin," *American Quarterly* 63, no. 4 (2011): 955–81.
11. Charles Darwin, *The Descent of Man, and Selection in Relation to Sex* (John Murray, 1922).
12. Her pamphlet biography in the Harvard Theatre Collection says she was born in 1831, while the Circus Museum's 1854 version at The Ringling says 1829. Madame Clofullia's life story in this chapter draws on "Biography of the Celebrated Swiss Bearded Lady Madame Ghio, and Her Son Esau," 1855, Harvard Theatre Collection, Houghton Library, Harvard University.
13. "American Museum Playbill," July 9, 1853, playbill, THE AS TCS 65 Box 317, Harvard Theatre Collection, Houghton Library, Harvard University.
14. Clofullia's examination is detailed in three articles Chowne wrote for *The Lancet*: W. D. Chowne, "Remarkable Case of Hirsute Growth in a Female," *The Lancet* 59, no. 1496 (May 1852): 421–22; W. D. Chowne, "Remarkable Case of Hirsute Growth in a Female," *The Lancet* 59, no. 1500 (May 1852): 514–16; W. D. Chowne, "Remarkable Case of Hirsute Growth in a Female," *The Lancet* 60, no. 1507 (July 1852): 51–53.
15. "The Bearded Lady of Geneva," *Athens Post*, June 17, 1853; Frederick Drimmer, *Very Special People: The Struggles, Loves and Triumphs of Human Oddities* (Bantam Books, 1976), 115. Drimmer further notes that "Doubting Thomases were always appearing who asserted the bearded lady was not all that she was advertised to be. Showing the skeptics a row of medical certificates might now be as convincing as allowing them to pull her whiskers or examine her more intimately—but it was a lot easier on the bearded lady's dignity, not to mention her chin."
16. Sean Trainor, "Fair Bosom/Black Beard: Facial Hair, Gender Determination, and the Strange Career of Madame Clofullia, 'Bearded

Lady,'" *Early American Studies: An Interdisciplinary Journal* 12, no. 3 (2014): 548–75.
17. Pamphlet biographies include *Life and History of Madame Howard* (Dewsbury: Samuel Dawson and Son, n.d.); *Facts Relating to Madam De Vere, the Kentucky Bearded Lady* (New York: Popular, 1887); and *A Wide World Wonder. Madame Viola, the Bearded Lady* (New York: Damon & Peets, 1884). All from the Harvard Theatre Collection, Houghton Library, Harvard University. Another playbill at the Wellcome Collection describes Madame Howard as the "African Lion-Faced Lady," which has led to speculation that she was a Black performer. Howard's pamphlet describes her as being of English parentage, though, suggesting that the leonine references are tied to her wild origin myth: "I am a native of Sierre Leone, in South Africa. My father being an English soldier travelling that part of the country in company with my mother. On the journey my mother was attacked by Lions, and in endeavouring to save her life, my father was killed by those ferocious animals. My mother lived for only a short time after the death of my father, and I was left alone in a foreign land."
18. *History of Miss Annie Jones, Barnum's Esau Lady* (New York: Popular, 1885), National Library of Medicine; and *Admiral Dot the Smallest Man in the World and Annie Jones, the Bearded Girl*, 1873, Bridgeport History Center.
19. *Admiral Dot the Smallest Man in the World and Annie Jones, the Bearded Girl*.
20. George C. D. O'Dell, *Annals of the New York Stage, 1850–1857*, vol. 6 (Columbia University Press, 1931).
21. "The Hybrid or Semi-Human Indian," *New York Times*, December 19, 1854.
22. *Hybrid Indian, the Misnomered Bear Woman, Julia Pastrana* (Concord, NH: Steam Job Press of McFarland & Jenks, 1855), Beinecke Rare Book & Manuscript Library, Yale University.
23. "The Hybrid or Semi-Human Indian," *New York Times*; *Hybrid Indian, the Misnomered Bear Woman, Julia Pastrana*.
24. "Grand & Novel Attraction: Miss Julia Pastrana, the Nondescript," 1857, Wellcome Collection; "Account of Miss Pastrana, the Nondescript and the Double-Bodied Boy" (London: Hancock, n.d.); *Hybrid Indian, the Misnomered Bear Woman, Julia Pastrana*.
25. "Account of Miss Pastrana, the Nondescript and the Double-Bodied Boy."
26. See Nicolai Tulpii, *Observationaes Medicae*, 5th ed. (Lugduni Batavorum, 1716).
27. Jacobius Bontius, "Historiæ Naturalis & Medicæ: Liber Quintus: De Quadripedibus, Avibus & Piscibus," in *De Indiæ Utriusque Re Naturali et Medica* (repr., Elsevier, 2013), 50–86.

28. Odoardo Beccari, *Wanderings in the Great Forests of Borneo: Travels and Researches of a Naturalist in Sarawak* (Constable, 1904). Regarding Ota Benga, see Pamela Newkirk, *Spectacle: The Astonishing Life of Ota Benga* (Amistad, 2015).
29. Silvia Sebastiani, "A 'Monster with Human Visage': The Orangutan, Savagery, and the Borders of Humanity in the Global Enlightenment," *History of the Human Sciences* 32, no. 4 (2019): 80–99.
30. "Mazurier, rôle de Joko," 1826, lithograph, Jerome Robbins Dance Division, New York Public Library.
31. R. L. Stevenson, *Strange Case of Dr. Jekyll and Mr. Hyde* (London: Longmans, Green, 1886), 131.
32. Rosemarie Garland-Thomson, "Julia Pastrana, the 'Extraordinary Lady,'" *Alter* 11, no. 1 (2017): 35–49.
33. "Local and Miscellaneous," *Daily Ohio Statesman*, July 3, 1855; "Julia Pastrana in Costume (Print)," n.d., TCS 50 (Pastrana, Julia), Harvard Theatre Collection, Houghton Library, Harvard University.
34. Jan Bondeson, "The Strange Story of Julia Pastrana," in *A Cabinet of Medical Curiosities* (Cornell University Press, 1997).
35. "Account of Miss Pastrana, the Nondescript and the Double-Bodied Boy."
36. "Grand & Novel Attraction: Miss Julia Pastrana, the Nondescript."
37. "The Bear Woman," *National Police Gazette*, January 26, 1856.
38. "Trouble About a Hybrid," *American and Commercial Advertiser*, November 12, 1855.
39. "Untitled," *Bangor Daily Whig & Courier*, November 17, 1855.
40. "In the Matter of False Pretenses against Theodore Lent," *New York Herald*, March 15, 1853. In locating information about Lent and in researching Pastrana generally, I am in tremendous debt to Kathleen Godfrey's digital humanities project Julia Pastrana Online (http://juliapastranaonline.com).
41. See Jan Bondeson, "The Strange Story of Julia Pastrana," in *A Cabinet of Medical Curiosities* (Cornell University Press, 1997).
42. "Julia Pastrana and Her Child," *The Lancet* 79, no. 2018 (1862): 467–69. The article is a translation from Sokolov's Russian.
43. Drimmer, *Very Special People*.
44. "Fair Time Arrives in the Valley," *Columbus Ledger*, October 7, 1972; "Apollo Ride Debuts at Fair," *Anderson Daily Bulletin*, August 17, 1972.
45. Laura Anderson Barbata, *The Eye of the Beholder: Julia Pastrana's Long Journey Home* (Lucia Marquand, 2017).
46. "'Krao', the 'Missing Link': A Living Proof of Darwin's Theory of the Descent of Man," n.d., playbill, EPH499A, Wellcome Collection; "Krao - the Missing Link. The Half-Way Point in the Evolution of Man

From Ape," poster, Performing Arts Collection, Harry Ransom Center, University of Texas at Austin.
47. "A Rich Scene at the Tombs," *New York Tribune*, July 2, 1853.

Chapter 10. Ella Zoyara, the "Boy-Girl"

1. Arthur Hornblow, *A History of the Theatre in America*, vol. 2 (J. B. Lippincott, 1919).
2. "An Old New Yorker Dead: William Niblo, the Theater Manager," *New York Times*, August 22, 1878.
3. "Niblo's Garden," *The Ladies' Companion, a Monthly Magazine; Devoted to Literature and the Fine Arts*, August 1837.
4. "Niblo's Garden," *New York Times*, January 17, 1860.
5. "A Romance of the Circus," *Indianapolis Journal*, March 14, 1888.
6. "The Reopening at Niblo's," *New York Times*, January 17, 1860.
7. "A Phenomenon on Horseback," *New-York Daily Tribune*, January 27, 1860.
8. See E. T. Whitney, *Gen. Tom Thumb in His Different Characters*, ca. 1850s, and photo of Jacob Driesbach, Barnum Museum. Driesbach photos are also found in the collections of the Art Institute of Chicago and in Philip B. Kunhardt, Philip B. Kunhardt, Jr., and Peter W. Kunhardt, *P. T. Barnum: The World's Greatest Showman*.
9. "Death Record: Samuel Omar Kingsley," India, Select Deaths and Burials, 1719–1948, Ancestry.com.
10. "A World-Famous Fraud," *National Police Gazette*, June 7, 1879; see also "Kingsley, Omar / Ella Zoyara," n.d., clippings file, Thayer Manuscript Collection, Circus Museum, The Ringling.
11. "Only a Memory," *Kansas City Star*, October 15, 1884.
12. Thomas Cringle, *Ella Zoyara, the Beautiful: The Fairy of the Magic Ring* (Melbourne: Clarson, Massina, 1866).
13. "Only a Memory," *Kansas City Star*.
14. "Kingsley, Omar / Ella Zoyara."
15. Cringle, *Ella Zoyara*.
16. Susanna Forrest, "The Horsewomen of the Belle Époque," *Paris Review*, January 9, 2020, https://www.theparisreview.org/blog/2020/01/09/the-horsewomen-of-the-belle-epoque.
17. Though pamphlets are often embellished, this appears to be true. See summary of court proceedings in, e.g., "Court Calendar," *Boston Daily Advertiser*, December 3, 1861.
18. Cringle, *Ella Zoyara*.
19. "Only a Memory," *Kansas City Star*.
20. "Kingsley, Omar / Ella Zoyara." See also the Theater Royal, Drury Lane playbill dated June 20, 1857, at the Circus Museum, The Ringling.

21. "Niblo's Garden," *New-York Daily Tribune*, January 28, 1860.
22. "City Summary," *New York Clipper*, February 4, 1860.
23. "City Summary," *New York Clipper*, February 11, 1860.
24. "Lines to Zoyara," *Vanity Fair*, February 11, 1860.
25. "City Summary," *New York Clipper*, February 11, 1860.
26. "Nimrod Sketches No. 2," *New York Clipper*, February 25, 1860.
27. Tana Wojczuk, *Lady Romeo, The Radical and Revolutionary Life of Charlotte Cushman, America's First Celebrity* (Avid Reader Press, 2020).
28. Dane Barca, "Adah Isaacs Menken: Race and Transgendered Performance in the Nineteenth Century," *MELUS* 29, no. 3–4 (2004): 293.
29. Shauna Vey, "The Master and the Mademoiselle: Gender Secrets in Plain Sight in Antebellum Performance," *Theatre History Studies* 27 (2007): 39–59.
30. Marcy Murray, "Strong Women and Cross-Dressed Men: Representation of Gender by Circus Performers During the Golden Age of the American Circus, 1860–1930," *Bandwagon* 48, no. 3 (2004): 18–23.
31. Vern L. Bullough and Bonnie Bullough, *Cross Dressing, Sex, and Gender* (University of Pennsylvania Press, 1993).
32. W. F. Wallett, *The Public Life of W. F. Wallett, the Queen's Jester: An Autobiography*, ed. John Luntley (London: Bemrose & Sons, 1870).
33. "Dan Rice's Great Show. Sixth Appearance of M'le Ella Zoyara in Her Unparalleled Scene of Equitation. Saturday Afternoon, March 3, 1860 . . . Philadelphia US Steam-Power Job Printing Office, Ledger Building," 1860, broadsheet, OCLC no. rbpe15700200, Library of Congress.
34. "Philadelphia Melodeon / City Summary," *New York Clipper*, April 14, 1860.
35. *The Theatre: An Illustrated Weekly Magazine*, vol. 3 (New York: Theatre Publishing, 1888), 329.
36. "American Theatricals," *The Era* (London), September 16, 1860.
37. "Miscellaneous News," *New Haven Daily Palladium*, September 28, 1863; "A Circus Performer's Legal Residence: An Attachment Against Ella Zoyara: Supreme Court Chambers," *New York Times*, December 20, 1863.
38. Mark St. Leon, "Novel Routes: Circus in the Pacific, 1841–1941," *Popular Entertainment Studies* 5, no. 2 (2014): 24–47.
39. Mark St. Leon, "Novel Routes," 31.
40. "A World-Famous Fraud," *National Police Gazette*.
41. Clare Sears, *Arresting Dress: Cross-Dressing, Law, and Fascination in Nineteenth-Century San Francisco*, Perverse Modernities (Duke University Press, 2015).
42. Fanny Fern, "A Law More Nice than Just," *New York Ledger*, July 10, 1858.

43. "LAW," *The Empire* (Sydney), November 28, 1867.
44. "Great Sensation Case," *Bell's Life in Sydney and Sporting Chronicle*, November 30, 1867.
45. "Equestrianism," *Punch* (Sydney), March 3, 1866.
46. "Amusements in China," *The Era* (London), July 12, 1868.
47. "A World-Famous Fraud," *National Police Gazette*.
48. Henry G. Langley, ed., *The San Francisco Directory for the Year Commencing December, 1865* (San Francisco: Excelsior Steam Presses, 1865).
49. "Amusements in California," *The Era* (London), May 17, 1874.
50. "Omar Kingsley," *Mayborough Chronicle, Wide Bay and Burnett Advertiser*, August 30, 1879.
51. "Mummer Memoirs No. 138," *Sydney Sportsman*, October 26, 1910: "His second wife was Miss Corbyn, daughter of the late Sherry Corbyn, who brought the first company of Georgia Minstrels to Sydney in 1876, before Hicks arrived." Also quoted: "I remember Zoyara with Cooke, Zoyara, and Wilson's Circus. Zoyara posed as a woman, but he came out here later with, I think, 'The Great World Circus' in propia persona as Omar Kingley. He had his wife with him then. They were both fairly tall, and so much alike that they would easily pass for brother and sister. On his last visit Omar Kingley acted as ringmaster. He died, I believe, somewhere in the colonies, and the widow married Walter Hawkins, a female impersonator, with a beautiful soprano voice."
52. "Only a Memory," *Kansas City Star*.
53. "Mummer Memoirs No. 139," *Sydney Sportsman*, November 2, 1910.

Chapter 11. New Women Join the Circus

1. Kathy Lee Peiss, *Cheap Amusements: Working Women and Leisure in Turn-of-the-Century New York* (Temple University Press, 1986).
2. Martha H. Patterson, ed., *The American New Woman Revisited: A Reader, 1894–1930* (Rutgers University Press, 2008).
3. Patterson, *The American New Woman Revisited*, 1.
4. Mrs. Booker T. Washington, "The New Negro Woman," in *The American New Woman Revisited: A Reader, 1894–1930*, ed. Martha H. Patterson (Rutgers University Press, 2008).
5. Lydia Hamessley, "Within Sight: Three-Dimensional Perspectives on Women and Banjos in the Late Nineteenth Century," *19th-Century Music* 31, no. 2 (2007): 131–63.
6. Lena Wånggren, *Gender, Technology and the New Woman*, Edinburgh Critical Studies in Victorian Culture (Edinburgh University Press, 2017).
7. "British Butterflies," *Cycling: An Illustrated Weekly*, August 7, 1897.

8. *Die Barnum & Bailey Groesste Schaustellung Der Welt—Lustige Szenen Auf Bicycles Und Rollschuhen*, 1900, lithograph, Prints and Photographs Division, Library of Congress.
9. *The Barnum and Bailey Greatest Show on Earth—L'Auto Bolide Thrilling Dip of Death*, 1905, lithograph, Prints and Photographs Division, Library of Congress.
10. Hamessley, "Within Sight."
11. See Anthony Comstock, O. B. Frothingham, and J. M. Buckley, "The Suppression of Vice," *North American Review* 135, no. 312 (1882): 484–501; Mark Irwin West, "A Spectrum of Spectators: Circus Audiences in Nineteenth-Century America," *Journal of Social History* 15, no. 2 (1981): 265–70.
12. Davis, *The Circus Age*, 88.
13. Peter J. Miller, "The Imaginary Antiquity of Physical Culture," *Classical Outlook* 93, no. 1 (2018): 21–31.
14. "The Charge of the Light Brigade," *Werner's Magazine*, 1898; George M. Gould and Walter L. Pyle, *Anomalies and Curiosities of Medicine* (London: Rebman, 1897).
15. This paragraph, see Bieke Gils, "Flying, Flirting, and Flexing: Charmion's Trapeze Act, Sexuality, and Physical Culture at the Turn of the Twentieth Century," *Journal of Sport History* 41, no. 2 (2014): 251–68; and "The Drama," *Democrat and Chronicle*, March 20, 1904.
16. "Woman's Marvelous Power Over Lions," *St. Louis Post-Dispatch*, December 24, 1899.
17. "Acts Daniel in Lion's Den," *Anaconda Standard* (Montana), January 30, 1900.
18. In Ellen Velvin's book *Wild Animal Celebrities* (Moffat, Yard, 1907), she refers to the lion Heliot carried as "Yula," but Sicchi is mentioned in Peta Tait's research as well as Heliot's own *Cosmopolitan* diary. It also very well could have been that Heliot trained multiple animals over time to do this act.
19. "Is a Daring Lion Tamer," *Decatur Daily Herald*, November 11, 1905.
20. "Claire Heliot - Most Daring of Lion Tamers," *New York Times*, October 29, 1905.
21. "Strange Beauty: Barbette and the Art of Transformation," *Missouri Review* 44, no. 3 (2021): 73–81.
22. Francis Steegmuller, "An Angel, A Flower, A Bird," *New Yorker*, September 27, 1969.
23. "Strange Beauty," *Missouri Review*.
24. Steegmuller, "An Angel, A Flower, A Bird."
25. Kat Vecchio, "Miss Suffie's Debut: Circus and the Suffrage Movement," *Bandwagon* 64, no. 1 (2020): 8–15.

26. "Enlist Suffragists For A Circus Holiday," *New York Times*, April 1, 1912.

Conclusion. Taming Savage Beasts

1. "Donnybrook Fair: Was It All That Bad?," *Dublin Historical Record* 34, no. 3 (1981): 103–9.
2. "The Lion Queen," *Weekly Standard and Express*, September 2, 1846.
3. "Glasgow Fair," *Glasgow Herald*, July 18, 1845.
4. William L. Slout, *Olympians of the Sawdust Circle: A Biographical Dictionary of the Nineteenth Century American Circus*, Clipper Studies in the Theatre, no. 18 (Borgo Press, 1998).
5. "Thrilling Incident at the Menagerie," *Camden Journal*, November 8, 1848.
6. Stuart Thayer, *The Performers: A History of Circus Acts* (Dauven & Thayer, 2005), 132. See also William L. Slout, *Olympians of the Sawdust Circle* (Borgo Press, 1998), for information on the Carroll family and the suggestion that young Marie was the girl in question.
7. "Zoological Institute," *Public Ledger* (Philadelphia), February 15, 1848.
8. Charles Dickens, *The Letters of Charles Dickens*, ed. Georgina Hogarth and Mamie Dickens (London: Chapman & Hall, 1882), 194–95.
9. Claire Heliot, "Diary of a Lion-Tamer," *Cosmopolitan: A Monthly Illustrated Magazine*, September 1906.
10. "Why it is Harder to Tame a Husband than a Lion," *Chicago Tribune*, April 1, 1906, p. 83.
11. "A Tit-Bits' Representative Enters a Lion's Den," *Grey River Argus*, January 8, 1897.
12. "Lions at the Aquarium," *Illustrated London News*, August 15, 1896; "The Lioness and Her Cubs at the Aquarium," *The Sketch: A Journal of Art and Actuality*, August 18, 1896.
13. "Royal Aquarium," *Daily Telegraph*, August 19, 1896; "Advertisements & Notices," *The Graphic*, October 10, 1896.
14. "Folies Bergère: La Comtesse de X et Ses Lions," *Le Petit Journal*, May 19, 1895.
15. "Royal Aquarium," *Financial Times*, August 10, 1896.
16. The circus scholar Steve Ward has written about Maccomo, a Black man who performed big-cat acts in the late 1800s, and there are a small number of images showing unidentified Black women with menagerie animals. See Steve Ward, "Martini Maccomo, the African Lion King," *Journal of Victorian Culture Online*, https://jvc.oup.com/2021/06/11/martini-maccomo-the-african-lion-king; "A Brilliant Star Will Appear," *Berrow's Worcester Journal*, June 26, 1869, p. 5.

17. Peta Tait, "Performed Identities as Circus Illusions," in *The American Circus* (Bard Graduate Center: Decorative Arts, Design History, Material Culture; Yale University Press, 2012).
18. "The Most Daring Man in All Europe to the Most Daring Woman in America," *San Francisco Examiner*, November 10, 1901.
19. "Mrs. Taylor Over the Falls and Is Living!," *The Buffalo Times*, October 25, 1901.
20. "A Female Blondin," *Selma Morning Times*, July 21, 1876.
21. See "The Most Daring Man in All Europe to the Most Daring Woman in America," *San Francisco Examiner*, and Annie Edson Taylor, *Over The Falls: Annie Edson Taylor's Story of Her Trip* (Mrs. Annie Edson Taylor, 1902).
22. Harry Houdini, *Miracle Mongers and Their Methods* (E. P. Dutton, 1920).

BIBLIOGRAPHY

This bibliography lists the primary writings and archival collections referenced in this book. The survey of archival collections is meant to introduce readers to the range of repositories that preserve the history of the American circus. The selected bibliography of secondary sources is intended to serve as an introduction to scholarly writings on the circus and nineteenth-century America.

ARCHIVAL COLLECTIONS

Barnum Museum, Bridgeport, CT
Beinecke Rare Book and Manuscript Library, Yale University
Bodleian Library, Royal Archives, Windsor, UK
Bridgeport History Center, Bridgeport, CT
Conjuring Arts Library, New York
Hargrett Rare Book and Manuscript Library at the University of
    Georgia Libraries
Harry Ransom Center, University of Texas at Austin
Harvard Theatre Collection, Houghton Library, Harvard University
The John and Mable Ringling Museum of Art, Sarasota, FL
   Thayer Manuscript Collection
   Tibbals Learning Center and Circus Museum
Library of Congress
   General Collections
   Prints and Photographs Division
National Archives, Washington, DC

New York Public Library
  Digital Collections
  Jerome Robbins Dance Division
  Miriam and Ira D. Wallach Division of Art, Prints and
    Photographs: Photography Collection
Wellcome Collection, London, UK

SECONDARY SOURCES

"Account of Miss Pastrana, the Nondescript and the Double-Bodied Boy." London: Hancock, ca. 1860.

Adams, Bluford. "'A Stupendous Mirror of Departed Empires': The Barnum Hippodromes and Circuses, 1874–1891." *American Literary History* 8, no. 1 (1996): 34–56.

Alger, Jr., Horatio. *Ragged Dick and Struggling Upward*. Penguin Books, 1985.

Allen, Robert Clyde. *Horrible Prettiness: Burlesque and American Culture*. Cultural Studies of the United States. University of North Carolina Press, 1991.

Anbinder, Tyler. *Five Points: The 19th-Century New York City Neighborhood That Invented Tap Dance, Stole Elections, and Became the World's Most Notorious Slum*. Plume, 2002.

Ancestry.com. Death Record: Samuel Omar Kingsley. India Deaths and Burials, 1719–1948.

Andersen, Kurt. *Fantasyland: How America Went Haywire: A 500-Year History*. Random House, 2017.

Anderson Barbata, Laura. *The Eye of the Beholder: Julia Pastrana's Long Journey Home*. Lucia Marquand, 2017.

Arnold, Richard A., ed. *Route of P. T. Barnum's Great Traveling Exposition and World's Fair through the Principal Cities and Towns in the U.S. Season of 1872*. Chicago: J. S. Thompson, 1872.

Ashby, LeRoy. *With Amusement for All: A History of American Popular Culture since 1830*. University Press of Kentucky, 2012.

Auerbach, Jeffrey A. "What They Read: Mid-Nineteenth Century English Women's Magazines and the Emergence of a

Consumer Culture." *Victorian Periodicals Review* 30, no. 2 (1997): 121–40.
Ballantyne, J. W. "Teratogenesis: An Inquiry into the Causes of Monstrosities." *Edinburgh Medical Journal* 42, no. 3 (1896): 240–55.
Barca, Dane. "Adah Isaacs Menken: Race and Transgendered Performance in the Nineteenth Century." *MELUS* 29, no. 3–4 (2004): 293–306.
Barker, Barbara. "Imre Kiralfy's Patriotic Spectacles: 'Columbus, and the Discovery of America' (1892–1893) and 'America' (1893)." *Dance Chronicle* 17, no. 2 (1994): 149–78.
Barnum, Phineas Taylor. *Humbugs of the World*. London: John Camden Hotten, 1866.
Barnum, Phineas Taylor. Letter to John Greenwood. May 14, 1864. Lost Museum Archive. https://lostmuseum.cuny.edu/archive/letter-from-p-t-barnum-to-john-greenwood.
Barnum, Phineas Taylor. "P. T. Barnum's Speech on 'Negro Suffrage,'" May 26, 1865. Lost Museum Archive. https://lostmuseum.cuny.edu/archive/p-t-barnums-speech-on-negro-suffrage-may-26-1.
Barnum, Phineas Taylor. *Struggles and Triumphs; or Forty Years' Recollections of P. T. Barnum*. Buffalo: Warren, Johnson, 1872.
Barnum, Phineas Taylor. *Struggles and Triumphs; or Forty Years' Recollections of P. T. Barnum*. Rev. ed. Buffalo: Warren, Johnson, 1873.
Bartlett, John Russell. *Dictionary of Americanisms*. Boston: Little, Brown, 1859.
Beccari, Odoardo. *Wanderings in the Great Forests of Borneo: Travels and Researches of a Naturalist in Sarawak*. Constable, 1904.
Becker, Jeffrey A. "The Ambition of Popular Control: Jacksonian Democracy and American Populism." In *Ambition in America: Political Power and the Collapse of Citizenship*. University Press of Kentucky, 2014.
Benedict, Barbara. *Curiosity: A Cultural History of Early Modern Inquiry*. University of Chicago Press, 2001.

Betancourt, Alvaro. *Route Book of P. T. Barnum's Greatest Show on Earth and the Great London Circus Since the Consolidation Seasons of 1881, 1882, 1883, 1884, & 1885.* 1885.

Betts, Raymond F., and Lyz Bly. *A History of Popular Culture: More of Everything, Faster and Brighter.* 2nd ed. Routledge, 2013.

"Biographical Sketch of Millie Christine, the Carolina Twin." Hennegen, n.d., ca. 1902–1912.

Blumenbach, Johann Friedrich. *The Anthropological Treatises of Johann Friedrich Blumenbach.* London: Longman, Roberts, & Green, 1865.

Bogdan, Robert. *Freak Show: Presenting Human Oddities for Amusement and Profit.* University of Chicago Press, 1990.

Bondeson, Jan. *A Cabinet of Medical Curiosities.* Cornell University Press, 1997.

Bontius, Jacobius. "Historiæ Naturalis & Medicæ: Liber Quintus: De Quadripedibus, Avibus & Piscibus." In *De Indiæ Utriusque Re Naturali et Medica.* Reprinted by Elsevier B.V., 2013. Originally published in 1648.

Braid, James. *Magic, Witchcraft, Animal Magnetism, Hypnotism and Electro-Biology: Being a Digest of the Latest Views of the Author on These Subjects.* London: John Churchill, 1852.

Braude, Ann. *Radical Spirits: Spiritualism and Women's Rights in Nineteenth-Century America.* 2nd ed. Indiana University Press, 2001.

Brown, Marilyn R. "Miss La La's Teeth: Reflections on Degas and 'Race.'" *Art Bulletin* 89, no. 4 (2007): 738–65.

Buckley, Matthew S. "Refugee Theatre: Melodrama and Modernity's Loss." *Theatre Journal* 61, no. 2 (2009): 175–90.

Bullough, Vern L., and Bonnie Bullough. *Cross Dressing, Sex, and Gender.* University of Pennsylvania Press, 1993.

Butler, Jon, Grant Wacker, and Randall Herbert Balmer. *Religion in American Life: A Short History.* 2nd ed. Oxford University Press, 2011.

Butler, Judith. "Foucault and the Paradox of Bodily Inscriptions." *The Journal of Philosophy* 86, no. 11 (1989): 601–7.

Butler, Judith. "Performative Acts and Gender Constitution: An Essay in Phenomenology and Feminist Theory." *Theatre Journal* 40, no. 4 (1988): 519–31.

Carlisle, Anthony. "An Account of a Family Having Hands and Feet with Supernumerary Fingers and Toes." *Philosophical Transactions of the Royal Society of London* 104 (1814): 94–101.

Carlyon, David. *Dan Rice: The Most Famous Man You've Never Heard Of.* Public Affairs, 2001.

Carlyon, David. "'Soft and Silky Around Her Hips': Nineteenth-Century Circus and Sex." *Journal of American Drama and Theater* 22, no. 2 (2010): 25–47, 107.

Chandler, H. S. "Miracles of the Past: The Invisible Girl." *Magicana*, October 1981. CA Id 22419. Conjuring Arts Library.

Childress, Micah. "Life Beyond the Big Top: African American and Female Circusfolk, 1860–1920." *Journal of the Gilded Age and Progressive Era* 15, no. 2 (2016): 176–96.

Chowne, W. D. "Remarkable Case of Hirsute Growth in a Female; With Observations on Certain Organic Structures and their Physiological Influences." *The Lancet* 59, no. 1496 (1852): 421–22.

Chowne, W. D. "Remarkable Case of Hirsute Growth in a Female; With Observations on Certain Organic Structures and their Physiological Influences." *The Lancet* 59, no. 1500 (1852): 514–16.

Chowne, W. D. "Remarkable Case of Hirsute Growth in a Female; With Observations on Certain Organic Structures and their Physiological Influences." *The Lancet* 60, no. 1507 (1852): 51–53.

Circus Annual: A Route Book of Ringling Brothers World's Greatest Shows Season 1902. Central Engraving & Publishing, 1902.

Circus Girl and Sunday-School Scholar. Philadelphia: American Sunday School Union, 1860.

Clair, Jean, Galeries nationales du Grand Palais (France), and National Gallery of Canada, eds. *The Great Parade: Portrait of the Artist as Clown*. Yale University Press; National Gallery of Canada, 2004.

Clarke, Sidney W. *The Annals of Conjuring*. The Miracle Factory, 2001.
Claudet, M. "No. VIII. The Progress and Present State of the Daguerreotype Art." *Transactions of the Society, Instituted at London, for the Encouragement of Arts, Manufactures, and Commerce* 55 (1843): 89–110.
Cliff, Nigel. *The Shakespeare Riots: Revenge, Drama, and Death in Nineteenth-Century America*. Random House, 2007.
Cogan, Frances B. *All American Girl: The Ideal of Real Womanhood in Mid-Nineteenth Century America*. University of Georgia Press, 1989.
Comstock, Anthony, O. B. Frothingham, and J. M. Buckley. "The Suppression of Vice." *The North American Review* 135, no. 312 (1882): 484–501.
Conklin, George, and Harvey W. Root. *The Ways of the Circus: Being the Memories and Adventures of George Conklin, Tamer of Lions*. Harper & Brothers, 1921.
Connor, Steven. "Talking Heads, Automaton Ears." In *Dumbstruck: A Cultural History of Ventriloquism*. Oxford University Press, 2000.
Cringle, Tom. *Ella Zoyara, the Beautiful: The Fairy of the Magic Ring*. Melbourne: Clarson, Massina, 1866.
Croly, David. *Miscegenation: The Theory of the Blending of the Races, Applied to the American White Man and Negro*. New York: H. Dexter, Hamilton, 1864.
Crowley, W. G., ed. *The Australian Tour of Cooper, Bailey, & Co.'s Great International Allied Shows 187*. Brisbane: Thorne & Greenwell, 1877.
Cummings, E. E. "The Adult, the Artist and the Circus." *Vanity Fair*, October 1925.
Dahlinger, Fred. "The American Circus Tent." In *The American Circus*, edited by Susan Weber, Kenneth L. Ames, and Matthew Wittmann. Bard Graduate Center; Yale University Press, 2012.
Dahlinger, Fred, Jr., "A Short Analysis of Steam Calliope History Before 1900," *Bandwagon* 17, no. 6 (1972): 25–27.

Darwin, Charles. *The Descent of Man, and Selection in Relation to Sex.* John Murray, 1922.
Davis, Janet M. *The Circus Age: Culture & Society under the American Big Top.* University of North Carolina Press, 2002.
Davis, Janet M. "The Circus Americanized." In *The American Circus*, edited by Susan Weber, Kenneth L. Ames, and Matthew Wittmann. Bard Graduate Center: Decorative Arts, Design History, Material Culture; Yale University Press, 2012.
Dennett, Andrea Stulman. *Weird and Wonderful: The Dime Museum in America.* New York University Press, 1997.
Desbonnet, Edmond. *Le Rois de La Force.* Libraire Berger-Levrault, 1911.
Dickens, Charles. *The Letters of Charles Dickens.* Vol. 1, *1833 to 1855*, edited by Mamie Dickens and Georgina Hogarth. London: Chapman & Hall, 1882.
Dickens, Charles. *Sketches by Boz.* Chapman & Hall, 1913.
Disher, M. Willson. *Blood and Thunder: Mid-Victorian Melodrama and Its Origins.* Haskell House Publishers, 1974.
Dobrow, Joe. *Pioneers of Promotion: How Press Agents for Buffalo Bill, P. T. Barnum, and the World's Columbian Exposition Created Modern Marketing.* William F. Cody Series on the History and Culture of the American West. University of Oklahoma Press, 2018.
"Donnybrook Fair: Was It All That Bad?" *Dublin Historical Record* 34, no. 3 (1981): 103–9.
Drewal, Henry John. "Beauteous Beast: The Water Deity Mami Wata in Africa." In *The Ashgate Research Companion to Monsters and the Monstrous*, edited by Asa Simon Mittman and Peter Dendle. Routledge, 2012.
Drewal, Henry John. *Mami Wata: Arts for Water Spirits in Africa and Its Diasporas.* Fowler Museum at UCLA, 2008.
Drimmer, Frederick. *Very Special People: The Struggles, Loves and Triumphs of Human Oddities.* Bantam Books, 1976.
Ellis, R. J., and Henry Louis Gates. "'Grievances at the Treatment She Received': Harriet E. Wilson's Spiritualist Career in Boston, 1868–1900." *American Literary History* 24, no. 2 (2012): 234–64.

Everett, Shaun. "The British Lion Queens: A History." Published by the author, 2013. http://www.georgewombwell.com/articles/TheLionQueens.pdf.

Family Search. "United States Census, 1900." Entry for Robert G. Austin and Rose E. Austin, 1900. https://www.familysearch.org/ark:/61903/1:1:MSNR-HSR.

Family Search. "United States Census, 1920." Entry for Robert G. Austin and Rose E. Austin, 1920. https://www.familysearch.org/ark:/61903/1:1:MHQJ-7SS.

Farini, G. A. *Through the Kalahari Desert: A Journey to Lake N'gami and Back.* London: S. Low, Marston, Searle, & Rivington, 1886.

Fausto-Sterling, Anne. *Myths of Gender: Biological Theories About Women and Men.* 2nd ed. Basic Books, 1992.

Fisher, George J. *Diploteratology.* Albany: Van Benthuysen's Steam Printing House, 1866.

Flint, Richard. "American Showmen and European Dealers: Commerce in Wild Animals in Nineteenth-Century America." In *New Worlds, New Animals: From Menagerie to Zoological Park in the Nineteenth Century*, edited by R. J. Hoage and William A. Deiss. Johns Hopkins University Press, 1996.

Foner, Eric. *The Second Founding: How the Civil War and Reconstruction Remade the Constitution.* W. W. Norton and Company, 2019.

Forbes, Erin E. "Do Black Ghosts Matter?: Harriet Jacobs' Spiritualism." *ESQ: A Journal of Nineteenth-Century American Literature and Culture* 62, no. 3 (2016): 443–79.

Foucault, Michel, and Jay Miskowiec. "Of Other Spaces." *Diacritics* 16, no. 1 (1986): 22–27.

Frost, Linda. "The Circassian Beauty and the Circassian Slave: Gender, Imperialism, and American Popular Entertainment." In *Freakery*, edited by Rosemarie Garland-Thomson. New York University Press, 1996.

Frost, Linda. *Never One Nation: Freaks, Savages, and Whiteness in U.S. Popular Culture, 1850–1877.* University of Minnesota Press, 2005.

Frost, Thomas. *Circus Life and Circus Celebrities*. London: Chatto & Windus, 1881.

Frost, Thomas. *Lives of the Conjurors*. London: Tinsley Brothers, 1875.

Frost, Thomas. *The Old Showmen and the Old London Fairs*. 2nd ed. London: Tinsley Brothers, 1875.

Gallagher, Winifred. *New Women in the Old West: From Settlers to Suffragists, an Untold American Story*. Penguin Press, 2022.

Garland-Thomson, Rosemarie. "Feminist Disability Studies." *Signs* 30, no. 2 (2005): 1557–87.

Garland-Thomson, Rosemarie. "Julia Pastrana, the 'Extraordinary Lady.'" *Alter* 11, no. 1 (2017): 35–49.

Garland-Thomson, Rosemarie. *Staring: How We Look*. Oxford University Press, 2009.

Gils, Bieke. "Flying, Flirting, and Flexing: Charmion's Trapeze Act, Sexuality, and Physical Culture at the Turn of the Twentieth Century." *Journal of Sport History* 41, no. 2 (2014): 251–68.

Gould, George M., and Walter L. Pyle. *Anomalies and Curiosities of Medicine*. London: Rebman, 1897.

Gould, Stephen Jay. *The Mismeasure of Man*. Rev. and exp. W. W. Norton, 1996.

Green, Timothy, ed. *Acts and Laws of the State of Connecticut, in America*. Hartford: Hudson and Godwin, 1784.

Greenberg, Amy S. *Manifest Destiny and American Territorial Expansion: A Brief History with Documents*. 2nd ed. The Bedford Series in History and Culture. Bedford/St. Martin's; Macmillan Learning, 2018.

Hagenbeck, Carl. *Beasts & Men: Being Experiences for Half a Century among Wild Animals*. Longmans, 1910.

Hagenbeck, Carl. *Von Tieren Und Menschen*. Vita deutsches Verlagshaus, 1909.

Haines, Michael. *The Population of the United States, 1790–1920*. National Bureau of Economic Research, 1994. https://doi.org/10.3386/h0056.

Halen, Don Juan van. *Narrative of Don Juan van Halen's Imprisonment in the Dungeons of the Inquisition at Madrid, and His Escape in 1817 and 1818; to Which Are Added, His Journey to

Russia, His Campaign with the Army of the Caucasus, and His Return to Spain in 1821. London: H. Colburn, 1827.

Hamessley, Lydia. "Within Sight: Three-Dimensional Perspectives on Women and Banjos in the Late Nineteenth Century." *19th-Century Music* 31, no. 2 (2007): 131–63.

Hamlin, Kimberly A. "The 'Case of a Bearded Woman': Hypertrichosis and the Construction of Gender in the Age of Darwin." *American Quarterly* 63, no. 4 (2011): 955–81.

Hardinge, Emma. *Modern American Spiritualism: Twenty Years' Record of the Communion Between Earth and the World of Spirits*. New York: Published by the author, 1870.

Harrington, Henry F. "Female Education." *The Ladies' Companion, a Monthly Magazine; Devoted to Literature and the Fine Arts*, 1838.

Harrington, Hugh T., and Susan J. Harrington. "Georgia's Dixie Haygood: The Original Annie Abbott and 'Little Georgia Magnet.'" *Georgia Historical Quarterly* 86, no. 3 (2002): 423–48.

Harris, Neil. *Humbug: The Art of P. T. Barnum*. Phoenix ed. University of Chicago Press, 1981.

Herrmann, Adelaide. *Adelaide Herrmann, Queen of Magic: Memoirs, Published Writings, Collected Ephemera*. Edited by Margaret Steele. Bramble Books, 2012.

Herzig, Rebecca M. *Plucked: A History of Hair Removal*. New York University Press, 2015.

Hirsch, Robert. *Seizing the Light: A Social & Aesthetic History of Photography*. 3rd ed. Routledge, Taylor & Francis Group, 2017.

"History and Medical Description of the Two-Headed Girl." Buffalo: Warren, Johnson, 1869.

"History of Miss Annie Jones, Barnum's Esau Lady." New York: Popular, 1885.

Hobson, Janell. *Venus in the Dark: Blackness and Beauty in Popular Culture*. 2nd ed. Routledge, Taylor & Francis Group, 2018.

Hocus Pocus Junior: The Anatomie of Ledgerdemain, or, The Art of Juggling set forth in his proper colours, fully, plainly, and exactly, so that an ignorant person may thereby learn the full perfection of the same, after a little practice: Unto each Tricke is added the figure, where it is needfull for instruction. London: T. H. for R. M. 1635.

Hornblow, Arthur. *A History of the Theatre in America: From Its Beginnings to the Present Time.* Vol. 2. J. B. Lippincott, 1919.

Horowitz, Helen Lefkowitz. *Attitudes toward Sex in Antebellum America: A Brief History with Documents.* The Bedford Series in History and Culture. Bedford/St. Martin's, 2006.

Houdini, Harry. *Miracle Mongers and Their Methods.* E. P. Dutton, 1920.

Huang, Minhua. "The 'Hundred Entertainments': China's 2,000-Year-Old Tradition of Acrobatics." *UNESCO Courier* 41, no. 1 (1988): 8–9.

Hybrid Indian, the Misnomered Bear Woman, Julia Pastrana. Concord, NH: Steam Job Press of McFarland & Jenks, 1855.

Illustrated News. "Uncle Tom's Cabin at Barnum's Museum." November 26, 1853. https://lostmuseum.cuny.edu/archive/uncle-toms-cabin-at-barnums-museum.

Irving, Washington. *Diedrich Knickerbocker's History of New-York.* Heritage Press, 1940.

Jacobs, Harriet. *The Deeper Wrong; or, Incidents in the Life of a Slave Girl.* London: W. Tweedie, 1862.

James, John Angell. *Female Piety: Or, The Young Woman's Friend and Guide Through Life to Immortality.* New York: Robert Carter & Brothers, 1853.

Jando, Dominique. *Philip Astley & the Horsemen Who Invented the Circus: 1768–1814.* Circopedia, 2018.

Jay, Ricky. *Celebrations of Curious Characters.* McSweeney's Books, 2011.

Jay, Ricky. *Extraordinary Exhibitions: The Wonderful Remains of an Enormous Head, the Whimsiphusicon, & Death to the Savage Unitarians.* Quantuck Lane Press, 2005.

Jay, Ricky. "The Gnome Fly." *Jay's Journal of Anomalies* 3, no. 3 (1997).

Jay, Ricky. *Many Mysteries Unravelled: Or, Conjuring Literature in America, 1786–1874.* American Antiquarian Society, 1990.

"John Palmer, 29, Marries Mathilde Marie Emilie Poupon, 24, in Walworth, Surrey." #177, April 20, 1886, London Metropolitan Archives; London, England; London Church of England Parish Registers; Reference Number: P92/JN/025 (via Ancestry.com), n.d., ancestry.com.

Johnson, Claudia D. "That Guilty Third Tier: Prostitution in Nineteenth-Century American Theaters." *American Quarterly* 27, no. 5 (1975): 575–84.

Johnson, Paul E. *Sam Patch, the Famous Jumper*. Hill and Wang, 2004.

"Julia Pastrana and Her Child." *The Lancet* 79, no. 2018 (1862): 467–69.

Kenny, Kevin. *The Problem of Immigration in a Slaveholding Republic: Policing Mobility in the Nineteenth-Century United States*. Oxford University Press, 2023.

King James I. *Daemonologie*. John Lane; E. P. Dutton, 1924. Originally published in 1597.

Kotar, S. L., and J. E. Gessler. *The Rise of the American Circus, 1716–1899*. McFarland, 2011.

Kraditor, Aileen, ed. *Up From the Pedestal: Selected Writings in the History of Feminism*. Quadrangle Books, 1968.

Kunhardt, Jr., Philip B., Philip B. Kunhardt III, and Peter W. Kunhardt. *P. T. Barnum: America's Greatest Showman*. Knopf, 1995.

Lady's Book. Vol. 10–11. Philadelphia: Louis A. Godey, 1835.

LaFleur, Greta, Masha Raskolnikov, and Anna Kłosowska, eds. *Trans Historical: Gender Plurality Before the Modern*. Cornell University Press, 2021.

Lamar, Howard Roberts. *The Far Southwest, 1846–1912: A Territorial History*. Rev. ed. University of New Mexico Press, 2000.

Langley, Henry G., ed. *The San Francisco Directory for the Year Commencing December, 1865*. San Francisco: Excelsior Steam Presses, 1865.

Larner, Christina. *Witchcraft and Religion: The Politics of Popular Belief*. Basil Blackwell, 1984.

Leak, Ann. *The Autobiography of Miss Ann E. Leak, Born without Arms; Containing an Interesting Account of Her Early Life and Subsequent Travels in the United States and Australia.* Melbourne: Azzopardi, Hildreth, 1867.

Lee, R. J. "Maternal Impressions." *The British Medical Journal* 1, no. 736 (1875): 167–69.

Lehman, Eric D. *Becoming Tom Thumb: Charles Stratton, P. T. Barnum, and the Dawn of American Celebrity.* The Driftless Connecticut Series. Wesleyan University Press, 2013.

Leonard, Thomas C. *News for All: America's Coming-of-Age with the Press.* Oxford University Press, 1995.

Lerner, Gerda. "The Lady and the Mill Girl: Changes in the Status of Women in the Age of Jackson." *American Studies* 10, no. 1 (1969): 5–15, back cover.

"Lions and Lion-Taming." *Every Saturday: A Journal of Choice Reading* 1, no. 7 (1872): 173–76.

Locke, Richard Adams, and J. N. (Joseph Nicolas) Nicollet. *The Moon Hoax; or, A Discovery That the Moon Has a Vast Population of Human Beings.* New York: W. Gowans, 1859.

Lockwood, John, and Charles Lockwood. "First South Carolina. Then New York?" *New York Times*, January 6, 2011. https://archive.nytimes.com/opinionator.blogs.nytimes.com/2011/01/06/first-south-carolina-then-new-york/.

Lorber, Judith. "Shifting Paradigms and Challenging Categories." *Social Problems* 53, no. 4 (2006): 448–53.

Lorde, Audre. "Age, Race, Class, and Sex: Women Redefining Difference." In *Sister Outsider: Essays and Speeches.* Crossing Press, 1984.

Lulu Hurst (The Georgia Wonder) Writes Her Autobiography. Rome, Georgia: Lulu Hurst Book Co, 1897.

Magri, M. Lavinia. *The Autobiography of Mrs. Tom Thumb (Some of My Life Experiences).* Edited by A. H. Saxon. Archon Books, 1979.

Marriage Certificate of Charles Stratton (General Tom Thumb) to Mercy Lavinia Warren Bump (Lavinia Warren). February 10, 1863. Collection of the Barnum Museum.

Martell, Joanne. *Millie-Christine: Fearfully and Wonderfully Made.* John F. Blair, 2000.
Martin, Charles D. *The White African American Body: A Cultural and Literary Exploration.* Rutgers University Press, 2002.
Maskelyne, John Nevil. *Automata.* Magic Circle Foundation, 1989.
Mayer, Joe. *Barnum and Bailey Show Route Book Season of 1888.* C. Lloyd & Joe Mayer, 1888.
Middleton, George. *Circus Memoirs: Reminiscences of George Middleton as Told to and Written by His Wife.* G. Rice and Sons, 1913.
Miller, Peter J. "The Imaginary Antiquity of Physical Culture." *The Classical Outlook* 93, no. 1 (2018): 21–31.
Milman, Rev. Henry Hart. *Nala and Damayanti and Other Poems.* Oxford: D. A. Talboys, 1835.
Moore, R. Laurence. "The Spiritualist Medium: A Study of Female Professionalism in Victorian America." *American Quarterly* 27, no. 2 (1975): 200–221.
Mounsey, Chris. "Speaking Forwards in History." In *The Variable Body in History*, vol. 6, edited by Chris Mounsey and Stan Booth. Queering Paradigms. Peter Lang, 2016.
Mrs. Harvey. *Turkish Harems and Circassian Homes.* London: Hurst & Blackett, 1871.
Murray, Marcy. "Strong Women and Cross-Dressed Men: Representation of Gender by Circus Performers During the Golden Age of the American Circus, 1860–1930." *Bandwagon* 48, no. 3 (2004): 18–23.
Newcomb, S. "The Georgia Wonder-Girl and Her Lessons." *Science* 5 (June 1885): 106–8.
Newkirk, Pamela. *Spectacle: The Astonishing Life of Ota Benga.* Amistad, 2015.
O'Dell, George C. D. *Annals of the New York Stage, 1850–1857.* Vol. 6. Columbia University Press, 1931.
Ogden, Emily. *Credulity: A Cultural History of US Mesmerism.* Class 200: New Studies in Religion. University of Chicago Press, 2018.
Osterud, Amelia. "The True Life and Adventures of Tattooed Performers: Tattoos, Captivity Narratives and Popular

Culture." In *Tattoo Histories: Transcultural Perspectives on the Narratives, Practices, and Representations of Tattooing*, edited by Sinah Theres Kloß. Routledge, 2019.

Pandora, Katherine. "Popular Science in National and Transnational Perspective: Suggestions from the American Context." *Isis* 100, no. 2 (2009): 346–58.

Paré, Ambroise. *On Monsters and Marvels*. Translated by Janis L. Pallister. University of Chicago Press, 1982.

Parkin, Andrew, ed. *Selected Plays of Dion Boucicault*. Catholic University of America Press, 1987.

Patmore, Coventry. *The Angel in the House*. Edited by Henry Morley. London, Paris & Melbourne: Cassell, 1891.

Patterson, Martha H., ed. *The American New Woman Revisited: A Reader, 1894–1930*. Rutgers University Press, 2008.

Paul, Heike. "Expressive Individualism and the Myth of the Self-Made Man." In vol. 1 of *The Myths That Made America: An Introduction to American Studies*. Transcript Verlag, 2014.

Peiss, Kathy Lee. *Cheap Amusements: Working Women and Leisure in Turn-of-the-Century New York*. Temple University Press, 1986.

Peters, Arthur King. *Seven Trails West*. Abbeville Press Publishers, 1996.

Plato. *The Republic of Plato*. 3rd ed. Translated by Benjamin Jowett. Oxford: Clarendon Press, 1888.

Popova, Maria. "'Venus with Biceps': A History of Muscular Women, in Pictures." *The Atlantic*, November 24, 2011. https://www.theatlantic.com/entertainment/archive/2011/11/venus-with-biceps-a-history-of-muscular-women-in-pictures/248820/.

Pratt, Julius W. "The Origin of 'Manifest Destiny.'" *The American Historical Review* 32, no. 4 (1927): 795–98.

Reynolds, David S. "Lincoln Walks a Tightrope." *American Heritage* 67, no. 2 (2022): 1–8.

Ringling Bros and Barnum & Bailey Combined Shows Route, Personnel and Statistics for the Season of 1952. Ringling Brothers and Barnum & Bailey, 1952.

Robinson, Ben. *Twelve Have Died: Bullet Catching—the Story & Secrets*. Ray Goulet's Magic Art Book Co., 1986.

Rogers, Kory W. "On the Covers." *Bandwagon* 60, no. 2 (2016): 5.

Rouse, Wendy. "The Very Queer History of the Suffrage Movement." *National Park Service* (blog), n.d. https://www.nps.gov/articles/000/the-very-queer-history-of-the-suffrage-movement.htm.

Route Book of the Great Forepaugh Show, Circus, Hippodrome and Menagerie Season 1883. Silbons, 1883.

Russett, Cynthia Eagle. *Sexual Science: The Victorian Construction of Womanhood*. Harvard University Press, 1991.

Samuels, Ellen. "Examining Millie and Christine McKoy: Where Enslavement and Enfreakment Meet." *Signs* 37, no. 1 (2011): 53–81.

Saxon, A. H. "P. T. Barnum and the American Museum." *The Wilson Quarterly* 13, no. 4 (1989): 130–39.

Saxon, A. H. *P. T. Barnum: The Legend and the Man*. Columbia University Press, 1989.

Schickel, Richard. *Intimate Strangers: The Culture of Celebrity in America*. Ivan R. Dee, 2000.

Scientific American. "The Umbrellas and Chairs of Lulu Hurst." 51, no. 1 (1884): 7.

Scientific American. "Walking on the Ceiling Head Down." 63, no. 1 (1890): 8.

Scot, Reginald. *Discoverie of Witchcraft*. Edited by Brinsley Nicholson. London: Elliot Stock, 1886.

Sears, Clare. *Arresting Dress: Cross-Dressing, Law, and Fascination in Nineteenth-Century San Francisco*. Perverse Modernities. Duke University Press, 2015.

Sebastiani, Silvia. "A 'Monster with Human Visage': The Orangutan, Savagery, and the Borders of Humanity in the Global Enlightenment." *History of the Human Sciences* 32, no. 4 (2019): 80–99.

Sellers, Charles Coleman. *Mr. Peale's Museum: Charles Willson Peale and the First Popular Museum of Natural Science and Art*. W. W. Norton, 1980.

Showalter, Elaine. "Killing the Angel in the House: The Autonomy of Women Writers." *The Antioch Review* 50, no. 1/2 (1992): 207–20.
Silvestre, Armand. "Le Monde Des Artes." *La Vie Moderne*, April 1, 1879, 52–53.
Singleton, Esther. *A Daughter of the Revolution*. Moffat, Yard, 1915.
The Sketch: A Journal of Art and Actuality. "The Lioness and Her Cubs at the Aquarium." August 18, 1896.
Skinner, J. E. Hilary. *After the Storm, or, Jonathan and His Neighbours in 1865–6*. London: R. Bentley, 1866. Microform.
Slout, William L. *Clowns and Cannons: The American Circus During the Civil War*. Emeritus Enterprise Book, 2000. Originally published in 1997 by Wildside Press, LLC.
Slout, William L. *Olympians of the Sawdust Circle: A Biographical Dictionary of the Nineteenth Century American Circus*. Clipper Studies in the Theatre, #18. Borgo Press, 1998.
Snyder, Clifford L. "Setting The Record Straight On Old Bet." *American Heritage* 25, no. 3 (1974).
Sontag, Susan. "Notes on Camp." In *Queer Aesthetics and the Performing Subject: A Reader*. Edited by Fabio Cleto. Edinburgh University Press, 1999.
St. Leon, Mark. "Novel Routes: Circus in the Pacific, 1841–1941." *Popular Entertainment Studies* 5, no. 2 (2014): 24–47.
Stevenson, R. L. *Strange Case of Dr. Jekyll and Mr. Hyde*. London: Longmans, Green, 1886.
"Strange Beauty: Barbette and the Art of Transformation." *The Missouri Review* 44, no. 3 (2021): 73–81.
Sturtevant, Charles Gates. "Who's Who in the American Circus: Sturtevant's List of Circuses 1880–1889." Circus Historical Society. https://classic.circushistory.org/History/Sturtevant.htm.
Susman, Warren I. *Culture as History: The Transformation of American Society in the Twentieth Century*. Pantheon Books, 1984. Reprint. Smithsonian Institution Press, 2009.
Tait, Peta. *Fighting Nature: Travelling Menageries, Animal Acts and War Shows*. Animal Publics. Sydney University Press, 2016.

Tait, Peta. "Performed Identities as Circus Illusions." In *The American Circus*. Edited by Susan Weber, Kenneth L. Ames, and Matthew Wittmann. Bard Graduate Center: Decorative Arts, Design History, Material Culture; Yale University Press, 2012.

Taylor, Annie Edson. *Over The Falls: Annie Edson Taylor's Story of Her Trip*. Published by the author, 1902.

Taylor, Tom, ed. *Life of Benjamin Robert Haydon, Historical Painter*. Vol. 2. New York: Harper & Brothers, 1853.

Thayer, Stuart. *Annals of the American Circus, 1793–1829*. Rymack, ca. 1976.

Thayer, Stuart. "The Anti-Circus Laws in Connecticut, 1773–1840." *Bandwagon* 20, no. 1 (1976): 18–20.

Thayer, Stuart. *The Performers: A History of Circus Acts*. Dauven and Thayer, 2005.

Theatre: An Illustrated Weekly Magazine. Vol. 3. New York: Theatre Publishing, 1888.

Thomas, Leonard C. *News for All: America's Coming-of-Age with the Press*. Oxford University Press, 1995.

Tocqueville, Alexis de. *Democracy in America*. Translated by Henry Reeve. Boston: John Allyn, 1873.

Todd, Jan. *Physical Culture and the Body Beautiful: Purposive Exercise in the Lives of American Women, 1800–1870*. Mercer University Press, 1998.

Toulmin, Vanessa. "'My Wife to Conclude Performs the Rest'—Patty Astley the First Lady of Circus." *Early Popular Visual Culture* 16, no. 3 (2018): 290–300.

Trainor, Sean. "Fair Bosom/Black Beard: Facial Hair, Gender Determination, and the Strange Career of Madame Clofullia, 'Bearded Lady.'" *Early American Studies* 12, no. 3 (2014): 548–75.

Tulpii, Nicolai. *Observationaes Medicae*. Editio Quinta. Leiden, Netherlands: Lugduni Batavorum, 1716.

Twain, Mark. *The Celebrated Jumping Frog of Calaveras County*. 3rd ed. New York: C. H. Webb, 1869.

Twain, Mark. *Life on the Mississippi*. Boston: James R. Osgood, 1883.

US Census Bureau. 1860 United States Census. Year: 1860; Census Place: District 1001, Spalding, Georgia; Roll: M653_136; Page: 173.

Vecchio, Kat. "Miss Suffie's Debut: Circus and the Suffrage Movement." *Bandwagon* 64, no. 1 (2020): 8–15.

Velvin, Ellen. *Wild-Animal Celebrities*. Moffat, Yard, 1907.

Vey, Shauna. "The Master and the Mademoiselle: Gender Secrets in Plain Sight in Antebellum Performance." *Theatre History Studies* 27, no. 2 (2007): 39–59.

Wallett, W. F. *The Public Life of W. F. Wallett, the Queen's Jester: An Autobiography*. Edited by John Luntley. London: Bemrose & Sons, 1870.

Walsh, Margaret. "The Democratization of Fashion: The Emergence of the Women's Dress Pattern Industry." *The Journal of American History* 66, no. 2 (1979): 299–313.

Wånggren, Lena. *Gender, Technology and the New Woman*. Edinburgh Critical Studies in Victorian Culture. Edinburgh University Press, 2017.

Ward, Steve. *Father of the Modern Circus "Billy Buttons": The Life & Times of Philip Astley*. Pen & Sword History, 2018.

Ward, Steve. "Martini Maccomo, the African Lion King." *Journal of Victorian Culture*, June 11, 2021. https://jvc.oup.com/2021/06/11/martini-maccomo-the-african-lion-king/.

Washington, Mrs. Booker T. "The New Negro Woman." In *The American New Woman Revisited: A Reader, 1894–1930*, edited by Martha H. Patterson. Rutgers University Press, 2008.

Watts, Edward. *Colonizing the Past: Mythmaking and Pre-Columbian Whites in Nineteenth-Century American Writing*. University of Virginia Press, 2020.

Welter, Barbara. "The Cult of True Womanhood: 1820–1860." *American Quarterly* 18, no. 2, pt. 1 (1966): 151–74.

West, Mark Irwin. "A Spectrum of Spectators: Circus Audiences in Nineteenth-Century America." *Journal of Social History* 15, no. 2 (1981): 265–70.

Whitney, E. T. *Gen Tom Thumb In His Different Characters*. Poster with photographs. Barnum Museum. ca. 1850s. http://hdl.handle.net/11134/60002:133.

Wildman, Daniel. *A Complete Guide for the Management of Bees, Throughout the Year*. London: T. Jones, 1802.

Williamson, Jefferson. *The American Hotel*. Leisure Class in America. Arno Press, 1975.

Wineapple, Brenda. *Ecstatic Nation: Confidence, Crisis, and Compromise, 1848–1877*. Harper Perennial, 2013.

Wittman, Matthew. *Circus and the City: New York: 1793–2010*. Bard Graduate Center, 2012.

Wojczuk, Tana. *Lady Romeo, The Radical and Revolutionary Life of Charlotte Cushman, America's First Celebrity*. Avid Reader Press, 2020.

Wollstonecraft, Mary. *A Vindication of the Rights of Woman*. Penguin Great Ideas. Penguin Books, 2006.

Wordsworth, William. *The Prelude: Or Growth of a Poet's Mind*. London: Edward Moxon, 1850.

World Health Organization. "Gender and Health." Accessed August 16, 2023. https://www.who.int/health-topics/gender.

Yale Law School. "Avalon Project - Journals of the Continental Congress - The Articles of Association; October 20, 1774." Accessed August 16, 2023. https://avalon.law.yale.edu/18th_century/contcong_10-20-74.asp.

Young, Kevin. *The Rise of Hoaxes, Humbug, Plagiarists, Phonies, Post-Facts, and Fake News*. Graywolf Press, 2018.

Young Ladies' Journal Complete Guide to the Work-Table. London: E. Harrison, 1884.

Younger, John G. "Bronze Age Representations of Aegean Bull-Leaping." *American Journal of Archaeology* 80, no. 2 (1976): 125–37.

BETSY GOLDEN KELLEM is a scholar of the unusual. Her writing on circus and entertainment history has appeared in venues including *The Atlantic*, *Vanity Fair*, *Washington Post*, *Public Domain Review*, *Smithsonian*, *Atlas Obscura*, and *Slate*. She has served on the boards of the Barnum Museum and the Circus Historical Society, and is an Emmy Award winner for her *Showman's Shorts* video series on P. T. Barnum. She is a columnist for JSTOR Daily and regularly teaches and speaks for academia and industry. If you ask nicely, she will juggle knives for you. She lives in North Haven, Connecticut.

The Feminist Press publishes books that ignite movements and social transformation. Celebrating our legacy, we lift up insurgent and marginalized voices from around the world to build a more just future.

See our complete list of books at
feministpress.org